Troubled Waters

PERSIAN GULF STUDIES

A CIRS/Cornell series

جـامـعـة جـورجـتـاون قـطـر
GEORGETOWN UNIVERSITY QATAR

Center *for* International *and* Regional Studies

TROUBLED WATERS

Insecurity in the Persian Gulf

MEHRAN KAMRAVA

CORNELL UNIVERSITY PRESS
ITHACA AND LONDON

First published 2018 by Cornell University Press

Printed in the United States of America

Library of Congress Cataloging-in-Publication Data

Names: Kamrava, Mehran, 1964– author.
Title: Troubled waters : insecurity in the Persian Gulf / Mehran Kamrava.
Description: Ithaca : Cornell University Press, 2018. | Series: Persian Gulf
    studies | Includes bibliographical references and index.
Identifiers: LCCN 2017038574 (print) | LCCN 2017041649 (ebook) |
    ISBN 9781501720376 (epub/mobi) | ISBN 9781501720369 (pdf) |
    ISBN 9781501720352 | ISBN 9781501720352 (cloth : alk. paper)
Subjects: LCSH: Security, International—Persian Gulf Region. | Human
    security—Persian Gulf Region. | Persian Gulf Region—Foreign
    relations.
Classification: LCC JZ6009.P35 (ebook) | LCC JZ6009.P35 K36 2018
    (print) | DDC 355/.0330536—dc23
LC record available at https://lccn.loc.gov/2017038574

Cornell University Press strives to use environmentally responsible
suppliers and materials to the fullest extent possible in the publishing
of its books. Such materials include vegetable-based, low-VOC
inks and acid-free papers that are recycled, totally chlorine-free, or
partly composed of nonwood fibers. For further information,
visit our website at cornellpress.cornell.edu.

Contents

ACKNOWLEDGMENTS

Work on this book was made considerably easier with the help of two superb research assistants, Leena Nady and Erika Thao Nguyen. The book was conceived, researched, and written under the auspices of the Center for International and Regional Studies at Georgetown University–Qatar. I am deeply grateful to my colleagues at CIRS for their support and for helping foster an intellectually rewarding environment for research and writing. Grateful acknowledgment also goes to the Qatar Foundation for its support of research and other scholarly endeavors. A generous research grant from Georgetown University–Qatar made it possible for me to meet with and interview a number of scholars, foreign policy experts, and policymakers across the Persian Gulf region. I gratefully acknowledge the insights and information shared with me by Abdulkhaleq Abdulla, Yusuf bin Alawi bin Abdullah, Saleh al-Rajhi, Turki M. Saud Al-Kabeer, Mohammad Farazmand, Behzad Khoshandam, Abbas Maleki, Kazem Sajjadpour, and Jamal Sanad al-Swaidi. A number of other interviewees requested anonymity but were equally helpful in sharing their insights and inside knowledge of issues related to security dynamics in the region. Once earlier drafts of the manuscript were finished, I was extremely fortunate to have had all or parts of it read by Zahra Babar, Robert Gallucci, Thomas Lippman, Mahmood Monshipouri, Gary Sick, Gary Wasserman, and Robert Wirsing. Their feedback and suggestions have been vital in shaping the manuscript into what it is, and in the process they saved me from many embarrassing mistakes big and small. At Cornell University Press, Roger Haydon was instrumental in helping me sharpen my arguments and in seeing the manuscript through to publication. Needless to say, whatever errors remain are my own responsibility.

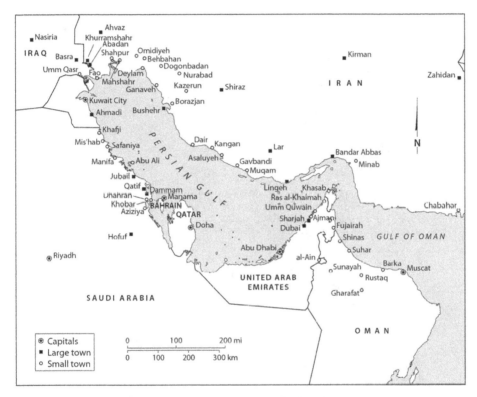

Map 1. Map of the Persian Gulf political area.

TROUBLED WATERS

INTRODUCTION

Why is the Persian Gulf so chronically insecure? This is the central question guiding this book. Today, the Persian Gulf remains one of the most heavily militarized and insecure regions in the world. This book examines, individually and collectively, the causes and consequences of these dynamics, which have made this small waterway and its surrounding areas one of the most volatile and tension-filled regions in the world. This pervasive insecurity, the book argues, is largely a product of four interrelated developments, the examination of which forms the central basis around which the book's arguments are organized. Briefly, the four developments are preoccupation with "conventional" security threats at the expense of pervasive, though largely intangible, nonconventional "critical security" issues; the flawed nature of the prevailing security architecture, which, ironically, perpetuates regional insecurity; the deliberate actions and policies of the regional and extraregional actors involved in the Persian Gulf; and the self-reinforcing nature of the region's security dilemma.

First, I argue here that security threats in the Persian Gulf emanate from two complementary sets of sources. One set may be broadly labeled as conventional security threats, arising out of actual physical and military challenges to states. Some of the primary ingredients of these sorts of threats involve armaments and weaponry, high politics, interstate tensions, international intrigue, proxy wars, and cross-border conflicts. Just as pervasive, though perhaps harder to grasp and to quantify, is another set of security threats, namely, those arising from the consequences of perceived threats to culture and identity. It is precisely these challenges to what are broadly defined as "human security" that in the post-2011 context have fanned the flames of sectarianism across the region. For the most part, discussions of human security, or what has also been more broadly called a critical security perspective, have largely been academic in nature. But in the post-2011 period, the Persian Gulf offers a paradigmatic example of the concrete consequences of perceived threats to human security. The nature of security threats, and perceptions of such threats, are fluid and tend to change over time. In the post-2011 Persian Gulf, I maintain, focusing on one category of threats and ignoring other threats, which may be out of sync with our conventional notions of security, only gives us an incomplete picture.

The research for this book took me to several regional capitals, where I would typically meet with fellow academics and whoever in the various government ministries was willing to talk to me. In addition to learning that the waiting halls of foreign ministries must all have the same decorator, or at least have their furniture delivered from the same store, I was particularly struck by two exchanges I had with two of the region's most prominent policymakers. In my interviews I always included the same question in my list of inquiries: "What is the biggest security threat your country faces today?" Most often, I would get the answer I expected. In Riyadh and Abu Dhabi, for example, the answer was always "Iran." In Tehran, it was "The Gulf Cooperation Council and its American backers." But on two occasions the responses surprised me, not so much for the answer itself but for the honesty and foresight of my respondents. In Muscat, asked to identify the biggest security threat to Oman, without even a pause Foreign Minister Yusuf bin Alawi bin Abdullah shot back, "Unemployment." When I asked the question again, thinking it might have been misunderstood, he repeated his answer.

Something similar happened in another regional capital, where in a confidential interview with the minister of defense I asked for reasons behind the recent introduction of compulsory military service in the country. The response: "to prevent boredom." "Our young are easily bored," the defense minister explained, "and they can fall prey to Daesh and its propaganda. Our goal is to keep them busy, give them discipline, and to instill in them a sense of hope in the future." The minister went on to confirm what those of us who live in the region feel viscerally, that there is a palpable sense of unease among many strata of society arising from perceived threats to cultural authenticity and to identity. If left unaddressed, such feelings have the potential of growing into serious threats to the state. That these worries were being expressed by no less than a defense minister, rather than by a sociologist or a social worker, was all the more interesting.

In the chapters to come, I place the importance of pervasive military threats in the Persian Gulf within the context of a broader array of security challenges that also include elements of human security. The prevailing security architecture of the Persian Gulf, I argue, has neglected some of the more pervasive security threats the region faces while exaggerating others for seemingly political and ideological reasons. Neglect of human security concerns, in particular, has given rise to issues of identity politics and sectarianism, which have in turn been manipulated by states for instrumentalist purposes.

A second, central argument of the book points to the role of agency in general, and individual policymaking and initiatives in particular, as one of the primary causes of the Persian Gulf's pervasive insecurity. Studying security in the Gulf reminds us of that simple truism in political science, that agency matters. Institutions may limit the range of choices available to policymakers, but not during critical junctures, as in the Arab Spring, or when leaders retain their supremacy over institutions, as is often the case in the Middle East.[1] Much of the pervasive insecurity in the Persian Gulf, I argue, is not only the product of larger structural dynamics built into the region's security architecture. It is also a result of deliberate policies followed by regional actors, in collusion with their foreign backers, meant deliberately to identify and to undermine opponents. Many regional actors, I maintain, are willful belligerents.

Agency and structure complement each other and compete for importance depending on prevailing circumstances and conditions, with agency being particularly consequential in moments of change and transition. The time frame this books covers, the period after the 2011 Arab uprisings, happens to be one of the most fluid and unpredictable in the history of the Persian Gulf. Not only did many Middle Eastern countries witness regime change; within the Persian Gulf itself a number of regional policymakers left office and were replaced by new ones. Qatar's reigning emir retired and was succeeded by his son in June 2013. Iran elected a new president the following August. A new king assumed power in Saudi Arabia in January 2015. Further, in the United States, Donald Trump pulled off a surprise victory over Hillary Clinton in the country's 2016 presidential elections.

Trump's presidential victory has been especially consequential for security dynamics in the Persian Gulf. Within a few months, the ripple effect of Trump's election sent tidal waves of change to the prevailing diplomatic and security arrangements of the Persian Gulf. Within days of the U.S. president's visit to Riyadh in May 2017 to meet with a group of Arab and Muslim leaders, Saudi Arabia and the United Arab Emirates (UAE) launched a massive and sudden campaign to isolate Qatar and to induce a "change in behavior" among its leaders. With Bahrain and Egypt as part of their alliance, the Saudi-Emirati campaign threatened to cause irreparable fractures in the very structure of the Gulf Cooperation Council.

Within days of spearheading the economic boycott and blockade of Qatar, Saudi Arabia's King Salman changed the line of succession within the kingdom's royal family. He removed his nephew Mohammed bin Nayef from the position of heir apparent and instead promoted his son, the ambitious Mohammed bin Salman, to the position.

Even in places where the top leadership did not necessarily change, as in Bahrain and especially in the UAE, new actors rose to influence, while others were eclipsed. In the UAE, Crown Prince Mohamed bin Zayed is generally seen as the country's ruler. In all these instances, new policies were put in place, the cumulative effects of which have further heightened regional tensions and insecurity across the Persian Gulf.

A third cause of regional insecurity lies in the very nature of the regional security architecture. This security architecture has two basic features: it relies on the objectives and components of U.S. power, and it is premised on excluding, containing, and marginalizing two of the region's largest and most important states, Iran and Iraq. However, in spite of extensive military commitment, coupled with crippling sanctions imposed on Iran because of its nuclear program, efforts at establishing an American-led security architecture in the Persian Gulf have failed to make the region more secure. Moreover, the resulting security architecture is inherently unstable, relying on actors who often do not share common objectives or even always see eye to eye.

A fourth cause of insecurity in the Persian Gulf results from the pervasiveness of the "security dilemma" among virtually all actors involved in the region. A security dilemma is a vicious cycle in which security-producing efforts by one state result in a sense of insecurity among another state, which then embarks on its own security-producing measures, in turn prompting the first actor to take additional steps to enhance its security. While by no means unique to the Persian Gulf, a number of factors have coalesced to make the region's security dilemma increasingly intractable in recent years. These factors include the growing sectarianization of foreign and security policy pursuits by countries such as Iran and Saudi Arabia, especially since 2011; the ever-expansive military cooperation between the United States and the Arab states of the region; and the spread of proxy wars in weak and fragile states such as Yemen, Iraq, and Syria.

My goal here is neither to offer a historical chronology nor to set forth a general theory of the international relations of the Persian Gulf. Instead, I will bring together the different components that explain the puzzle of Persian Gulf insecurity. There are four pieces to the puzzle, each explored in greater detail in chapter 1. The chapter has two primary objectives. First, it presents a broad outline of some of the most salient historical, political, and military factors that have shaped the international relations of the Persian Gulf. Second, the chapter problematizes the notion of security, arguing that the concept ought to be broadened to include a wider category of threats and challenges that go beyond merely military and physical dimensions.

This sets the stage for chapter 2, which examines the Persian Gulf's prevailing security architecture. More specifically, the chapter traces the historic evolution of the architecture, and then analyzes the ways in which the very arrangements meant to make the region secure are largely responsible for its insecurity. The chapter points to the dominant role of the United States in fostering and maintaining the architecture; its reliance on regional allies; and its exclusion, initially of both Iran and Iraq and now largely of only Iran, as the primary causes for the flaws in which it inheres.

Structures such as security architectures are not immutable. They are only as robust as the actions and commitments of the actors that are influenced by them in one form or another. Chapter 3 looks at the cast of characters—more specifically the state actors—whose foreign and security policies have so greatly contributed, both intentionally and unintentionally, to the perpetual insecurity of the Persian Gulf. These actors include the United States, the Gulf Cooperation Council (GCC) as a collective security or political and economic organization, Saudi Arabia, Qatar, the UAE, and Iran. The deepening security dilemma of the region and the resulting pervasive insecurity, the chapter contends, are as much the result of deliberate policies pursued by each of these actors as they are an outcome of structural dynamics inherent in the region's security architecture.

Chapter 4 turns the book's attention to the Persian Gulf's security dilemma. Since the 2011 Arab uprisings, the strategic landscape of the Middle East in general, and the Persian Gulf in particular, has witnessed unprecedented levels of securitization.[2] This pervasive securitization has only deepened the region's security dilemma and the resulting insecurity of many regional and extraregional actors. In my efforts to better understand regional threat perceptions, I interviewed many technical experts and other key policy figures in foreign ministries in Abu Dhabi, Doha, Riyadh, Muscat, and Tehran. Without fail, everyone I interviewed expressed apprehension and fear about the intentions of neighboring states, regardless of whether or not they were a part of the GCC. Mistrust and skepticism about the intentions of others deepens the region's security dilemma, only aggravating the pervasiveness of the Persian Gulf's insecurity.

The book's final chapter brings together the main arguments of the previous chapters. It ends with an examination of possible win-win scenarios that are likely to reduce tensions and security threats in the Persian Gulf. There has been no shortage of such scenarios offered over the years, meant to reduce tensions in the region. But these are, unfortunately, only possible *scenarios*, the plausibility of which policymakers and politicians are seldom willing to entertain. At least for the foreseeable future, the realities of the Persian Gulf are likely to keep it insecure.

The book offers several key takeaways. One has to do with the very nature of the security threats as perceived inside the region. Perceived threats and anxieties in the Persian Gulf are not just regional and international; they are also domestic, rooted in patterns of economic development and processes of social change. A broadened conception of security needs to take into account feelings of social and economic unease produced by demographic imbalances and the dizzying pace of socioeconomic transition.

In many ways, this broadening of notions of security can no longer be avoided in the post-2011 era, when Persian Gulf states have securitized the individual and collective identities of their citizens. Long resonant but largely dormant in their societies, it was the Persian Gulf states themselves that awakened sectarian impulses in their populations in order to instrumentally frame an us-versus-them narrative. Even when the flames of sectarianism no longer needed fanning by the state and had assumed dynamics of their own, policymakers and other key actors refused to back down, capitalizing on the utility of sectarianism for "struggles" of various kinds against one enemy or another. Today, the scourge of sectarianism creeps through Persian Gulf societies in multiple dimensions and many forms.

Sectarianism only reinforces exclusivist assumptions of regional security that revolve around zero-sum calculations. These calculations, and the institutional arrangements meant to protect and reinforce them, make the region more rather than less insecure. More specifically, excluding Iran from regional security arrangements—as the United States and its chief regional ally, Saudi Arabia, have sought to do—has only made Iran all the more determined to safeguard its security interests in the Persian Gulf and elsewhere in a manner that has been conflictual in relation to the other actors and has often destabilized the region.

The ensuing dialogue of the deaf has in turn perpetuated a region-wide security dilemma, the only way out of which appears to be the courage to engage in diplomacy and statesmanship. Held back by their domestic constituents and stakeholders, and even more tightly by their own myopia and tunnel vision, policymakers both in the region and in the United

States appear singularly incapable of stepping out of and beyond measures that merely aggravate the pervasive insecurity around them. Structures do indeed define the parameters of action. But they are not unchangeable, and policymakers have the agency to act outside what may have become established norms and conventions. Whether or not actors have the foresight or the wherewithal to act outside these constraints is a different matter.

The one attempt at regional integration, that of the GCC, resembles more a temporary marriage of convenience fostered by the ebb and flow of external threats than a meaningful institutional means of coordinating the foreign and security policies of its members. There are structural issues that undermine the GCC's efficacy in the long term and under normal circumstances. By virtue of its size, history, economy, and military power, Saudi Arabia assumes itself to be the first among equals in the GCC, a designation not always accepted by the other members. For the Saudis, the wars in Syria and Yemen have afforded the opportunity to foster a measure of Gulf unity under the auspices of the GCC, a unity cemented further by Iran's own deliberate sectarian otherness. But civil wars do not last forever, and the collective will of the other five states to yield to Saudi wisdom in matters of security and diplomacy is unlikely to outlast periods of regional crisis.

It is unclear whether the GCC can withstand its self-inflicted wounds of 2017. In June that year, sharp chasms emerged within the organization with Saudi Arabia, the UAE, and Bahrain on one side, Qatar on the other, and Kuwait and Oman in the middle. As an institutional forum for summitry and pleasant talk, the GCC is likely to be a long-term feature of the regional landscape. And the organization may even make headway in issues related to uniform taxation, currency exchange rates, and monetary union. Beyond that, however, the GCC is unlikely to transform regional preferences for bilateral trade and security relations into impulses of multilateralism and defense and security coordination.

Perhaps the biggest takeaway, the central thesis of the book, is, I am afraid, an unhappy one. Given all that is happening in the region—the deepening hold of sectarianism, the intransigence of the belligerents involved, the pervasiveness of zero-sum calculations, and the perpetuation, rather than receding, of the region-wide security dilemma—the Persian Gulf is likely to remain both heavily militarized and highly insecure for the foreseeable future. This is an insecurity with multiple causes and dimensions, unlikely to be remedied by quick fixes or more militarization. It requires sustained attention, buy-in on the part of the many actors and states involved, and, perhaps more than anything else, diplomacy and dialogue. These two necessary ingredients, diplomacy and dialogue, are what the Persian Gulf is currently missing the most.

1

THE TROUBLE WITH THE PERSIAN GULF

The Persian Gulf has emerged as one of the most heavily armed, securitized, and highly volatile regions of the world. For more than a half century, the shallow waterway has been of critical strategic importance because of the rich oil deposits spread among its littoral states, as well as, more recently, the enormous natural gas fields beneath its seabed. For the global great powers, especially at first the United Kingdom and then the United States, this was a region of tremendous strategic significance, a real estate of considerable worth and value, a place to dominate and govern either directly through colonial means or indirectly via pliant local rulers. Throughout the twentieth century, in one form or another, the West viewed the Persian Gulf through proprietary lenses. In the words of U.S. president Jimmy Carter, as he enunciated what came to be known as the Carter Doctrine, "An attempt by any outside force to gain control of the Persian Gulf region will be regarded as an assault on the vital interests of the United States of America, and such an assault will be repelled by any means necessary, including military force."[1]

The Soviets, and once they collapsed whoever else threatened Western interests, were to be kept out of the region or kept weak so as not to challenge a status quo that favored the West's dominance of the Persian Gulf. Volatility across the region or in the constituent states was tolerated as long as it did not threaten access to oil and its flow out of the region—the wounds of the Iran-Iraq War, for example, festered for eight years, from 1980 to 1988, until the two sides had exhausted each other and themselves. When international tensions threatened friendly suppliers with ample oil resources, as happened when Iraq invaded Kuwait, the threat was resolutely countered and put down by the United States.

The end of a globally menacing Cold War and the arrival of a new millennium did little to calm the Persian Gulf's turbulent waters and its even more chaotic shores. If anything, the September 2001 terrorist attacks on American soil and the ensuing global War on Terror ushered in a new era of turmoil across the Middle East and specifically in the Persian Gulf region. It soon emerged that both the mastermind and the foot soldiers of the 9/11 terrorist attacks hailed from the countries of the Persian Gulf—of the nineteen who took part in the attacks, fifteen were from Saudi Arabia and two from the United Arab Emirates (UAE).

What larger environmental factors would prompt some of the richest countries in the world to breed such fanatically dedicated mass killers? Reason had little chance of addressing such existential questions in the hurried rush for vengeance. A new order descended upon the region, engulfing not just the Arabian Peninsula but also much of the Levant and North Africa. Securitization assumed new dimensions. Stability, enforced through gun barrels if necessary, became an all-consuming search. Meanwhile, wars of varying intensities were prosecuted by the Western powers against those belonging to an "Axis of Evil," two members of which, Iran and Iraq, were located in the Gulf region.[2]

Just as the world was getting accustomed to a new security consciousness in the post-9/11 era, a new malady descended upon the Persian Gulf and the larger Middle East region. What began as a hopeful Spring in late 2010 soon spiraled into a nightmare of religious extremism, civil wars, repressive despotism, and bloody sectarianism. And, in almost every form and in every dimension, the Persian Gulf was once again at the center of regional and global crosscurrents, affecting not just security but also politics, society, and life in general in places near and far. If there is a new order emerging out of the ashes of what began as the Arab Spring, nearly a decade on, it is yet another era of chaos and insecurity.

It is the study of the root causes of this insecurity to which this book is devoted. The puzzle I have set for myself is to decipher the underlying causes of the chronic insecurity of the Persian Gulf region. While my specific focus is the post–Arab Spring period, it is obvious that many of the underlying dynamics have deeper and older roots, spanning specific developments and arbitrary dates. Thus while my attention is primarily drawn to the contemporary era, at times a longer historical horizon is necessary.

The broad outlines of the argument I make here are as follows. I argue that the Persian Gulf's chronic insecurity is rooted in four interrelated, reinforcing sets of factors. First, the prevailing security architecture in the Persian Gulf contains a dual characteristic that makes it inherently insecure. This dual characteristic includes a flawed or at best incomplete *conception of security*, on the one hand, and, on the other, an equally *untenable evolution of security arrangements* as they have come to prevail across the region on the other. Security in the Persian Gulf has come to be understood in exclusively military and territorial terms. Later on in this chapter I will make the case—building on what is by now a well-established strand of security studies—that there are dimensions of security that go beyond balance-of-power equations and issues related to military affairs and instead revolve around the core human sense of security. These "critical" dimensions of human security, particularly germane in a region where matters of identity and belonging have assumed a central importance to individuals and communities, have long been neglected and, in fact, have often been suppressed.

Second, for decades this dogged neglect of human security issues has been built on an externally engineered and sustained regional security architecture that was, and remains, fundamentally unstable and unsustainable. This instability and unsustainability derived from the security architecture's main premises of overt reliance on an external balancer, the United States, and the exclusion of two major regional actors, Iran and Iraq. Near the end of its tenure, the administration of President Barack Obama developed somewhat of a businesslike relationship with Iran that was no longer premised on the containment and isolation of the

Islamic Republic. But mistrust and tensions remained, and were in fact heightened with the coming to office of Donald Trump's administration in January 2017. President Trump and his foreign and security policy team were initially slow to articulate clear goals and objectives in relation to the Persian Gulf, or the larger Middle East for that matter. But soon they reverted to pre-Obama policies designed to isolate and marginalize Iran from regional and global affairs. Trump's secretary of state, Rex Tillerson, even went as far as to admit to his country's willingness to affect regime change in Iran.[3]

A third reason for chronic insecurity in the Persian Gulf is the policies and priorities of the region's policymakers. These policymakers, I argue, pursue security-producing programs that ultimately perpetuate their own insecurity. Moreover, they are often adventurous and expansionist. Their motivations are guided by a combination of agency and structure. In terms of agency, they are often motivated by a desire to project power and influence abroad in order to maintain regime security at home. As far as structural dynamics are concerned, since their countries are actually secondary global powers or see themselves as such, they have aspirations of regional dominance and hegemony. Whatever the cause, local actors often act as belligerents. Mistrust marks their interactions even in good times, and cooperation is rare and fleeting when it happens. This is a region with far too many local states aspiring to dominate it in one form or another, some on their own but most with outside help. These clashing aspirations are yet another cause of regional insecurity.

The fourth and final cause of insecurity in the region revolves around the vicious cycle of security-insecurity that is commonly referred to in the discipline as a security dilemma. Because of pervasive insecurity, each of the states in the region has embarked on vigorous security-producing efforts of one form or another. All have engaged in massive arms purchases save for Iran, which instead has long compensated for the international sanctions it faces on weapons imports by building a robust domestic military industry of its own, especially in the form of a ballistic missile program. In turn, the flood of arms, be they domestically manufactured or imported, increases the insecurity of neighbors, which then acquire more arms, only to prompt others to do the same thing. And the cycle continues. The essence of the security dilemma traces back to mistrust, of which there is plenty all around the Persian Gulf. As the following chapters argue, alliances are all too often marred by an innate transience that reigns as soon as a uniting security threat recedes. Interstate politics in the Persian Gulf remains largely a zero-sum game and, as such, perpetuates a security dilemma from which it is all but impossible to escape.

I will elaborate on these arguments in the chapters that follow. For now, in the remainder of this chapter I will lay the groundwork for that discussion more fully by covering two additional, related topics. First, I will examine some of the more consequential developments in the international relations of the Middle East, and more specifically the Persian Gulf, and the security predicaments of its constituent actors. The countries of the region have been subject to many of the broader dynamics under way in or affecting the Middle East, from state building to war making, arms races, power projection, revolutions, civil wars, and multiple other catalytic events. The security architecture of the Persian Gulf as it has evolved over the past several decades and the current priorities and objectives of regional leaders and state actors—their fears and threat perceptions, and their efforts to carve out for themselves spheres of influence near and far—all have been invariably shaped and influenced by broader region-wide developments, including those in the Levant and North Africa.

Once the general landscape of the international relations of the Middle East and the Persian Gulf has been painted, I will turn to an examination of the concept of *security*. Building on a well-established strand within security studies, I argue that one-dimensional conceptions of security that focus exclusively on its physical and territorial facets are at best incomplete and at worst oblivious to deeper and more salient and consequential dynamics. Conventional understandings of security need to be broadened to include social and political anxieties with potential for unease and instability. Not all threats and challenges come from the barrel of a gun or from tilts and imbalances in power equations. Some are harder to discern at first, and may emanate from phenomena as nebulous as identity and sense of belonging. But they may be no less threatening to political order and stability, no less compelling as motivators for foreign policy behavior, and no less pernicious as a security challenge. Security, in short, is multidimensional, far more complex and complicated than reducible to military and defense matters only, and is an issue not just of power and influence but also of popular perceptions, collective anxieties, and a sense of unease.

The Landscape

Three broad themes or developments characterize the overall background within which Persian Gulf security is currently unfolding. The first has to do with the weight and continuing consequences of historical developments. History is far from static, and the ramifications of events that constitute it often cascade onto subsequent eras and periods. For the larger Middle East and the Persian Gulf in particular, processes of state formation and critical historical junctures continue to unfold and shape major developments. This relates to a second development, namely, the long-standing nexus between domestic politics and foreign policy. Across the Middle East and especially in the Persian Gulf, as elsewhere, foreign policy behavior is all too often influenced by considerations revolving around domestic politics. In the Gulf region, foreign policy is often directly tied to issues of regime security.

A third and final development has to do with the steady shift of power and focus within the Middle East, away from the Levant and North Africa and in the direction of the Arabian Peninsula. Over the past two decades or so, actors once considered insignificant and at best marginal in regional affairs have now taken center stage. These include the likes of Qatar and the UAE, which now house aspiring global cities, host mega-events and showcase projects geared to audiences throughout the world, and have emerged as global hubs for commerce and transport. Both Qatar and the UAE have ambitions of influence and power projection that are wholly incommensurate with their brief history as independent states and with their small size. Even Saudi Arabia, which has long been a key player in regional affairs, is now far more assertive than perhaps at any other point in its history, seeking to complement its hegemonic ambitions within the Arabian Peninsula with leadership roles in the larger Middle East and beyond.

Let us delve a little deeper into each of these developments, beginning with the unfolding ramifications of major historical events and processes of state formation in the region. Raymond Hinnebusch has distinguished five phases of state formation in the contemporary Middle East: the period of oligarchy (1945–1955), the era of populist revolutions (1956–1970), authoritarian state consolidation (1970–1990), post-populist authoritarianism (1990–2011), and the age of Arab Spring (2011–).[4] Each of these eras left its own indelible mark on the Middle East, building on and adding to layers before and after, and setting into motion developments with domestic and regional consequences. The oligarchs' control by foreign masters, mostly British and French, gave way in the early 1950s to populists who assumed that strength rested in numbers and that power and progress could be had through uniting under the banner of a common Arab nation. But by the early to the mid-1970s the pan-Arabists' compelling slogans had failed to put food on the table or to accomplish any victories on the battlefield, and for the following four decades or so the region descended into an abyss of authoritarianism and stale, despotic rule. The Arab Spring was the hopeful answer, but only briefly. It soon turned into a nightmare of religious extremism, sectarianism, civil wars, and weak and collapsing states.

Each of these eras saw its own tenor and rhythm of foreign policy and international relations, and each gave rise to its own host of security challenges and threat perceptions. The days of the oligarchs witnessed the last gasps of overt colonialism in the Middle East, replaced by the revolutionary populism of Nasser, and in later forms of Qaddafi and Saddam, which sought to smash old orders and re-create new, supposedly progressive ones. The Persian Gulf, at the time governed by pro-Western, conservative rulers on both sides, did not take too kindly to the revolutionary tenor of the times. It was, instead, far more welcoming of the pro-order and stability-focused 1970s and its trenchant authoritarianism.

The façade of stability did not last long, however, as Iran's 1978–1979 revolution once again upset any semblance of balance the Middle East, and especially the Persian Gulf region, had come to assume. Anoushiravan Ehteshami identifies the Iranian revolution as the first of five "catalytic events" that left the Middle East deeply scarred and its security arrangements in turmoil.[5] Revolutions are seldom content to remain in their own home; they have an impulse to export themselves. Iran's export of its revolution in the early days shook the remaining monarchies of the Middle East and compelled them to action, prompting support for Saddam Hussein's war on Iran for eight bloody years. The exhaustive war ended in 1988, but Saddam's campaign was not over yet. Turning his tanks toward former allies, in August 1990 he invaded Kuwait. What had started out in the 1950s and the 1960s as an international relations system focused on liberating Palestine had become fragmented into self-motivated pieces in the 1970s and the 1980s and was in utter chaos by the 1990s.[6] Arab brethren had turned on each other. The regional order was turned on its head.

Other catalytic events followed: the September 11 attacks in the United States; the 2003 U.S. invasion of Iraq; the Arab Spring; and, still in the making, the changing global distribution of power eastward and away from the Euro-Atlantic bloc.[7] By now the region was in constant flux, its security arrangements seldom remaining static for more than a few years at a time. The Iranian revolution had ended the tacit agreement among regional states that they did not challenge each other's domestic legitimacy.[8] The three major wars that followed in relatively rapid succession—the Iran-Iraq War of 1980–1988, Iraq's invasion and expulsion from Kuwait in 1990–1991, and the U.S. invasion and occupation of Iraq in 2003—each arose out of and was meant to change the regional balance of power.[9] In the 1990s, U.S. efforts to curtail Iranian ambitions and Iraqi mischiefs resulted in a policy called "dual containment," the premises of which—marginalizing two of the region's largest and most pivotal actors—only further exacerbated regional tensions and insecurity.

Ironically, despite the U.S. desire to contain and marginalize Iran, the American invasion and occupation of Iraq increased Iran's strategic significance, as well as that of the region's other non-Arab states: Turkey and Israel.[10] This expansion of Iran's strategic influence continued even after the outbreak of the 2011 Arab uprisings, paradoxically at the same time as actors on the other side of the Gulf have been seeking to assert their own leadership role in the Middle East. I will return to this topic shortly. First, given the fluidity and uncertainty of regional power alignments, and the degree and depth to which power balances in the region shift, I want to highlight the connection in the Middle East between foreign policy, and more broadly international relations, on the one hand, and domestic politics, on the other.

Given the constant turmoil and unpredictability of international relations in the Middle East, coupled with brittle or nonexistent sources of domestic political legitimacy, throughout the region foreign policy is frequently used as a source of domestic legitimacy.[11] Bahgat Korany has used the term "intermestics" to refer to the intermeshing of local and domestic dynamics with international and global ones. Intermestics, he maintains, "is a reflection of creeping globalization, characterized by the retreat of exclusive state sovereignty, and the rise instead of the intensity of societal interconnectedness and speedy circulation of ideas, but without wiping out the impact of local features."[12] In the specific context of the Persian Gulf region, intermestics has come to assume an intertwining of the internal and external dimensions of security. This is largely because across the Gulf, the paramount objective of foreign policy is regime security.[13] And, consequently, in the region "regime" security and "national" security remain conflated.[14]

This conflation, and the broader, intimate interconnectedness of domestic politics and international relations in the Persian Gulf has a number of consequences for constructing a theoretical framework applicable to the region. I do not wish to engage in theory building here, a task to which a number of perceptive works have already made significant contributions.[15] Based on the foregoing analysis, however, I do want to draw on some important, relevant theoretical insights related to the international relations of the Middle East and the Persian Gulf.

In general, international relations theory has not fared well in the Middle East. The region has in fact been a "graveyard" for many contemporary international relations theories.[16] This is mainly because international relations in the Middle East remain largely complex and unpredictable.[17] Across the region, given the pervasiveness of authoritarian, personalist systems that feature weak or nonexistent input from professional foreign policy technocrats, foreign policy tends to reflect the personality and worldview of the chief policymaker and is therefore subject to periodic changes in tenor, direction, and outlook.[18] As Louise Fawcett has observed, understanding the behavior of Middle Eastern states therefore demands "a flexible and inclusive theoretical framework" that takes into account the politics of power and influence, the role of diverging ideas and norms, and domestic influences.[19] This "flexible and inclusive theoretical framework," I believe, must necessarily take into account the roles of both *agency* and *structures*. As this and subsequent chapters demonstrate, once in place, structures provide frameworks within which a range of individual choices become possible. But when structures are not yet fully formed or have less strength and resilience as compared with individuals, choice and agency assume much greater significance and salience.[20]

Along similar lines, Gregory Gause has asserted that most of the conflicts in the Middle East can be understood only in the context of the incentives and transnational platforms that powerful local leaders have to appeal to in order to advance their interests. These transnational platforms could include the Arab-Israeli conflict or may be inter-Arab, Arab-Iranian, or sectarian in dimension.[21] The international politics of the Middle East is often conditioned by the imperative of regime survival and threat responses that are formulated in a very complex, threat-filled environment.[22] Understanding this environment requires taking into account three interrelated elements: transnational ideological and identity factors, the constraining and enabling effects of threats and opportunities posed by the international environment, and the structures of decision making and the decision makers' perceptions and role conceptions.[23]

It has been precisely this combination of structural dynamics on the one side and the agency and choices of regional leaders on the other that has turned the Persian Gulf region into the new center of economic, political, and diplomatic gravity within the Middle East. There is no denial that the early decades of the twenty-first century have witnessed a steady shift in the leadership of the Arab world away from North Africa and the Levant and toward the Persian Gulf region.[24] This is part of a broader historical trend in which the distribution of power in the Middle East has been constantly changing.[25] The structural factors that facilitated the latest shift included the development of a number of economic and political constraints that eroded the ability of the Middle East's traditional powerhouses to continue to project power and influence—in places such as Algeria, Egypt, Syria, and Iraq—at a time when the Persian Gulf states successfully translated windfalls from the second oil boom, in the early 2000s, into influence in the international and especially regional political economies. By the first decade of the 2000s, the GCC states had emerged as what some saw as "strategic and commercial pivots" by leveraging their international profile, oil resources, foreign policies, and international investments and their position as "super connectors" in hubs of global aviation.[26]

This wider regional context opened political space for a number of ambitious personalities to try to propel their countries, hitherto marginal players in regional politics, into positions of prominence. Qatar's former emir Sheikh Hamad, in power from 1995 to 2013, was a paramount example of a man with outsized ambitions and visions of power and influence for his small country.[27] Following Hamad's retirement, it was the Saudis' turn to make their mark on regional politics in their neighborhood and beyond. Within a few months of ascending to power in January 2015, the kingdom's new ruler, King Salman, had not only changed the succession order in his own household, but also revolutionized traditional patterns of Saudi foreign policy behavior by waging war on Yemen shortly after assuming office.[28] His ambitious son, defense minister and later Crown Prince Mohammed Bin Salman (b. 1985), was seen as equally instrumental in effecting profound changes in the kingdom's foreign and security policies.[29] Not to fall too far behind, the UAE, effectively led by Crown Prince Mohammed bin Zayed Al Nahyan (b. 1961) since the mid-2000s, hurriedly joined the Saudi campaign in Yemen. Again, the militarization of the UAE's foreign policy is a radically new development.[30]

The consequences of this shift in power and activism toward the Arabian Peninsula entails more than the mere emergence of Saudi Arabia as one of the Arab world's most influential countries.[31] It is, as Hussein Sirriyeh has observed, part of a recent effort by Saudi Arabia to place itself as the leading force in a new, region-wide pan-Arabism. With the pan-Arabism of the Nasserist kind dead after 1967, and especially with the 1973 war, some wondered if the 1990–1991 war in the Persian Gulf had ushered in a new version of pan-Arabism that called for the formation of a new Arab order.[32] Such was not to be. In fact, it was only after the Arab Spring reached the shores of the Persian Gulf itself, in the form of a popular uprising in Bahrain, that Saudi Arabia sprang into action and, for reasons of regime survival more than anything else, decided to take matters into its own hands and to lead a counterrevolution of sorts.[33]

Such was the genesis of, and the reasons for, the latest Saudi campaign to assert leadership over a chaotic region that by mid-2011 seemed to be sinking even deeper into the abyss. Motivated by reasons of regime security, and in order to delegitimize the Bahraini uprising and to deflate any prospects for its expansion, the Saudi state joined the Bahraini royal court in portraying the protests as manifestations of an Iranian export of revolutionary Shiᶜism.[34] Bahrain and Saudi Arabia colluded to frame the Bahraini uprising in decidedly sectarian terms, joined before too long by a host of quasi-academic pundits, all-too-eager clerics, and an assortment of other opinion makers peddling their sectarian views through satellite television, the Internet, and the official media. That Syria's bloody civil war was popularly perceived to be shaping up along the country's sectarian divides, with Iran supporting the Alawite regime and most GCC states supporting the regime's opposition, only lent credence to what soon became a regional framing of foreign policy and security issues along sectarian lines.

Hussein Sirriyeh, the scholar who back in 2000 originally theorized about a "Gulf-advocated conception of Pan-Arabism," was far too sanguine about the shape of things to come. He maintained that the new iteration of pan-Arabism would feature the restoration of Arab solidarity, coordination, and respect for individual Arab states; tolerance of subregional arrangements such as the GCC by the new Arab system; increasing harmonization of the position of Arab states on the Arab-Israeli conflict around the two-state solution; and a realization that "the Arab regional order can be made to work without a hegemonic power that would take it upon itself to establish order."[35] So far, however, the historical record has had a decidedly different account of the new alliance. Just as the pan-Arabism of yesteryear was a cover for Nasserism and the centrality of Egypt to all affairs Arab, the new version, spearheaded by Saudi Arabia, seeks to place the desert kingdom at the center of regional affairs, as the pacesetter for the political life and rhythm of the whole region. In reality, the kingdom's allies are part of this broader coalition out of convenience or compulsion, not genuine belief that the region's salvation lies in Saudi ways. Within the fractured GCC itself, in fact, states have exhibited a decided preference for internationalization over enhanced and deepened regionalization, among themselves fearing Saudi ambitions for hegemony.[36] In 2014 and again in 2017, when fellow GCC member Qatar appeared to be balking at Saudi hegemony, it incurred Riyadh's wrath, in the first instance with a temporary withdrawal of ambassadors, and in the second with a comprehensive boycott of all commercial and diplomatic activities, an air and land blockade, and the expulsion of Qatari citizens from Saudi soil. A list of demands was subsequently presented to Qatar by Saudi Arabia and its three other allies (the UAE, Bahrain, and Egypt). Among others, the demands included the closure of the Al Jazeera network and the severing of diplomatic ties with Iran.

Finally, what there is of a new pan-Arab order has a strong hint of Sunni sectarianism, feeding off of and in turn fueling Syria's civil war, on the one hand, and Iranian rhetoric and intransigence, on the other. It is this strategic competition—one over allies and centered around balance-of-power rivalries—that is at the core of Saudi-Iranian tensions.[37] Sectarianism is only the window dressing through which this strategic rivalry manifests itself. Just as the Bahraini and Saudi states framed Bahrain's national uprising in sectarian, anti-Shia terms, the Syrian and Iranian states presented the Syrian uprising through a sectarian framing. Bahrain and Syria are both pawns in a larger, region-wide strategic rivalry. This strategic rivalry in turn fuels competing sectarian rivalries. There is, indeed, a real and tangible fear of a supposed "Shia crescent" among the region's Sunni rulers. Not surprisingly, developments in Iraq—and more recently in Syria—continue to be seen through sectarian lenses. But such fears rest on flawed assumptions, conflating and confusing strategy with identity as a prime motivator.[38]

All this, ultimately, only deepens and further perpetuates insecurity across the region. Not surprisingly, the Middle East and especially the Persian Gulf are among the most highly securitized—and militarized—regions in the world today, and yet they remain among the most insecure as well. Part of the problem lies in the security dilemma alluded to earlier and elaborated on more fully in chapter 4, as well as in the fondness of regional leaders for bigger and more effective lethal weapons available for purchase from the West.[39] But another side of the coin is that they are looking at the problem of security mostly through a one-dimensional, militarized perspective. There is much more to security than matters of hard power and military defense. That most political leaders the world over, especially Persian Gulf leaders and their patrons in the West, perceive of security in militarized terms does not mean there aren't equally important, nonmilitarized dimensions to the concept as well. It is to an examination of this aspect of the security phenomena that the chapter turns next.

What Security?

Security is about survival, existential threats, and extraordinary measures designed to counter such threats.[40] In this section I argue that without an adequate broadening of the concept of security, its utility in understanding the full range of threats facing the Persian Gulf is limited. I have adopted here most—but not all—of the insights offered by critical security studies, which argues against an exclusive focus on the military dimensions of state behavior and instead calls for greater attention to the individual, the community, the political economy, and notions of identity.[41] Security should not be defined exclusively in terms of the state or its borders. Security is a human condition, with a security issue being one that threatens, or appears to threaten, one's sense of safety.[42] The Copenhagen School of security studies in particular has sought to "widen" the definition of security threats to include nonmilitary dynamics as long as they pose an "existential threat" to a referent object.[43] Instead of relying on conventional notions of security, the Copenhagen School argues, we should be "broadening," "deepening," "extending," and "focusing" conceptions of security.[44]

The conception of security that I adopt here revolves around four specific dimensions: military matters, human security, migration, and state weakness. Persian Gulf security has been, and for the foreseeable future will continue to be, influenced by any one or a combination of threats and challenges that may be rooted in military matters, human insecurity, migration, and state weakness. Critical security studies points to two additional dimensions of security, one of which may be broadly labeled as "emancipation" and the other arising from environmental factors. While in certain contexts issues revolving around the environment and lack of freedom may emerge as serious sources of security threats, in the Persian Gulf region they are either unimportant or ancillary to threats arising from military matters, human insecurity, migration, and state weakness.

Emancipation, it should be noted, is at the heart of critical security studies. This school of thought sees itself as a "discourse of human self creation and the politics of trying to bring it about." It seeks to free "people, as individuals and collectivities, from contingent and structural oppressions."[45] Many proponents of critical security studies view security politics in terms of the transformation of society and the emancipation of individuals from those shackles that impede human development.[46] Emancipation for them has three roles: it serves as a philosophical anchor; it is a strategic process; and it is a guide for tactical goal setting.[47] "Security," its proponents maintain, "is inextricably linked with membership of a political community in which all members respect one another and in which all of them have some say in shaping a form of life that they regard as their own."[48] From a critical perspective, security requires a form of political community in which the only constraints on actors are voluntary, made possible through the establishment of structures that guarantee political participation in dialogic arrangements. "An ideal security community will take the form of an unlimited speech or communication community in which the right to participate in dialogue is possessed by one and all."[49]

While there may be positive connections between security and emancipation, possible co-occurrences need to be critically examined. As Hayward Alker has argued, "culturally sensitive concepts of emancipation should be linked in a posthegemonic way to similarly culturally sensitive, concretely researchable conceptions of existential security."[50] Moreover, the absence of democracy does not translate into a security threat in every case. Especially in extreme cases of rentierism, such as the ones we find in countries such as Qatar, Kuwait, and some of the bigger emirates in the UAE, concerns for democracy do not have the same urgency, or the same ramifications, that they might in other contexts.[51]

In the sense employed here, the threats posed by environmental insecurity are also subsumed under the broader rubric of human security issues or military threats. In general terms, environmental threats to human security are often seen in terms of ozone depletion, global warming, persistent organic pollutants (POPs), and desertification.[52] These and other related security threats posed by environmental factors can be caused by disruptions in the ecosystem, population, and energy and food supplies, as well as by economic problems and civil strife.[53] The Persian Gulf is the location of one of the world's most strategically significant choke points, namely, the Strait of Hormuz, a possible closure of which could lead to major disruptions to commerce, especially to the flow of oil and other commodities in and out of the region. During the Iran-Iraq War, near the end of the hostilities, in April 1988 Iranian forces laid mines near the strait in an effort to close shipping lanes to Iraq and its allies, including Saudi Arabia, Kuwait, and the United States. When a U.S. warship operating in the area was damaged by an Iranian mine, the United States destroyed two Iranian oil rigs and sank eight Iranian ships in what it called Operation Praying Mantis.[54] Any similar future scenarios to close the Strait of Hormuz would have much more drastic military consequences and result in heightened military insecurity, rather than threaten environmental security.

It is this military dimension of security threats, in fact, that has predominated in both the study and the reality of the Persian Gulf's past and present. This builds on a long and rich tradition in the security studies scholarship. Stephen Walt, for example, states emphatically that "security studies may be defined as *the study of the threat, use, and control of military force.*"[55] John Mearsheimer similarly views security in military terms, both in relation to what he sees as "offensive realism"—noting that "the best guarantee of survival is to be a hegemon, because no other state can seriously threaten such a mighty power"[56]—and in terms of "nonoffensive defense," premised on defending one's territory while rejecting any means of invading or attacking others.[57] Power maximization, after all, is a natural goal of states, Mearsheimer maintains, especially for great powers, which are motivated by aspirations of hegemony and dominance over others.[58] For Mearsheimer, and for other realists, the military, in its both defensive and offensive functions, remains elemental to international relations in general and to security studies in particular.

As the examples of naval altercations between Iran and the United States in the 1980s demonstrate, most of the security challenges pervading the Persian Gulf region have been military in nature. The region has witnessed one military conflict after another in the past several decades: the 1980–1988 Iran-Iraq War, the Iraqi invasion and occupation of Kuwait in 1990, military tensions between the United States and Iraq throughout the 1990s and between the United States and Iran in the 2000s, the U.S. invasion and occupation of Iraq in 2003, Iranian-Saudi strategic competition in Syria and elsewhere after 2011, and the Saudi war on Yemen beginning in 2015. There is no reason to believe that the trend toward pervasive military threats all across the Persian Gulf region is about to recede anytime in the near future.

Military threats and geopolitical issues will still continue to shape security challenges worldwide for the foreseeable future. But, especially in the more affluent countries of the West as well as elsewhere, the key security threats are likely to be nonmilitary and revolve around issues such as population movements, pandemics, transboundary pressures, and the like.[59]

"We are currently confronted by a world in transition," writes Graeme Cheeseman, with "new sources of unease and insecurity."[60] New conceptions of security, therefore, revolving especially around issues of human security, are critically important.

There are widely varying interpretations of human security, both in academic discourse and in the policy arena.[61] This is largely because military security is tangible and easily identifiable, whereas human security is not. In broad terms, human security has traditionally included issues of poverty, underdevelopment, hunger, and other assaults on human integrity and potential.[62] While these issues center mostly on financial and economic security, human security is also influenced by developments or phenomena that are not strictly economic, such as the prevalence of crime, the state of healthcare services, poor governance, civil turmoil, and corruption. At the broadest level, therefore, attention to human security means ensuring "the satisfaction of basic material needs of all humankind."[63] In the human security context, the notion of security is then recast as a social construct. As such, insofar as it can constrain liberties and limit individuals, the pursuit of state security can often undermine human security.[64]

Definitions of human security have frequently been criticized as imprecise, overly broad, and opaque. In fact, Roland Paris argues that while there is little policy or academic utility in the concept of human security, it may be useful as a broad *label* to refer to "the safety of societies, groups, and individuals, in contrast to more traditional approaches to security studies that focus on protecting states from external threats."[65] But the nebulous definition and nature of human security do not detract from its universality, or the interdependence of its components. And, given that its focus is on "how people live and breathe," it is easier to achieve through earlier rather than later interventions.[66]

In the context of the Persian Gulf, it would be difficult to argue that the emergence and spread of religious extremism, and its latest manifestation, Daesh, is not an issue of human security. Daesh is indeed a military threat to countries such as Syria and Iraq. But the larger phenomenon it represents, religious extremism, is a fundamental threat to human security in the countries of the Persian Gulf, across the Middle East, and beyond. Daesh may be defeated on the battlefield; no amount of zealous determination can withstand the full force of regional armies and their Western partners. But Daesh's ideology will not, and cannot, be defeated on the battlefield. It is, in fact, only likely to gain strength from its military confrontation with those it regards as infidels.

Less nebulous than human security but very much related to it is the issue of migration. Insofar as threats from migration are concerned, they often revolve more around *perceptions* than around *reality* and can easily spill over into racism and xenophobia.[67] States often fear that refugees who are too many or too poor may overwhelm services and generate local resentment. In addition to apparent strains on existing resources, migration and the preponderance of "migrants can be perceived as a threat to the major societal values of the receiving country."[68]

In the Persian Gulf region, it is not the consequences of migration on resources that is generally viewed as an issue but migration's contribution to the erosion of identity that is seen as an important, though often overlooked, potential threat. Given the considerable political and economic resources deployed by both national and transnational actors to construct national and international identities, identity as a security issue should not be ignored.[69] Not surprisingly, discussions of identity have long been important to conceptions of security.[70] But these discussions are generally focused on extraterritorial threats to one's identity—and are often framed in the form of societal security—rather than on threats to identity from within borders.[71] "Societal security is about large, self-sustaining identity groups."[72] It can also be understood as "identity security."[73] For societal insecurity to emerge, the "we" has to be threatened *in its identity*.[74] Societal insecurity emerges when communities feel threatened in the very identity that defines them as a community. In other words, "societal insecurity exists when communities of whatever kind define a development or potentiality as a threat to their survival as a community."[75]

Traditional discussions of security threats posed by national identity have revolved around issues such as nationalism, minority rights, and ethno-religious conflicts.[76] Of these, as the discussion of sectarianism here makes clear, there are plenty in the Persian Gulf. But much less studied and understood are threats to identities arising from the need to import armies of migrant workers into such small demographics as those found in Qatar and the UAE and even Kuwait, Oman, Saudi Arabia, and Bahrain. Being a very small minority in one's own country, as Emiratis and Qataris are in their countries, is quite unsettling. The feeling of being besieged is often seen as an existential threat, a perceived human security threat of the highest magnitude.

There is a "profound feeling of vulnerability among an important segment of GCC Arabs in the twenty-first century."[77] The flood of expatriates into the GCC states often exacerbates long-felt existential fears about identity. As one observer has noted, "In particular, Gulf Arabs worry that international institutions, the prevalence of the English language, European conceptions of gender, and marriage to expatriates are so influential that they will compel everyone to conform to Western social norms and to abandon the traditions and social practices that define Gulf life. Despite their wealth and their distance from military conflicts in the Middle East, Gulf Arabs often view themselves as unable to combat forces that are altering life in their societies."[78] Not surprisingly, Gulf intellectuals are often "concerned about the possibility of what amounts to national dispossession."[79]

Dubai's developmental model, having deliberately positioned the city into the crosscurrents of globalization, has been especially instrumental in marginalizing the city's local population. The preponderance of expatriates in Dubai has led to the geographic marginalization of Emiratis as they move out of the city center and into the suburbs, as well as their cultural marginalization, in turn prompting the government to take deliberate steps to strengthen Emirati national identity.[80] According to one Emirati intellectual, "[We] fear that we may lose everything that we have built. . . . This feeling comes from the fact that we are a small minority in a city that's full of foreigners. We are very scared."[81] Another writer, Mishaal Al Gergawi, speaks of a deep sense of "melancholy" at a loss of national identity.[82] The same sense of identity loss is pervasive in Qatar. Abdullah Ghanem Albinali Mohannadi, a vocal Qatari writer, often complains in the press about the excessive level of Western cultural content in the country. "Are we really in a Muslim country or one that has been taken over by non-Muslim foreigners?" he asks. "By celebrating Christmas in our streets, we feel like we're in a Christian European country."[83]

Perceptions of being overwhelmed by non-nationals have been further magnified in recent years by the collapse of weak and fragile states in nearby Syria, Iraq, and Yemen. But, especially in the context of the Persian Gulf, where Al Qaeda in the Arabian Peninsula (AQAP) operates with relative impunity in Yemen's broken polity, state collapse is a particularly threatening security challenge. In failed or collapsing states, the state loses its capacity to deliver basic social services, from public schools to traffic control, sanitation services, the provision of security and law enforcement, or employment opportunities. Informal networks, many with criminal or at least extralegal intentions, spring up to fill ensuing vacuums, providing perfect opportunities for warlordism, human trafficking, smuggling, piracy, extremism, and connections with transnational criminal networks.[84] These and other threats abound all around the vicinity of the Persian Gulf region: piracy in Somalia; human trafficking in Afghanistan; risks to public health in Afghanistan, Yemen, Somalia, and elsewhere; and extremism in Yemen, Iraq, and Syria. Given that these security challenges often easily traverse territories and do not always stop at national boundaries, the danger of spillover from security challenges arising out of state weakness is both tangible and real.[85]

As this summary analysis demonstrates, I have adopted a multidimensional approach to the study of security in the Persian Gulf. Building on insights offered by critical security studies—that a full understanding of the range of security threats needs to go beyond state-centered and state-exclusive approaches to security issues[86]—I point to security threats in areas of defense and military matters, as well as in the economic, political, and economic sectors. I agree with Buzan, Waever, and de Wilde that security threats may be military, political, economic, or societal.[87] In the military sector, a security threat is usually posed to the state or, at times, to other military entities. In the economic sector, a security threat is often in the form of bankruptcy or sharp economic declines leading to widespread dislocations and unease. In the political sector a security threat is posed to the sovereignty, or at times the ideology, of the state. Political security is about threats to internal legitimacy or to external recognition. In the societal sector, a security threat is often to "large-scale collective identities that can function independent of the state, such as nations and religions."[88]

In the post-2011 Persian Gulf, there has been a confluence of two sets of different but complementary security challenges. One set of security challenges has been military and diplomatic, rooted in balance-of-power considerations, multiple interstate competitions and tensions, and competing aspirations of regional hegemony and power projection. These challenges are not new to the region and have long featured in the international relations of the Persian Gulf and the larger Middle East. A second, new set of security challenges has largely emerged and spread after the 2011 uprisings. These nonconventional security threats revolve around identity politics in general and sectarianism in particular. Falling under the broad rubric of human security, the widespread growth of sectarian sensitivities across the Persian Gulf has given rise to previously nonexistent social anxieties, and specifically to feelings of "otherness" in the face of pervasive threats of having one's primordial religious identity overrun by hostile "others." This sectarianism is fanned and deepened by complementary political and military developments in and around the region. In the post-2011 era, conventional and nonconventional security challenges in the Persian Gulf, and more broadly in the Middle East, have developed a symbiotic relationship with one another.

Perceived security threats, in whatever domain, lead to "securitization," that is, when something is seen as an existential threat. More specifically, securitization "is constituted by the intersubjective establishment of an existential threat with a saliency sufficient to have substantial political effects."[89] Securitization can be either ad hoc or institutionalized. If a type of threat is recurrent or persistent, then securitization is institutionalized (as in the pervasiveness of migrants and expatriate workers in the GCC). Securitization can be in the form of a spectrum running from nonpoliticized (an issue not being seen as political) to politicized (a matter of public policy) to securitized (seen as an existential threat).[90] "Actors and their audiences securitize certain issues as a specific form of political act" as part of what is "politics of existential threats."[91] As we shall see in the chapters to come, the Persian Gulf is one of the most securitized regions of the world, with securitization pervading most aspects of economic and political life.

Another marked security feature of the Persian Gulf is its interdependent and aggregate nature. Actors act in terms of aggregate security, letting security concerns in one sector color their security definitions in other sectors, adding everything up to come up with one security narrative.[92] Traditional security dynamics often arise from and are located at the regional level. In the Persian Gulf's highly securitized environment, and in light of the pervasive nature of multiple security challenges and threat perceptions, it is small wonder that states feel so besieged.

This sense of besiegement is all the more magnified given that the Persian Gulf region represents a "regional security complex." The Gulf Cooperation Council is the most representative organizational expression of a regional security complex, which may be defined as *"a set of states whose major security perceptions and concerns are so interlinked that their national security problems cannot reasonably be analyzed or resolved apart from one another."*[93] The security perceptions of states within a security complex, and their interactions with each other, shape the internal dynamics and infrastructures of a security complex. There is a considerable amount of security interdependence among actors within the same regional security complex "both to establish them as a linked set and to differentiate them from surrounding security regions."[94]

An example of reinforcing threat perceptions within the same regional security complex would be assumptions across the GCC about the spread and threat of sectarianism after 2011. Almost uniformly, political elites in the GCC view Iraq and Syria through sectarian lenses.[95] But while sectarianism is an ever-present factor, it is only one of the drivers of the international relations of the region.[96] Throughout the GCC, in fact, uneven distribution of wealth is creating pockets of poverty in otherwise wealthy and affluent societies. Large numbers of unskilled and skilled migrant workers dwarf local populations in many countries and give nationals a distinct sense of being small minorities in their own countries. Real or potential challenges arising from human insecurity pervade the political landscape, yet they go unaddressed and often even unnoticed. Very few GCC states, if any of them at all, are in a position to make difficult political decisions in the post-rentier era.[97] The multiple dimensions of security, and the complexities of addressing them, all appear to local policymakers as negligible and marginal as compared with more immediate and more ominous military threats.

I will end this chapter with a note of caution by Gary Sick, a veteran observer of the Persian Gulf. The Middle East and especially the Persian Gulf, he wrote in 2010, exhibit an uncanny predilection toward having "Black Swans," or developments that are "not only surprising but [also have] the capacity to disrupt or severely alter the anticipated course of events." He warns that "the future of the Persian Gulf and the wider Middle East is impossible to discern. But in any serious discussion of strategy, it is imperative to recognize that we are in uncharted waters, beset with Black Swans on all sides. Old formulas will not work and should be regarded with suspicion."[98]

2

The Persian Gulf
Security Architecture

The Persian Gulf region has long been one of the key flashpoints for conflict in the Middle East. The rise of the Islamic State in Iraq and al-Sham (ISIS, or Daesh in Arabic), and the involvement of and consequences for several regional state and nonstate actors in relation to Daesh, is only likely to keep the region as a security flashpoint for the foreseeable future. But even before the rise of Daesh and the effective dismemberment of Syria and Iraq in 2013–2014, the security arrangement that had evolved in the Persian Gulf included several structural features that made the Gulf inherently unstable. In fact, the region's prevailing security arrangement, as it has evolved since the 1980s and is currently in existence, has itself been the cause of much of the region's instability and insecurity. This security arrangement has also been highly unstable as several key actors and components subject to it have set out to challenge its basic premises and its various manifestations. Despite these challenges, thanks largely to the overwhelming power and commitment of the United States, the security arrangement has held. But it has neither made the region secure nor addressed the root causes of Gulf insecurity. Unless this prevailing security architecture fundamentally changes in nature and focus, the Persian Gulf's chronic insecurity and unstable security situation is unlikely to improve anytime soon.

This chapter examines the root causes that underlie the instability of the security architecture that has evolved in the Persian Gulf. The discussion begins with a brief historical overview of this architecture's development, looking specifically at the replacement in the 1980s of a relatively stable, tripolar security arrangement based on a rough balance of power between Iran, Iraq, and Saudi Arabia, with an American-centered architecture. The new architecture, the chapter's next section argues, is inherently unstable and itself a source of chronic insecurity because of four primary reasons. First, America's heavy-handed presence in the region and its multiple "footprints" across the Arabian Peninsula and Iraq are a source of chronic tension and resentment by both state and nonstate actors throughout the region. Second, especially insofar as the southern rim of the Persian Gulf is concerned, the state actors involved feel highly vulnerable to external threats and also conflate regime security with the security of the country. They thus foster, and in turn operate in, highly securitized and unstable national and therefore regional environments. This insecurity is reinforced especially at the regional level by a third development, namely the rise of identity politics across national boundaries. Identity politics has always had a measure of salience across the Middle East in general and the Persian Gulf region in particular. But the 2011 Arab uprisings and the appearance of next-generation Al Qaeda groups such as Daesh have injected new vigor into the appeal of transnational currents and organizations. This appeal would most likely not have been as powerful had it not been for the widespread inattention of state actors to elements of human security—the fourth reason for the instability of the prevailing security architecture. Unless and until these four elements of the region's security arrangement begin to change, the Persian Gulf is likely to remain unstable and insecure.

In the Persian Gulf, local and external actors alike have constantly contested and reshaped geopolitics, therefore undermining the possibility of a collective security arrangement.[1] The distinct regional security complex that has emerged has been driven by three interrelated drivers of change in the Persian Gulf: political economy, conflict, and revolution.[2]

The strategic significance of this regional security complex has been magnified by the region's rich oil resources, which have in turn increased the likelihood of conflict and have made cooperation more difficult.[3] Across the Persian Gulf, oil has configured the national security thinking of state elites and has directed their survival strategies. At the same time, it has also shaped the strategies of outside powers toward the security of the region.[4] All this at a time when parts of the Arabian Peninsula have been emerging as a new center of gravity in the Middle East over the past several decades, with regional actors such as Qatar and the United Arab Emirates becoming new hubs of globalization, seeking to construct global cities, and fostering rapid and fundamental social and infrastructural changes.[5]

In the process, the region's security dynamics have been shaped by a number of interrelated macrotrends. These have included the flows of people, information, and money; the internationalization of the Persian Gulf; continuing dominance of hydrocarbons; and an absence of strong centripetal forces within the states of the Gulf Cooperation Council.[6] The resulting continued strategic importance of the region, coupled with the emergence of Iran as a challenger to U.S. regional interests and objectives, have prompted the United States to take a proactive role in devising and sustaining the security architecture that has come to prevail in the region since the 1980s. That the architecture has been precarious and unstable at best, and that it fosters further insecurity itself, has so far not prompted its primary architects, that is, the United States and its regional allies, to rethink its fundamental premises.

In the sections to come, I begin by sketching the historical evolution of the security architecture that currently prevails in the Persian Gulf, highlighting in particular America's sustained, and over time steadily deepening, attention to and engagement with the region. I argue that the emerging security arrangement, which relies on the United States as an external balancer through overwhelming dependence on U.S. military force projection, is inherently unstable and volatile. At the same time, the arrangement's premise of marginalizing and isolating Iran has prompted the Islamic Republic to try to counter U.S. regional hegemony through expanding its own influence over nonstate allies across the region. Near the end of the Obama administration's tenure in office it appeared as if slight improvements in U.S.-Iranian relations would change, or at least somewhat modify, prevailing regional security arrangements. But those improvements in U.S.-Iranian relations proved ephemeral and were reversed by the Trump administration. The old order was never given a chance to be modified. What we have in the Persian Gulf today is a middle power refusing to abide by the desired regional security arrangements of the world's only superpower. The resulting security arrangement is inherently unstable and volatile.

I further argue that these structural contradictions are compounded by the security architecture's neglect of some key threats and challenges facing the Persian Gulf region. These include the inherent sense of vulnerability by regional actors and a deep, mutual suspicion of other neighbors; the rise in salience and potency of identity politics and intrasocietal sectarian tensions; and an increasing rise in human and resource insecurity, especially insofar as food and water security and demographic imbalances are concerned.

The Evolution of Persian Gulf Security

The contemporary political history of the larger Middle East and the Persian Gulf region within it have featured the uninterrupted interference of extraregional actors for nearly a century now, with the very birth of many of the region's states a product of foreign machinations and map-making.[7] This is largely because Middle Eastern states, especially those in the Persian Gulf, on the whole have been weak hegemons and poor balancers, resulting from the absence of a strong and durable hierarchy, the presence of entrenched and powerful identities, and the pervasiveness of external influences. A number of states in the Middle East have vied for regional leadership at one time or another. Middle Eastern leaders have tried to eclipse one another with promises of spearheading a liberation around the corner, or a milestone of epic proportion here, another one there. But none of the states or the larger-than-life leaders have been able to construct a regional order to their own liking, their aspirations constrained by a combination of their own regional isolation, external dependence, and domestic structural shortcomings.[8] The international relations of the Middle East, therefore, have been routinely shaped and reshaped by multiple, often overlapping and reinforcing local, regional, international, and transnational pressures.

Within and because of this broader context of fluidity and flux, the Persian Gulf has long been especially subject to foreign, particularly American, military presence. In fact, while there have never really been any serious challenges to U.S. hegemony in the Persian Gulf, or in the larger Middle East for that matter, the United States continues to view the region as most threatening to its national security.[9] This overwhelming U.S. attention to and military presence in the region, reinforced by the political and strategic preferences of many local political elites, has resulted in the conflation of notions of regime and national security among most regional states. In turn this has given rise to a dynamic interplay between internal and external forces that have combined to shape the region's modern state system and influenced its domestic political dynamics.[10]

In this respect, the decades of the 1960s and the 1970s were particularly significant in shaping many of the security dynamics that still prevail in today's Persian Gulf. The period of British withdrawal from the region, between 1961 and 1971, presented many of the smaller, emerging states of the Persian Gulf with an existential threat, most feeling abandoned at birth. The end of British hegemony was, in fact, a watershed in the evolution of the Gulf's security structure. In particular, the smaller sheikhdoms of Kuwait, Bahrain, Qatar, and the UAE felt structurally insecure on their own to withstand the territorial ambitions and ideological and political currents emanating from regional capitals such as Riyadh, Baghdad, and Tehran. When promises from the smaller sheikhdoms of financial assistance to underwrite Britain's continued presence and protection failed to have desired results, they searched for an alternate protector. The United States was only too happy to oblige.

Initially, in the early to mid-1970s, the United States was reluctant to get involved in the Persian Gulf's security architecture. Under the auspices of the Nixon Doctrine, the United States preferred instead to rely on a "twin pillars" policy of supporting Iran and Saudi Arabia as the primary bastions and conservators of the regional status quo. This corresponded with a time when a "new pragmatism" marked the foreign policies of a number of Middle Eastern states that now began to see the world through comparatively nonideological lenses. This new pragmatism—born out of "a triumph of realpolitik over vision, and of tactics over strategy"—had three primary causes: doubts and pessimism about the attainability of lofty goals such as Arab unity and the liberation of Palestine, the departure from the scene of old-school politicians and activists who promised deliverance and liberation (but only brought national ruin and dashed hopes), and "emphasis on managerial and technocratic decision-making" in preference over sloganeering and showmanship.[11]

Before long, however, a confluence of events and developments drew the United States deep into Persian Gulf matters in unprecedented ways. First, the signing of the Egyptian-Israeli peace treaty confirmed the United States' "strategic primacy" throughout the Middle East region, especially in the Persian Gulf.[12] Reinforcing this was the overthrow in Iran of the shah and the loss of a trusted ally in January 1979, soon followed by the storming of the U.S. embassy in Tehran the following November, the Soviet invasion of Afghanistan a month later, and Iraq's invasion of Iran in September 1980. It was during these multiple crises that President Jimmy Carter outlined what came to be known as the Carter Doctrine:

> Let our position be absolutely clear: An attempt by any outside force to gain control of the Persian Gulf region will be regarded as an assault on the vital interests of the United States of America, and such an assault will be repelled by any means necessary, including military force.[13]

The 1980s saw a deepening of American military, economic, and diplomatic ties with the Persian Gulf. As the decade wore on, this gave rise to a new security architecture that relied overwhelmingly on increasingly direct American military involvement in the region. In this evolving security arrangement, it was at first America's regional allies that played the most prominent military role. Beginning in 1981, in reaction to the Iranian Revolution and the Iran-Iraq War, the Saudis were able to consolidate their position as the leading power within the Arabian Peninsula thanks largely to almost unqualified military and political support from the United States. Similarly, Iraq capitalized on U.S.-Iranian tensions in order to receive American military assistance and billions of dollars' worth of aid from its pro–United States, regional allies. At the same time, the development of expansive, bilateral economic and military ties between the United States and the smaller oil monarchies afforded the latter a measure of maneuverability in relation to both the Saudis and the Iraqis.[14] These ties expanded dramatically in the second half of the 1980s. As late as 1986, in fact, the U.S. military presence in the Persian Gulf was still not substantial. The "tanker war" that started in 1987, however, and then Iraq's invasion of Kuwait in 1990 changed all that, substantially increasing America's direct military presence in the region. This occurred especially after the U.S.-led ejection of Iraq from Kuwait was accomplished the following year.

The end of the Cold War in the waning years of the 1980s did not fundamentally alter the security arrangement in the Persian Gulf, especially insofar as the nature and intensity of U.S. attention to, and therefore direct involvement in, the region was concerned. If anything, "the end of the Cold War actually encouraged the subsystem's anarchical tendencies and intensified its dynamism."[15] To preserve its regional and global interests amid the reigning anarchy, the United States had already assumed a direct military role in the region beginning in the late 1980s.[16] If anything changed it was the intensity and size of this American involvement, ranging from several hundred thousand troops at the height of the occupation of Iraq to several tens of thousands during peacetime.

As in the previous decades, region-wide developments were not unimportant in shaping the nature and extent of America's involvement in the Persian Gulf. Of particular importance was the continued fragmentation of the Middle East's once-focused system in the post–Cold War period, leaving regional actors unable to forge a common strategic position on their own on such core security issues as extremism and the role and policies of the United States. "The region seems rudderless," Louise Fawcett wrote in the 2000s, "without an obvious core."[17] In fact, there was very little cooperation and alliance-making across the region anchored in institutional arrangements, trade, and security, "no longer perhaps even a core community of shared ideals."[18]

Developments in the decade of the 2000s, and now especially during the post-2011 period, have only made the once-fragmented system chaotic and ill at ease with itself. These include the emergence and increasing potency of nonstate actors (Al Qaeda and Daesh), civil wars in Libya and Syria, the de facto partition of countries such Syria and Iraq, chronic instability in Yemen, and increased tensions among regional actors for influence and leverage. Recent decades have witnessed a dissolution of "relatively regular and intense patterns of interactions, recognized internally and externally as a distinctive arena," once identifiable at the Middle East system level.[19] Instead, there has been a proliferation of "regional security complexes," of which the Persian Gulf constitutes a distinctive one.

One of the main developments that was emblematic of the emergence of this regional security complex was the establishment in 1981 of the Gulf Cooperation Council. According to the GCC's own statement of objectives, "while, on one hand, the GCC is a continuation, evolution and institutionalisation of old prevailing realities, it is, on the other, a practical answer to the challenges of security and economic development in the area."[20] In fact, the GCC was born out of a "sense of deep unease" with the security situation in the Gulf region. But from the very beginning of its formation, the GCC suffered from a lack of internal cohesion and the suspicion of the smaller sheikhdoms toward the intentions of Saudi Arabia.[21] This lack of cohesion, and the corresponding inability to articulate a common set of region-wide security objectives, further facilitated, and from Washington's perspective necessitated, the United States' deepening role in the region's security architecture.

In addition to increased military commitments to its regional allies, one of the primary reasons for America's deepening involvement in Gulf security in the 1990s was the policy of President Bill Clinton's administration of "dual containment" toward Iran and Iraq, designed to isolate both countries regionally, cut them off from world trading and economic systems, and encourage wholesale regime change in Iraq and, somewhat more modestly, regime behavior change in Iran. But, as Gregory Gause argued at the time, the policy's implementation was highly problematic, and it offered "no guidelines for dealing with change in the gulf and it tie[d] American policy to an inherently unstable regional status quo." Worst yet, "the policy could end up encouraging the very results, regional conflict and increased Iranian power, that the United States seeks to prevent."[22] Gause's prediction turned prophetic a decade later when the United States invaded and occupied Iraq under the George W. Bush administration's banner of the "global war on terror" and under the pretext of dismantling Iraq's weapons of mass destruction.

Up until that point, the Persian Gulf had been something of a tripolar regional system, with Iran, Iraq, and Saudi Arabia each constituting one of the poles.[23] The U.S. invasion of Iraq, however, destroyed a system that had assumed a measure of stability through its own balance-of-power dynamics. The emergent security arrangement is highly volatile and unstable. As Gause observes, "Unlike the three-cornered structure of Gulf international relations" that had prevailed before the U.S. invasion of Iraq, "this new disposition does not appear to be at all stable."[24] This instability was—and remains—rooted in several developments, some of the most important of which include the eruption of centrifugal forces tearing apart Iraq's collapsing state, the scramble by Iran to preempt an American attack by leveraging its influence over allied nonstate actors in Afghanistan and Iraq, and an unprecedented arms race entailing the proliferation of military forces up and down the Persian Gulf meant to contain possible spillovers from the Iraq war.

After the 2003 regime change in Iraq, Saudi Arabia and Iran became the Persian Gulf's dominant local powers, jockeying for position and dominance in the Levant and the Arab-Israeli conflict and competing both locally and beyond the region.[25] In the contest between the two for greater regional influence, the Saudis enjoyed the near-unqualified support of the United States and Western allies. More generally, the purchasing of billions of dollars' worth of weaponry from the West propelled the region's arms race into new, unprecedented heights (table 2.1).[26] In the process, by virtue of being the main anchor for the West's diplomatic, economic, and military presence in the Persian Gulf, Riyadh emerged as a real force to be reckoned with.[27] For its part, a sanctions-ridden Iran boosted its own domestic arms production and cultivated ties with local nonstate actors, especially the Lebanese Hezbollah, the Palestinian Hamas, and the Mahdi Army militia in Iraq, in addition, of course, to close ties with the Shia-led central government in Baghdad. Unconfirmed rumors also reported Iranian influence over the Houthis in Yemen.

This is the security predicament in which the Persian Gulf finds itself today. We can detect four broad trends in the evolution of the prevailing security arrangement in the Gulf. First, there has been a steady deepening of U.S. predominance in the Gulf's security arrangement, either directly through the stationing of forces or indirectly through arms sales and various forms of military-military cooperation. In addition to the United States' pursuit of its own strategic objectives in the region, U.S. policy in

TABLE 2.1 Military personnel and expenditures in the Persian Gulf

	Military expenditure (% of GDP)[a]	Military expenditure (% of central government expenditure)[b]	Military expenditure (current USD)[c]	Military expenditure 2005–2015 aggregate (current USD)[d]	Armed forces personnel, total (2014)[c]	Armed forces personnel (% of total labor force) (2014)[f]	Arms imports (1990 $ millions) (2015)[g]	Arms imports 2005–2015 aggregate (1990 $)[h]
Iraq	2015—7.3%	2014—16.2%	2015—12.9 billion	56.1 billion	209,000	2.4%	1215	5.3 billion
Iran	2014—2.3%	2009—15.4%	2015—9.2 billion	53.3 billion	563,000	2.1%	13	1.3 billion
KSA	2015—13.5%	NA	2015—87.2 billion	565.7 billion	251,500	2.1%	3161	12.7 billion
Bahrain	2015—4.6%	2011—16%	2014—1.4 billion	10.6 billion	19,460	2.6%	10	403 million (excluding 2009)
Qatar	2010—1.5%	2010—8.0%	2010—1.9 billion	10.4 billion (2004–2010 only)	11,800	0.7%	655	1.6 billion (2009–2015 only)
Kuwait	2014—3.7%	2012—10.7%	2014—5.6 billion	47.2 billion (2004–2014 only)	22,600	1.1%	366	1.7 billion
UAE	2014—5.7%	2014—144.9%	2014—22.8 billion	156.5 billion (2004–2014 only)	63,000	1.0%	1289	12.4 billion
Oman	2015—14.2%	2013—42.9%	2015—9.9 billion	77.5 billion	47,000	2.1%	148	2.2 billion
Yemen	2014—4.0%	1999—23.9%	2014—1.5 billion	11.6 billion (2004–2014 only)	20,000	0.3%	12	846 million

[a] http://data.worldbank.org/indicator/MS.MIL.XPND.GD.ZS/countries/AE-YE-IQ-IR-SA?display=graph
[b] http://data.worldbank.org/indicator/MS.MIL.XPND.ZS/countries/AE-YE-IQ-IR-SA?display=graph
[c] http://data.worldbank.org/indicator/MS.MIL.XPND.CN/countries/1W-IR?display=default (29/1/2017 rates used)
[d] http://data.worldbank.org/indicator/MS.MIL.XPND.CN/countries/1W-IR?display=default (29/1/2017 rates used)
[e] http://data.worldbank.org/indicator/MS.MIL.TOTL.P1?display=default
[f] http://data.worldbank.org/indicator/MS.MIL.TOTL.TF.ZS?display=default
[g] http://wdi.worldbank.org/table/5.7
[h] http://databank.worldbank.org/data/reports.aspx?source=2&series=MS.MIL.XPND.GD.ZS,MS.MIL.XPND.ZS,MS.MIL.TOTL.P1,MS.MIL.TOTL.TF.ZS,MS.MIL.XPRT.KD,MS.MIL.MPRT.KD

the Persian Gulf has been shaped by the conduct of local actors.[28] As I will argue in the following section, whatever the causes of this predominant role, its consequences have actually eroded the region's security and have made the Gulf more unstable.

Second, beginning with the eruption of the Iran-Iraq War in 1980 and reinforced through additional, successive conflicts, regional actors have sought the support and protection of outside, more powerful patrons. Except for Iran, whose nuclear program and support for nonstate actors made it a pariah in the West, and Qatar, which opted for a policy of hedging, regional actors sought shelter in the security embrace of more powerful, invariably Western, patrons, choosing to bandwagon with the United States and its primary regional ally, Saudi Arabia.[29] The unpredictable and intense nature of each violent eruption fed unilateralist tendencies among regional actors and further undermined the prospect for comprehensive and meaningful cooperation among the more powerful states, especially Iran and Saudi Arabia.

This has fed into a third development. The domestic insecurity and political paranoia of the region's various authoritarian regimes have prompted them to become increasingly more reliant on their security apparatus and the military for staying in power. Insecurity has bred militarism at home and belligerence abroad, perpetuating a regional security arrangement that, despite its own inherent instability, is intimately tied to equally tenuous political systems across the region. This has resulted in the development of a new form of security dilemma: politically insecure regimes maintaining a structurally unstable regional security arrangement. Any sudden shift in one is likely to have ripple effects in the other.

Reinforcing the other three trends has been a fourth one, the proliferation and increasing potency of various nonstate actors, some of which are directly or indirectly supported and sustained by states—the Hezbollah, Hamas, and the Houthis being prime examples—and some seeking to supplant and replace existing states altogether, with Al Qaeda and Daesh being the most deadly ones.[30] So far, as of 2018, none of these groups have been a direct (counter)force in the security architecture of the Persian Gulf basin. But they have nonetheless jolted central governments near and far, with Baghdad and Sanaa most directly threatened insofar as the Gulf's security is concerned. Which way Daesh's future will go is, at this point, anyone's guess. What is certain is that Daesh and similar groups pose a danger to regional security that is not easily countered, never mind being completely discounted.

The Insecurity of the Persian Gulf's Security Arrangement

Combined together, the trends in the evolution of the Persian Gulf's security architecture have in turn fostered four distinct but interrelated sources of regional insecurity. These sources of regional insecurity include, first and foremost, the consequences of the heavy-handed military presence of the United States as, ironically, the region's biggest and most powerful security provider; the structural weaknesses of many authoritarian states in the region; the reinforcing role of identity politics; and the challenges and threats posed by human insecurity. Each of these threats have been magnified in recent decades because of the spread of globalization and information technology, the increasing internationalization of the Persian Gulf, uneven rates of depletion of hydrocarbon resources, and the continuing weakness of internal consensus within the GCC.[31] As Kristian Coates Ulrichsen has correctly observed, "Each individual problem feeds off the others and acts as a threat multiplier that has assumed interregional and international dimensions and constitutes the most urgent security challenge to the stability of the Arabian Peninsula."[32]

The American Factor

In the period soon after the advent of the Iranian Revolution and the Soviet invasion of Afghanistan, and capped by Iraq's invasion and occupation of Kuwait, the United States decided that instead of reliance on regional allies to guarantee its own security interests and those of the Persian Gulf, it would directly station forces and military hardware in the region. Since then, beginning especially in the early 1990s, the United States has developed a comprehensive military and security strategy for the Gulf, the primary components of which include "a militarily focused counterproliferation approach based upon a flexible mix of deterrence, coercive diplomacy, global military superiority, and the preventive or preemptive use of military force."[33] This approach to regional security is subsumed under "a grander global vision of spreading liberal democracy and preventing the rise of a strategic competitor" at the regional level, whether that competition may be ideological, technological, or military.[34] At its height, in 2009, U.S. forces in the Persian Gulf numbered no less than 230,000, drawing down to 50,000 by 2014, still quite substantial by any measure.[35]

After 9/11, buoyed by global unipolarity, the United States sought to remake the region's domestic and regional arrangements.[36] Even though highly selective and careful not to upset America's authoritarian allies, the administration of President George W. Bush adopted "imposed democracy as a central plank of US's security strategy in the Gulf."[37] This selective imposition of democracy on the Middle East, at least in rhetoric if not in substance, led to a significant strengthening of conservative and radical forces across the Muslim world, including and especially in the Persian Gulf.[38]

Not surprisingly, the Obama administration soon abandoned the democracy-imposition drive and reverted back to efforts aimed at bolstering regional allies (i.e., the GCC) and undermining competitors through isolation and marginalization (i.e., Iran). In the words of Obama's former secretary of defense Chuck Hagel, the United States views the GCC as "an anchor for regional stability."[39] As such, according to the U.S. Defense Department, "U.S. policy will emphasize Gulf security, in collaboration with Gulf Cooperation Council countries when appropriate, to prevent Iran's development of a nuclear weapon capability and counter its destabilizing policies. The United States will do this while standing up for Israel's security and a comprehensive Middle East peace. *To support these objectives, the United States will continue to place a premium on U.S. and allied military presence in—and support of—partner nations in and around this region.*"[40]

Despite its massive commitment of personnel and resources, U.S. strategy in the Persian Gulf "has failed to reach all the primary goals enunciated by its supporters."[41] In fact, far from having its intended consequences, U.S. policy has actually had negative security implications for the region, the reasons for which fall into three interrelated categories. The first has to do with the United States' tendency to overestimate its ability as an external balancer to unilaterally organize the Gulf's security architecture. Although this is done in collaboration with regional allies, these allies tend to be small and treat their own military capabilities as if they are nonexistent.[42] The United States has been content to shoulder the overwhelming bulk, if not the entirety, of the commitments to its conception of Gulf security. As Robert Johnson observed some time ago, "while it has a role to play in the Gulf, the United States cannot play the role the British played in the colonial era. No nation can play that role anymore because the game in the Gulf has changed. It is much less the politico-military game of the colonial and immediate post-colonial past than it is a politico-economic game. As recent experience suggests, there may be a role for U.S. force, but it will be quite limited."[43]

The existing security arrangement in the Persian Gulf depends on the United States' commitment to wage large-scale and dangerous wars and to maintain a massive military presence in the region, despite local ambivalence to it.[44] As early as the late 1980s, however, observers were arguing that in relation to the Persian Gulf, "a rapid deployment force capable of large-scale intervention on the ground is very unlikely to be useful in dealing with either the more probable or the more unlikely threats" the region faces.[45] As an external security guarantor for the Persian Gulf, the United States has sought to have peace in the region either through complete "victory" and unchallenged hegemony over the various regional forces or through fostering a rough balance of power among regional actors. More commonly, it has pursued what amounts to a combination of both strategies. Regardless of whichever element has been more dominant, the resulting strategy has created not security but, rather, insecurity.[46]

A second problem associated with the U.S. security strategy in the Persian Gulf arises from the challenges inherent in the United States' role as an external balancer. Although political elites in the Arab states of the Gulf want the United States to remain an external balancer, "popular support within the region for continuing this arrangement simply does not exist."[47] Ironically, the current U.S.-dominated security system poses threats to the U.S. forces and bases located in the region, as well as to local allies, and even exposes the U.S. territory to threats posed by weapons of mass destruction.[48] More specifically, while the United States may enjoy "command of the commons"—sea, space, and air—it has far less leverage in "contested zones," which Barry Posen defines as "arenas of conventional combat where weak adversaries have a good chance of doing real damage to U.S. forces."[49] In these contested zones, as in Iraq for example, weak adversaries can inflict damage to U.S. forces because for them the stakes are higher, they have home-court advantage, their forces are more numerous, and they have weapons that may be simple but can still kill and inflict damage.[50]

A third source of insecurity arising from the U.S.-engineered security architecture has to do with U.S. efforts at excluding Iran from any regional security arrangements, despite the country's 1,100 mile (1,800 km) border with the Persian Gulf. The United States and Iran do not see a role for each other in the Persian Gulf.[51] As a result, the region's security arrangement has been organized on the basis of realpolitik but without the precondition for success, that is, the ability to find balance or general acceptance of the status quo.[52] The United States is relying on a risky and costly strategy that depends on Saudi Arabia, the weakest of the three local powers, the other two having either been effectively militarily neutralized (Iraq) or internationally isolated (Iran).[53] Since Iran is unwilling to relegate its own security or the security of the Persian Gulf to the United States and the latter's regional allies, the region remains at best prone to outbreaks of tension and at worst exposed to the possibility of accidental or even intentional military conflict. As far back as 1979, when Iran was in the throes of revolutionary upheaval, scholars argued that the country could not be ignored or isolated as far as the security of the Gulf was concerned.[54] But zero-sum and bunker mentalities continue to characterize the assumptions of most regional actors, especially in Iran, Saudi Arabia, the United States, and Israel. The result has been a security dialogue of the deaf, leading to the emergence of what Anoushiravan Ehteshami sees as an unstable—and dangerous—multipolarity in the Persian Gulf.[55]

Fragile Polities

In addition to the security threats arising from the pervasiveness of the U.S. military presence, the Persian Gulf faces the challenge of the inherent fragility of regional states. The security threat emanating from weak and fragile political systems is twofold. First, most regional states are institutionally weak, their political stability overwhelmingly, if not entirely, dependent on their continued ability to use oil revenues to generate and sustain legitimacy among social actors. The resulting authoritarian rentierism remains structurally vulnerable to internal and external economic or political shocks.[56] Moreover, nearby weak states that have already collapsed (Afghanistan and Iraq) or have been on the verge of collapse (Syria and Yemen) have served as fertile incubators for extremist groups such as Al Qaeda and Daesh, further aggravating the fragility of vulnerable, highly securitized states.

Not all threats necessarily come from the outside. As the Iranian Revolution demonstrated, the sources of domestic conflict in the Persian Gulf region are often far more pressing and more powerful than anticipated.[57] Across the Gulf, threats are as political as they are military.[58] While authoritarian states are structurally vulnerable to violent overthrow, over the course of the past several decades, in fact, a number of domestic and external security threats have converged to become especially threatening to the security of Persian Gulf states. They include, most notably, the emergence of Islamist oppositional movements and their spread through the use of information and communication technology.

In response, regional states initiated a number of cosmetic domestic political reforms in the early 2000s in order to undermine oppositional tendencies within their societies.[59] In fact, as Michael Kraig has observed, "the greatest danger in the Gulf is not a nuclear Iran or the traditional threat of conventional invasion, but rather internal socioeconomic and political changes that might be increasingly difficult for leaders to direct or control. Regionally, the greatest threat is not strategic WMD attacks, but Saudi fragmentation and weakening of the central state, Iraqi civil war and dissolution, and growing radicalism via violent forms of politicized Islam in Gulf Arab states—including increased levels of transnational violence and terrorism."[60] Equally threatening are vast swathes of "ungoverned" areas in Yemen that are outside the control of the central government.[61]

Threats to regime security have been magnified by the Internet, the proliferation of satellite television, and the widespread availability of social media.[62] Even more threatening is the danger posed by Daesh, particularly to Saudi Arabia, not just in the group's carrying out terrorist activities inside the kingdom but also, more ominously, in its attracting sympathizers to its cause. Ethan Bueno de Mesquita's research in this regard is instructive. According to de Mesquita's analysis of aggregate public opinion data from a number of Muslim majority countries, "the strongest correlates of support for terrorism were respondents' attitudes toward the United States as a threat to Islam and respondents' views of the role of Islam in politics." Perceptions of the existence of a threat to Islam are one of the main correlates of support for terrorism, and "among the possible threats to Islam, the perception of the United States as a threat to Islam was the largest correlate." Along the same lines, "among those who perceive there to be significant threats to Islam, those who believe the United States and the West pose such a threat are more likely to support terrorism." And, "those who view the United States as a threat are more likely to be strong supporters of terrorism."[63]

The postcolonial states of the Persian Gulf have endured three wars and, in the process, within each state a genuine attachment to national symbols has emerged. But this seeming durability and resilience mask several existing and latent fault lines that link internal security to regional and international events. Across the Arabian Peninsula, Ulrichsen claims, "security is fragile and based on a transient stability linked to the possession of substantial reserves of hydrocarbons."[64] But current levels of welfare spending across the GCC are not sustainable, and these states cannot buy off opposition groups and impulses in society in the post-oil future. In these oil monarchies, the younger generation is unable to relate to and comprehend a post-oil era.

The current, structural dependence on resources as a primary means of guaranteeing domestic stability and security has made regional states inherently fragile, causing them to be particularly vulnerable to exogenous, regional shocks.[65] This largely accounts for Saudi Arabia's hasty reactions to the uprisings in Bahrain in 1994 and again in 2011. This in turn has heightened regional weariness over chronic instability and the possible disintegration of central authority in Yemen, and the emergence of Syria after 2011 as one of the most important geopolitical battlegrounds between the various regional and extraregional actors. Because regime security is a central factor in determining foreign policy across the Persian Gulf, we have seen the "articulation of security in zero-sum, instead of collective or even cooperative, terms."[66]

Identity Politics

Partly arising from and in turn compounding this fragility is the rise of identity politics across the Persian Gulf in the post-Iraq invasion period. Identity has long been an important feature of the international relations of the Middle East, its importance, both among the popular classes and political actors, having been increasingly magnified through a series of successive events dating back to the Iranian revolution of 1979. The regional reverberations of the Iranian Revolution were framed more and more in sectarian terms by neighboring conservative, Sunni kingdoms that hoped to contain and defeat the Islamic Republic through their support of Saddam Hussein and his war effort against Iran.

In the meanwhile, within regional states, nonstate religious, ethnic, and linguistic identities began to have greater salience and appeal among populations who found themselves steadily more alienated from and disenchanted with the state and the official identities it promoted. As official narratives and discourses began to lose their efficacy as instruments of political rule and legitimacy, alternative, nonstate identities—many of which have deep commonalities across national boundaries—became more widespread among the urban middle classes.[67] Resort to political repression at home in turn deepened the appeal of extremist, transnational ideologies based on sectarian identities, facilitated by the spread and availability of satellite television channels and other means of communications technology. The introduction of the Internet in Saudi Arabia in 1999, as a case in point, played a central role in the spread of jihadist propaganda across the kingdom.[68] As de Mesquita's research demonstrates, "people who support a strong role for Islam in politics are more likely to also support terrorism. . . . [And] people who perceive Islam to play a large role in the politics of their home country also seem to be slightly more likely to support terrorism."[69]

The transnational rise in identity politics was compounded by developments within the Iraqi political landscape after 2003, which saw the rise and increasing hold on power by the country's once-repressed Shia majority, along with assumptions about Iran's assistance to and influence within the Iraqi Shia population.[70] Baghdad's fall also increased tensions, both locally and regionally, among the Sunnis and the Shia. Although it has little validity in historical fact, it was around this time that the theory of a "Shia crescent" running from Iran through Iraq and eastern Saudi Arabia and Lebanon gained popularity among the conservative, Sunni sheikhdoms of the Persian Gulf, who saw their domestic legitimacy and hold on power threatened by a rising tide of Shia empowerment.[71] Compounding fears of an ominous Shia tide after 2003 were the 2011 uprisings in countries such as Syria and Bahrain, whose preexisting sectarian divides had only been masked through authoritarianism. However, political upheavals brought these divides to the surface both at the street level and among political elites.

Identity has long played an important role in the international relations of the Middle East, and transnational identities continue to have particular salience in the Persian Gulf region, especially in the post-2003 and post-2011 periods.[72] It was, in many ways, with the Bahraini uprising—initially led mostly by the disaffected Shia who were nonetheless largely secularist—that the current sectarianization of regional politics began. This would be a sectarianism "by political instrumentalization of latent social group divisions, foreign military intervention, and unwitting entanglement by local forces in the broader regional competition for influence between Saudi Arabia and Iran."[73]

The appearance and uncompromising Sunni sectarianism of Daesh in Iraq and Syria, and political and military successes on the ground among Yemen's once-repressed Shia Houthis, have only reinforced the perceived and actual threats of sectarian and transnational identities across the region. These transnational identities give access to other populations by national leaders and are therefore perceived as threats by local political elites.[74] As Toby Matthiesen has demonstrated in specific relation to Bahrain and Saudi Arabia, sectarianism "was encouraged by sectarian identity entrepreneurs, namely people who used sectarian identity politics to bolster their own positions. . . . sectarianism was not just a government invention but the result of an amalgam of political, religious, social, and economic elites who all used sectarianism to further their personal aims."[75]

Human Insecurity

A fourth set of security challenges confronting the Persian Gulf may be clustered under the rubric of human security. These threats to human security can be divided into two broad categories of insecurity: resources and demographics. Resource insecurity refers to insufficient supplies of water and food across the Arabian Peninsula. Despite their location in one of the world's most arid regions, countries such as Kuwait, Qatar, and the UAE tend to have some of the highest per capita rates of water and energy usage in the world. According to World Bank data, of the world's top-ten energy consumers per capita, exactly half are located in the Arabian Peninsula (Qatar, Kuwait, Bahrain, the UAE, and Oman), with Qatar ranking as the world's second-highest energy user per capita in 2012 (17,419 kg of oil equivalent per capita) behind Iceland (18,755).[76]

The picture is even more bleak in relation to water usage, with Qatar having one of the world's highest per capita water consumption levels at around

500 liters a day.[77] Across the GCC, average renewable water resources are only 92 m³ per capita per annum (pcpa), whereas average consumption is at 816 m³ pcpa. Not surprisingly, on average 58 percent of the total water consumed in the GCC comes from desalination plants, ranging from a high of 79 percent in Bahrain to 14 percent in Saudi Arabia.[78] As part of the social contract, regional states keep water costs artificially low, with an average 92 percent gap between water costs and revenues across the region.[79] According to a 2014 study, on a per capita basis water consumption in the GCC is approximately 65 percent higher than the world average.[80]

Neither water scarcity nor steady increases in its consumption are likely to change in the foreseeable future. Throughout the GCC, in fact, domestic water demand is expected to double by 2025, while industrial water usage is estimated to triple in the same period.[81] Moreover, in order to perpetuate their legitimacy, the GCC states will continue to fund expensive and environmentally unfriendly programs and projects meant for the entertainment of their nationals, only deepening the environmental stresses with which they will have to contend in the future.

Based on almost purely political considerations, all the GCC states have made decisions to develop their own domestic agricultural production despite the fact that they can import food supplies far more cheaply. A staggering 85 percent of the groundwater in the GCC states is used for food production.[82] Not surprisingly, the GCC's ecological footprint is significantly higher than the global average, with the UAE having the world's largest per capita ecological footprint.

Increasing food insecurity is another major threat facing the states of the Persian Gulf, particularly the countries of the GCC, where the size of arable land available for agriculture ranges from a low of 0.1 percent in Oman to at most 2.9 percent in Bahrain.[83] Meanwhile, the total annual demand for food commodities is estimated to triple between 2010 and 2050, with annual demand for meat, for example, going from $4 billion in 2010 to just under $14 billion in 2050.[84] Throughout the region, governments spend hundreds of millions of dollars every year on food subsidies, reaching as high as $2.3 billion a year in Iraq (in 2009), $1.2 billion a year in Kuwait (in 2011), and $1.1 billion a year in Saudi Arabia (in 2010).[85] Still, according to a joint study by the United Nations Economic and Social Commission for Western Asia (ESCWA) and the International Food Policy Research Institute (IFPRI), at least one-fifth of the people in

Bahrain, Oman, Qatar, and Saudi Arabia consider themselves food insecure, and, despite astonishing levels of wealth across the region, childhood malnutrition persists within the GCC.[86]

The various policy responses that have been instituted in reaction to food inflation and regional unrest in 2007–2008 and 2011–2012—mostly in the form of expansive government price subsidies and substantial salary increases for state employees—are only likely to aggravate levels of food insecurity in the long term. For the time being, at least in the Arab states of the Gulf, the uninterrupted flow of oil and gas revenues into state coffers has enabled political elites to ameliorate most of the negative repercussions of their states' structural food insecurity. But their ability to continue doing so in the post-oil era is open to serious question.

Another element of human insecurity in the Persian Gulf, one that is unique to the region, arises out of vast demographic imbalances between national and non-national residents throughout the GCC states. Across the Arabian Peninsula, non-nationals constitute significant portions of the total population, ranging from extremes of 88.5 and 85.7 percentages in the UAE and Qatar, respectively, to a low of 32.4 percent in Saudi Arabia (table 2.2). In at least four of the six GCC states, nationals are minorities in their own countries.

TABLE 2.2 National and non-national populations in the GCC

Country	Total population	Percentage nationals	Percentage non-nationals
Bahrain	1,377,000 (2015)	48.9	51.1
Kuwait	3,892,000 (2015)	31.2	68.8
Oman	4,491,000 (2015)	56.3	43.7
Qatar	2,597,453 (2016)	11.5	88.5
Saudi Arabia	31,540,000 (2015)	67.3	32.7
UAE	9,157,000 (2015)	14.8	85.2
Total	49,551,653	51.5	48.5

Note: Data ranges between years 2014 and 2015.

Source: Data collected from United Nations, http://esa.un.org/unpd/wpp/Download/Standard/Population/; Gulf Labor Markets and Migration, Gulf Research Center, http://gulfmigration.eu/gcc-total-population-and-percentage-of-nationals-and-non-nationals-in-gcc-countries-latest-national-statistics-2010-2014/; and, Qatar Ministry of Development Planning and Statistics, http://www.mdps.gov.qa/en/statistics1/StatisticsSite/Pages/Population.aspx.

Not surprisingly, especially in cities such as Doha, Abu Dhabi, and Dubai, where the national population can be as low as 10 percent of the total, nationals often feel besieged and marginalized in their own countries. Despite the segregation of large proportions of migrant worker populations employed in the construction and services industries, the cultures of Western expatriates often predominate in most aspects and areas of social life.[87] Urban spaces, and even private domains, reflect the cultural preferences of the city's planners and architects, armies of whom are imported from the West. Despite robust heritage industries across the GCC and concerted efforts by each GCC state to foster and deepen processes of nation building, the realities of life in places such as Qatar and the emirates of Dubai and Abu Dhabi bear little resemblance to the national image being crafted and promoted by the state. English is the default lingua franca of daily life, necessary for conducting the most routine of daily transactions.

Sentiments decrying the erosion of national identity and the marginalization of cultural norms and values are not uncommon. Parents often deeply resent the fact that their children are far more fluent in English than in Arabic. Especially among intellectuals and the learned elite, there is a pervasive sense of unease and discomfort at what appears to be wholesale abandonment of all things local and traditional in favor of ways and means imported from abroad. The state's compensatory efforts—such as sponsorship of traditional falconry shows, patronage of national museums, and construction of grand mosques—only go so far in allaying perceptions of national cultures being eroded or altogether abandoned.

Only rarely do these sentiments of unease and resentment make it to the surface, kept in check by pervasive state authoritarianism across the GCC. In a 2012 tract published in Beirut, Qatari intellectual Ali Khalifa Al Kuwari called the "population imbalance" of his country "the most serious and pressing challenge in need of radical reform and the most deserving."

> If Qataris are unable to apply pressure to halt this growing imbalance and begin gradual reform, their natural position at the head of society will fall away and they will be rendered incapable of reforming the other and newer problems. Indeed, they will be transformed into a deprived and marginalised minority in their own land.
>
> The perpetuation of this growing imbalance threatens to uproot Qatari society, to erase its identity and culture, to take its mother tongue,

Arabic, out of circulation, and erode the role of its citizens in owning and running their own country. Local citizens constitute the leaders and administrators in every other country in the world, particularly in the public administration.[88]

Prior to 2011, the topic was also widely discussed in the UAE, at times in terms of "sharp criticism of the government's lack of seriousness in attending to the demographic nightmare in the country" and the impending "national suicide."[89] Despite its significance, much of the discussion, in both Qatar and the UAE, was at best ignored and at worst soon stifled by the state. The emboldening consequences of the 2011 uprisings in North Africa and in places such as Oman, Bahrain, and Saudi Arabia were met by reinvigorated authoritarianism and severe—in Bahrain and Saudi Arabia, brutal—crackdown by the authorities.[90] Today, what "chatter" on the topic does exist is overwhelmingly expressed in private gatherings—in the *diwaniyya* or *majlis*—or, on rare occasions, in social media, on microblogs, Twitter, and Facebook.

As in the case of food and water insecurity, GCC states, particularly those flush with oversized hydrocarbon revenues and cash reserves, have had little reasons to attend to the social, economic, cultural, and political consequences of their countries' demographic imbalances. For now, states have employed a combination of public policy and economic tools to ameliorate the discomforting consequences of having ever-shrinking national populations. These have included segregating low-skilled foreign workers from the rest of the population as much as possible, patronizing heritage industries and deepening efforts at nation building, and bestowing official largesse on the national population in order to further ensure its dependence on state patronage. Again, the sustainability of these efforts in the post-oil era, and the state's ability to contain the consequences of demographic insecurity at that time, are questionable.

Since the 1970s, the security architecture of the Persian Gulf has been increasingly shaped and influenced by the global as well as regional strategic considerations and objectives of the United States. As it has currently evolved, this security architecture contains two fundamental flaws. First, through and because of its overwhelming reliance on the U.S. military's large-scale presence in the region, the security architecture itself is, paradoxically, cause for much insecurity in the Persian Gulf and beyond. Not only has the prevailing security arrangement not made the Persian Gulf more secure than it would otherwise have been; it has, in fact, caused much domestic and regional insecurity across the strategic waterway, throughout the Arabian Peninsula, and beyond.

The basic premise of this American-engineered security arrangement has rested on a zero-sum assumption in which the United States and its GCC allies have assumed for themselves the exclusive role of acting as the Persian Gulf's security providers. Iran, in their eyes a source of regional instability, is seen to have no part to play in this security arrangement, its eleven-hundred-mile border with the Persian Gulf seemingly not a factor in its threat perceptions or its strategic calculations. The ensuing name-calling between Tehran on the one side and Washington and its regional allies on the other has only brought added tensions, mistrust, and the potential for at least an accidental eruption of hostilities. If the successful negotiations between Iran and the so-called P5+1 over the Islamic Republic's nuclear program were one day to extend to a substantive security dialogue, a win-win scenario might emerge that would significantly reduce tensions in the region and enhance its security. For now, such a possibility seems highly unlikely.

A second, related flaw in the prevailing Persian Gulf security architecture is its neglect of some of the more subtle but nonetheless salient security challenges the region faces. These include the inherent, structural fragility of existing polities across the region, especially in the Arabian Peninsula; the growing salience of identity politics and the spread of transnational, extrastate actors and identities and loyalties; and issues related to human security, especially connected to food and water security and popular perceptions of cultural identity erosion and unease over being a minority in one's own country. So far, the continued flow of oil and gas revenues into state coffers, and the robustness of the rentier social contract, have alleviated the need for serious attention to these and other related threats to domestic and regional security. Perhaps the good times will last indefinitely. But they are just as likely not to. Once the oil runs out and the revenues dry up, or at least decline precipitously, these salient security challenges will no longer be able to be ignored. At that point, the very foundations of the Persian Gulf's security architecture will be bound to change. Or, alternatively, the region's regimes are likely to.

3

THE BELLIGERENTS

Over the past several decades, the Persian Gulf has been home to a confluence of several complementary, overlapping, and mutually reinforcing
developments, of which two have been particularly consequential for the
current ordering of the regional architecture. One development has revolved around the evolving self-perceptions of regional actors in terms
of their own importance in global affairs and their influence both in their
immediate vicinity and in the broader Middle East. A number of Middle
Eastern states have come to see themselves as global middle powers, with
expansive aspirations of increased regional influence and power projection capacities. These goals and aspirations have often differed and have
brought the states into direct and at times open conflict.

A second, complementary development has been the growth of identity and sectarian politics across the region. Beginning especially with the
Arab Spring, sectarianism was deliberately employed, chiefly by Saudi
Arabia and Bahrain, as a useful tool for justifying domestic and, particularly, foreign policy pursuits. But the instrumentalization of sectarianism

tapped into and built on its own innate resonance among marginalized city dwellers for whom the uprisings had reawakened deeply held resentments against pervasive political inequality, elite corruption, and institutional weakness.[1] Before too long, sectarianism had grown in scale and scope, also influencing policymakers for whom domestic sensibilities and pressures could not be ignored.

This chapter examines the foreign policies of six key actors in the Persian Gulf in light of middle power rivalries and sectarian tensions. The actors include Iran and Saudi Arabia, which the chapter argues are today perhaps the Middle East's most significant middle powers, in addition to Turkey, of course. There are two other states in the area with aspirations of being middle powers, Qatar and the United Arab Emirates, despite their small geographic size and equally small populations. Even if Qatar and the UAE cannot be conceptually perceived as anything other than small states, their foreign policy behavior, buttressed on the two states' significant wealth, resembles middle power behavior more than anything else. A fifth actor includes the Gulf Cooperation Council, which in its own right as a multilateral, cooperative security and economic organization has been somewhat consequential in the international politics of the Persian Gulf. I will make the case here that while its individual members have indeed shaped and greatly influenced regional politics, several structural features have undermined the efficacy and objectives of the GCC as a multilateral organization. A last actor to consider is the United States, which is neither a middle power nor necessarily a sectarian actor, and not for that matter a part of the region. But no analysis of the international politics of the Persian Gulf, or that of the larger Middle East, is complete without reference to American policies toward and presence in the region.

In the pages to come, I argue that preferences by individual policymakers have combined with a number of structural dynamics to result in often aggressive and outright belligerent foreign policy outcomes. The United States, Iran, and Saudi Arabia each has different, at times sharply conflicting, ambitions—Iran wants to be the dominant power in Iraq and the Levant; Saudi Arabia regards Iranian aspirations as threatening to its own interests and objectives and at the same time has hegemonic aspirations of its own in the Persian Gulf and the Arabian Peninsula; and the United States, the only global superpower, seeks to contain and neutralize Iran and to ensure that the other regional actors remain within the U.S.

sphere of influence. Not to be left behind, the UAE has also embarked on a significant military buildup over the past decade or so, joining forces with Saudi Arabia out of convenience, to counter growing Iranian confidence and influence and to also ensure that its own interests are protected. Over time, the UAE, Saudi Arabia, and Qatar have had tensions with one another also, each at different times using its financial prowess to influence regional politics.

The outcome has been a region filled with tension and insecurity arising from diametrically opposing or at least conflicting foreign policies. Not surprisingly, the regional actors have often been at odds, at best coming together mostly in temporary alliances during moments of necessity and crisis. Before analyzing these foreign policies and their consequences, I will briefly examine middle power rivalries and sectarian impulses in the region.

Sectarianism and Middle Powers Rivalries

The roots of middle power rivalry in the region can in many ways be traced to the regional consequences of Iran's 1978–1979 revolution, which radically redrew the security maps of both the Persian Gulf and the Middle East. The ensuing Iran-Iraq War heralded the start of deep, systemic insecurities across the region at the same time as enabling leaders in Baghdad and Tehran, and later in Riyadh, to view themselves as the rightful protectors of an ideal regional order to be imposed on all others.

This roughly coincided with the time that Egypt, that other historic protector of the Middle East regional order, was experiencing precipitous marginalization throughout the region and economic and political decay at home. The trend toward middle power rivalry continued into the 1990s, but increasingly without Iraq, whose ill-fated invasion of Kuwait in 1990 had resulted in its de facto partition and the central government's inability to project power in the northern and southern parts of the country, never mind beyond its borders. But Riyadh and Tehran continued apace with assumptions of their growing importance and power, Tehran because of developments in Afghanistan and Iraq and its own internal reconstruction, and Riyadh because of its deepening special relationship with the United States and the European Union. Increasingly, the two regional actors saw themselves as global middle powers, not quite powerful enough to project power globally but still with enough clout and influence to shape and influence regional outcomes. Two aspiring regional hegemons with relative geographic proximity, vastly different worldviews, and conflicting goals and objectives—the outcome was hardly conducive to regional stability.

This was the predicament in which the Persian Gulf region entered the twenty-first century. Although by now reintegrated back into the Arab fold, Egypt's aged kleptocracy had gotten the better of the country's leading position in the Middle East. Iraq for its part was now deep into a civil war that even an American troop surge could not unwind, and the other potential regional powers—Algeria, Libya, and Syria—were too immersed in domestic problems to be able to meaningfully project any power beyond their own borders. The one true middle power in the region, Turkey, was focused westward, at this point willing to give far-reaching concessions to become a member of the European Union. Left standing were Iran and Saudi Arabia, each with its own aspirations. And biting at their heels were two new upstarts, Qatar and the UAE, also with different aspirations, unwilling to accept that their small geographic and demographic size undermined their prospects of becoming middle powers.

The century's first decade ended with a whimper for the region's states and a rare bang for social movements, beginning in North Africa and then spreading to the Levant. Tunisia led the way, its spontaneous revolution soon spreading to Egypt, Libya, Syria, and Bahrain. True to form, the regional heavyweights left standing busily sought to capitalize on the instability they witnessed around them, ensuring that their interests were not harmed and were at least preserved. Turkey saw the Arab Spring as its moment in history, a time to add "the Turkish model" to its arsenal of soft power for the likes of Egypt and Tunisia to emulate.[2] Qatar also saw the uprisings as an opportunity, not to become a model of sorts but to use its financial and economic prowess to turn yesterday's powerhouses into dependencies.[3] For Iran and Saudi Arabia, the Arab Spring played even more defining roles. Since Syria offered Iran ready logistical access to Hezbollah, the Syrian civil war and the possible overthrow of Assad represented a threat to Iran's ability at strategic deterrence against Israel. For Iran, as chapter 4 argues, the loss of Assadism was not an option.

For Saudi Arabia, however, the possibility of Assad's fall offered the prospects of expanding its own sphere of influence and in the process curtailing Iran's. Moreover, with the Arab Spring now threatening the monarchy next door in Bahrain, the Saudis could simply not afford to sit idly by and let events take their own course. The Saudis believed Bahrain's nascent revolution needed to be crushed before it spread any further. The uprising needed to be fought on two levels, one military and the other ideological. Militarily, in March 2011 a combined force of Saudi and Emirati troops entered Bahrain and effectively put down the uprising. Ideologically, the Bahraini and Saudi states, and to a lesser extent that of the UAE, set out to debunk and debase the rebellion by portraying it as a Shia disturbance guided and directed by Tehran.

The uprising was presented by the monarchies of Bahrain and Saudi Arabia not as the outcome of the social marginalization of Bahrain's populations or the monarchy's political despotism but as the result of machinations by Iran. Evidence by an independent commission to the contrary, the Islamic Republic was presented to domestic and international audiences as the chief culprit behind the popular uprising, an aggressor unable to do away with old habits and instead increasingly meddling in internal Bahraini affairs.[4] Thus began the process whereby national identity in general and sectarianism in particular were securitized. The sectarian framing of the uprisings and the securitization of identity may have started for purely instrumental purposes in Saudi Arabia and Bahrain, but, fueled by complementary developments in Syria, Iraq, and elsewhere, they soon developed a self-reinforcing momentum of their own.

Scholars have already masterfully studied the spread of sectarianism in the Persian Gulf.[5] I will only briefly mention here its evolving consequences for the region's international relations. Beginning with Bahrain and Saudi Arabia and reinforced by the twists and turns of the Arab Spring, social norms and identities in the Middle East and in the Gulf region have undergone changes. The post–World War II rallying cries of Palestine, Israel, and the West are no longer as resonant with "the Arab street" as they once were prior to 2011. Instead, what animates both the public and policymakers appears to be issues such as legitimate forms of rule and splits along fault lines such as Sunni versus Shia, Muslim Brotherhood versus Salafi, and Islamist versus secularist lines.[6]

The current Sunni-Shia divide, which has come to feature so prominently in the international relations of the region, can be best understood through what may be called an instrumentalist approach, whereby it is in the interest of leading regional actors to prop up sectarian divides—as Saudi Arabia has done by presenting the Syrian civil war as a manifestation of a deep and innate Sunni-Shia conflict.[7] At the same time, it is no longer just the political leaders who seek to advance a sectarian narrative for purposes of enhancing their own legitimacy. Many civil society organizations and clerics are just as vocal and convinced of the validity of sectarian perspectives on domestic politics and international affairs. Religious identities can be produced and securitized while still taking the character of the religious referent seriously. In the larger Middle East and especially in the Gulf region, multiple leaders are engaged in securitizing identity and religion at multiple levels—from Daesh fighters calling for jihad to Sunni and Shia clerics seeing an existential threat to their identity, to political leaders seeking to secure and further their own and their countries' interests.[8]

The combination of middle power rivalry and sectarianism, especially among two regional powers in close proximity, has proved destabilizing for the Persian Gulf region. Here I borrow the conceptualization of middle powers by Barry Buzan and Ole Waever, who propose a three-tiered scheme for the classification of states in the international system: superpowers and great powers at the systems level, and regional (or middle) powers at the regional level. Superpowers have "broad-spectrum capabilities exercised across the whole of the international system," including first-class militaries, economic capabilities, and the political reach to exercise their powers. Great powers have "the clear economic, military, and political potential to bid for superpower status in the short or medium term." As for regional powers, "their capabilities loom large in their regions but do not register much in a broad-spectrum way at the global level. Higher-level powers respond to them as if their influence and capability were mainly relevant to the securitisation processes of a particular region."[9]

Although they are economically and technologically dependent on other core states, and need to diversify their economies out of necessity, middle powers can on their own resist domination by the great global powers.[10] Middle powers may be therefore defined as those "countries that are neither at the apex nor the bottom of the international power structure. They are not so powerful as to be able to exert decisive influence on major issues of international security and economy. Nor are they so powerless as to be unable to protect themselves from the undesirable impacts of other countries' actions. They have considerable resources and capabilities, but are not dominant in international relations."[11]

Middle powers may be dominant regionally, but at the global level they are still subject to influence by globally dominant powers.[12] Much of the literature on "rising" or regional middle powers has focused on their role in and relationship with global governance institutions.[13] But in the developing world the greatest significance of middle powers is often at the regional level and is frequently felt within their immediate vicinity. Middle powers often explicitly challenge the hegemony of established, great powers, not so much at the global level but more specifically, and more immediately, within the regions in which they are located.[14]

Ian Lustick has traced the absence of great powers in the Middle East, and by implication the inverse prevalence of middle powers, to historical patterns through which state-building processes in the region have unfolded. Lustick argues that European state-building—the development of the state, its expansion, consolidation, war-making, victories, defeats, or its contraction and disappearance—occurred in an atmosphere of "moderated but violent disorder." In the Middle East, extraregional powers and international norms were consequential in the region's political development, or lack thereof. "The League of Nations," for example, "stood for nothing more than the European state system, which had, in any case, long since emerged as the decisive force in Middle Eastern political affairs."[15] By the time Middle Eastern states were being formed, the system of colonial domination and externally enforced norms to which they were subjected did not allow cross-border wars to change the number, size, and internal regimes of states. According to Lustick, *"These historical sequence-linked differences in the geopolitical context of European and Middle Eastern state system development constitute not the only but the single most important explanation for the contemporary absence of a Middle Eastern great power."*[16]

International dynamics were, and no doubt continue to be, of great significance in preventing the emergence of great powers in the Middle East. But also important, perhaps equally so, have been limitations on demography and agriculture. Following the breakup of the Ottoman Empire, none of the countries of the Middle East have had the human resources or the agricultural base needed to emerge as a great power. The natural resource that has brought them riches—oil—is by nature perishable and finite. In fact, in the process of developing their oil wealth, these countries have undermined and eroded their agricultural capabilities, and therefore their ability to feed themselves and others with a resource that can be replenished. More consequentially, oil wealth has ushered in an "institutions curse," whereby oil revenues can undermine the efficacy and development of institutions and cause political stasis.[17] Iran and Saudi Arabia, the Persian Gulf's two middle powers, also have human resources that are miniscule compared with those of Russia, the United States, and China. And, regardless of the policies or alliances they pursue, neither Iran nor Saudi Arabia has the potential of the likes of India or Brazil to emerge as a great power.

The absence of a regional great power opened up space for those from the outside to enter and try to shape the region's global orientation. Rich natural resource endowments only exponentially deepened the Gulf's strategic importance. First Britain and then the United States became outside hegemons in the Persian Gulf, Britain through direct and later indirect rule over many regional states, and, in the post-independence era, the United States through heavy reliance on its military might. As long as all littoral states acquiesced to the American presence, which was initially largely through proxies anyway, tensions were minimal. But with the Iranian Revolution, conditions changed and the American military presence in the Persian Gulf was no longer uniformly welcomed by all local stakeholders. Thus began a new phase of regional tensions and insecurity, with the United States and its regional allies on the one side, and Iran, and for a time, also Iraq, on the other.

The United States

As the Iranian Revolution was unfolding in the 1970s, the United States was still relying on the Nixon Doctrine's "twin pillars" policy of employing Iran and Saudi Arabia as "America's surrogates" in the region. While twin pillars relied more extensively on Iran, which was the presumptive "gendarme" of the Persian Gulf, the policy's goal was to bring the Middle East's largest repository of oil and one of the largest militaries, Saudi Arabia and Iran, respectively, into the American orbit, underpinned by U.S. weaponry.[18] The revolution naturally changed the strategic and military calculations of the United States and its regional allies. The United States first replaced Iran with Iraq as the recipient of its logistical, military, and diplomatic support during the Iran-Iraq War. But when Iraq proved an unreliable ally, the United States itself became more involved in the region through its military sales to its allies and the stationing of its own troops and hardware across the Arabian Peninsula and the Persian Gulf. Having been an offshore balancer in the region since the 1970s, the United States began to rely also on its preponderant military presence in the Persian Gulf in order to influence regional outcomes.[19]

It was beginning in the 1990s that the United States became deeply enmeshed in the Persian Gulf's regional security order.[20] As late as 1986, the U.S. military presence in the Persian Gulf was not substantial. But the 1987 tanker war and Iraq's invasion of Kuwait in 1990 drew the United States into the region more directly, and the U.S. military presence in the Persian Gulf only expanded after the 1990–1991 Gulf War ended. In October 1991, the United States and Bahrain signed a ten-year bilateral defense cooperation agreement. In October 2011, as the Bahraini state was busily suppressing internal dissidents, instead of renewing the agreement at an embarrassing time, its terms were secretly amended to include another five years, to 2016.[21] Throughout, tensions with Iran continued, and American policymakers frequently reminded their Iranian counterparts that "all options remained on the table" and that at any time the United States might unleash the full force of its formidable arsenal on the Islamic Republic and its intransigent leaders. In the meantime, as the Iranian leadership doggedly refused to change course in its pursuit of a nuclear program, the United States, both unilaterally and in cooperation with its allies in the European Union and the United Nations, spearheaded the imposition of ever more stringent and more punishing international economic and commercial sanctions on Iran.[22]

The administrations of Ronald Reagan, Bill Clinton, and George W. Bush did not change the essence of U.S. policy toward Iran and the rest of the region, a trend that continued well into President Obama's second term in office. The United States continued to perceive Iran as a threat to Gulf security, and containing "the Iranian threat" was seen by Washington as a central pillar of its global leadership. Both on its own and in cooperation with its European and especially also its regional allies, the United States sought to counter the influence of Iran's expanding, and increasingly more effective, missile program. One way of doing so was through strengthening the American military presence in the area. By 2015, there was a U.S. military force numbering no less than thirty-five thousand stationed in the Persian Gulf region.[23]

In light of broader U.S. military objectives, the emphasis on American military might was unabated. As the U.S. Defense Department stated,

> U.S. policy will emphasize Gulf security, in collaboration with Gulf Cooperation Council countries when appropriate, to prevent Iran's development of a nuclear weapon capability and counter its destabilizing policies. The United States will do this while standing up for Israel's security and a comprehensive Middle East peace. *To support these objectives, the United States will continue to place a premium on U.S. and allied military presence in— and support of—partner nations in and around this region.*[24]

The Pentagon continued: "*Whenever possible, we will develop innovative, low-cost, and small-footprint approaches to achieve our security objectives,* relying on exercises, rotational presence, and advisory capabilities."[25]

The U.S. military's bluster notwithstanding, Obama felt stung by George W. Bush's misadventures in Afghanistan and Iraq. As the journalist Jeffrey Goldberg rightly maintained near the end of Obama's tenure in office, the American president "was not looking for new dragons to slay. And he was particularly mindful of promising victory in conflicts he believed to be unwinnable."[26] In fact, the withdrawal of U.S. forces from Iraq was an early priority for the Obama administration.[27] Nevertheless, for Obama three types of threat warranted U.S. military action: the threat of Al Qaeda; threats to Israel; and the threat of a nuclear-armed Iran.[28] These perceived threats were not that different from the perceptions of previous administrations toward the Persian Gulf and the broader Middle East. Like his predecessors, Obama believed that "very little is accomplished in international affairs without U.S. leadership."[29] This had given rise over time to a widespread assumption among American policymakers that any changes to the security arrangement of the Persian Gulf could and should be stage-managed by Washington.[30] That the assumption is fundamentally flawed did little to lessen its hold on the logic of American policymakers, or that of regional leaders for that matter.

If reelected, U.S. presidents usually have a freer hand in their second term to pursue foreign policy objectives that may not have widespread popularity among domestic voters and even allies. For President Obama, the U.S. role in the Middle East has always been fraught and complicated. The Obama administration had had a vision of reducing U.S. political involvement in the Middle East, including in the Persian Gulf. Obama came to office wanting to extricate the United States from ongoing wars and to avoid involvement in new ones.[31] More fundamentally, he sought to rebalance and "rightsize" the American presence there by reducing both material presence and diplomatic restraint. The opportunity came with the Arab Spring, which Obama saw as a historic moment that could put an end to the Middle East's "toxic structure."[32]

Historic as it may have been, the Arab Spring made the Middle East's structure even more toxic. Now in his second term, however, and with the added impetus of thinking about his long-term legacy, Obama set out to tackle the U.S. tension with Iran over the Islamic Republic's nuclear program. What followed was a diplomatic marathon, conducted in secret first in Muscat and then alternating between Geneva and Vienna, in which diplomats from Iran, the United States, China, Russia, and the European Union huddled and haggled, threatened and cajoled, and eventually, after many weeks, reached a landmark deal. Historic as it initially was, however, the nuclear deal did not change much. Soon after Donald Trump's assumption of office, in fact, U.S.-Iranian tensions, both in rhetoric and in action, reverted back to pre-Obama days.

The nuclear deal with Iran was limited in scope to the Islamic Republic's *nuclear program*, as a result of which there was a *partial* lifting of international sanctions on Iran and the country's slow—very slow—reintegration back into the global economy. The nuclear agreement was not, and in the near future is unlikely to be, a prelude to close or even tension-free relations between the Islamic Republic and the United States. As articulated by Susan Rice, President Obama's national security adviser, "The Iran deal was never primarily about trying to open a new era of relations between the U.S. and Iran. . . . It was far more pragmatic and minimalist. The aim was very simply to make a dangerous country substantially less dangerous. No one had any expectation that Iran would be a more benign actor."[33]

Both sides have consistently downplayed the role of the nuclear agreement as a potential game changer in the security arrangement of the

Persian Gulf. Nevertheless, if oil supplies are generally secure, and if a modus vivendi of sorts with Iran is reached, then the need for the U.S. presence in the Persian Gulf may gradually decline.[34] For a time, in fact, it seemed as if a new strategic reality was shaping up in which the U.S. strategic presence in the Persian Gulf might have been lessening.[35] But such assumptions were laid to rest with the coming to office of the Trump administration, many of whose key figures, including Secretary of Defense James Mattis and CIA Director Mike Pompeo, are well known for their consistently hard line against Iran.

The deal with Iran was the culmination of what came to be called "the Obama Doctrine." Insofar as the Persian Gulf is concerned, President Obama sought to reduce regional tensions and avoided what he saw as the adventurism of the Bush administration.[36] In an effort to reduce regional tensions, especially as the Saudi leadership became increasingly alarmed over Iran's apparent reintegration into the international community following the conclusion of the nuclear deal, President Obama began encouraging the Saudis to enter into dialogue with the Islamic Republic. In an April 2016 interview, Obama urged the Saudis to share the Middle East with Iran: "The competition between the Saudis and the Iranians—which has helped to feed proxy wars and chaos in Syria and Iraq and Yemen—requires us to say to our friends as well as to the Iranians that they need to find an effective way to share the neighborhood and institute some sort of cold peace."[37]

Another aspect of the doctrine was "burden sharing," especially as a way to partner with regional actors to fight terrorism.[38] This was notably the case in the Obama administration's approach to Saudi Arabia. As noted by Jeffrey Goldberg, a reporter who observed him closely for a number of months, Obama was "clearly irritated that foreign-policy orthodoxy compels him to treat Saudi Arabia as an ally."[39] Claiming that "free riders aggravate me," Obama was keen to get other countries to take action on their own rather than wait for the United States to take the lead.[40] Beginning in 2013 and 2014, in fact, the United States actively sought to give substance to the joint missile defense system for the GCC as a way of enhancing the organization's self-reliance.[41]

In a deliberate contrast with George W. Bush's forward-leaning and bellicose unilateralism, when U.S. military action proved unavoidable, Obama demonstrated a penchant for assembling multinational coalitions in which the United States played an equal or even supporting role instead of taking the lead. A presidential adviser called the policy "leading from behind," a feature that came to be one of the defining premises of the Obama Doctrine. As a senior American diplomat explained, Obama "will put together a coalition, and he will try to keep them out front. . . . It will still be an American fight, but it will look less like one, and that's actually a strength. People will be less worried that it's a slippery slope if he's in charge because he's reluctant to be where he is."[42] Leading from behind stood for coalition building and assuming to be equal to other members of the coalition; those accustomed to America taking a global leadership role saw it as a sign of declining American power.[43]

"Leading from behind" came into being in the wake of the multinational effort to overthrow the truculent Muammar Qaddafi from power in 2011. But its most consequential application for the Persian Gulf can be attributed to the American reluctance to delve head-on into the Syrian civil war. Mindful of the American quagmire in Iraq, and keenly aware that Syria was no Libya and that the Assad regime would not be dislodged without a massive commitment of American troops and ground forces, Obama sought instead to combine relatively moderate military pressure on the Assad regime with spirited efforts at diplomacy and local and regional armed involvement. In the process, however, such seemingly hesitant policy ran contrary to widespread expectations of U.S. power, in turn triggering outsized fears among U.S. allies with vested interests in the overthrow of the Assad regime.[44]

Obama's doctrine may have had internal logical consistency, but the American president failed to effectively communicate his vision to policymakers and to publics in the Middle East and elsewhere. Although the president and top U.S. diplomats said all the right things and sent the right signals to their intended audiences, the message that was received in friendly Middle Eastern capitals was one of America's steady departure, or at least drifting attention, away from the region. Especially in relation to the Middle East, the United States neither provided security guarantees nor restrained or even guided its allies in such hotspots as Syria, Libya, and Yemen. According to the scholar Marc Lynch, in the post–Arab Spring era, many of the assumptions by regional leaders toward Obama's policy in the Middle East were informed by the U.S. administration's policies in Syria.[45] What the president must have seen as prudent, his detractors, including in Riyadh, saw as indecision and weakness.

In response to the Obama Doctrine and his perceived "weakness," in fact, the Saudis went so far as to offer their own version of the "Salman Doctrine," named after King Salman. One Saudi observer defined the doctrine thusly:

> The Saudi leadership believes that Assad must be removed from Syria; that Iran's regional and nuclear ambitions must be denied; that the Shia militias of Iraq, Syria, Lebanon and Yemen are terrorist groups and must be destroyed; that the world needs to recognize a Palestinian state; and every global effort must be made to defeat ISIS and Al Qaeda. At the center of many of these doctrinal differences is the Saudi assertion that Iran is at the root of numerous security problems now plaguing the Middle East. Obama's assertion that Saudi Arabia should "share" the region with Iran is patently absurd, given Tehran's vast and unending support for terrorism.[46]

Rhetoric is one thing; concrete policy steps are quite another. And the musings of a president about to leave office, no matter how reflective of his wishes, are even less translatable into action. If the United States were indeed about to reduce the depth and breadth of its military engagement with and commitment to the Persian Gulf, the empirical signs on the ground of such a development were nonexistent. As is demonstrated in chapter 4, the Arab states of the Gulf, accustomed since the late 1970s to benefiting from U.S.-Iranian tensions, mistook the signing of the nuclear deal as a signal of America's lessening commitment to their military and political security and a victory for Iran in which zero-sum games have become the norm. Quite to the contrary, in fact, the 2015 *National Military Strategy of the United States*, prepared by the U.S. Joint Chiefs of Staff, reiterated the centrality of the Persian Gulf region to the U.S.'s regional and global strategic calculations. "In the Middle East," it states, "we remain fully committed to Israel's security and Qualitative Military Edge. We also are helping other vital partners in that region increase their defenses, including Jordan, Saudi Arabia, Kuwait, Qatar, Bahrain, UAE, Egypt, and Pakistan."[47] In light of the United States' multi-billion-dollar arms sales to the states of the GCC, U.S. efforts to ensure Israel's Qualitative Military Edge and the security of its Gulf allies only perpetuates the region's arms race, especially in relation to Iran, thus further deepening a region-wide security dilemma for the multiple actors involved.

Not surprisingly, practically all the Arab states of the Gulf welcomed Obama's departure from office and his replacement with Donald Trump. Almost as soon as presidential elections results in the United States were announced, voices from inside the region began disparaging Obama's foreign policy as an "unmitigated disaster" and a "resounding failure."[48] Within months of Trump's assuming office, he was visited by the Saudi Deputy Crown Prince Mohammed bin Salman, who hailed the "historical turning point" in U.S.-Saudi relations during the new administration.[49] In a radical departure from past practice, President Trump's first official trip outside the United States was to Saudi Arabia, signaling a renewed commitment to strengthening relations between the two countries.

It was during this Riyadh trip in May 2017 where Trump appears to have outlined what may be shaping up as a Trump Doctrine. In a speech to the assembled leaders, the U.S. president enunciated the tenets of his foreign policy approach to the Middle East and the Persian Gulf. Giving it the label "Principled Realism," Trump outlined a balance-of-power vision of regional politics (realism) in which the primary yardstick for relations with the United States is a government's position toward Islamic extremism and terrorism (principle). The struggle against extremism and groups such as Daesh—what Trump called "the battle between Good and Evil"—is the organizing principle of contemporary regional politics.

America is committed to adjusting our strategies to meet evolving threats and new facts. We will discard those strategies that have not worked— and will apply new approaches informed by experience and judgment. We are adopting a Principled Realism, rooted in common values and shared interests.

Our friends will never question our support, and our enemies will never doubt our determination. Our partnerships will advance security through stability, not through radical disruption. We will make decisions based on real-world outcomes—not inflexible ideology. We will be guided by the lessons of experience, not the confines of rigid thinking. And, wherever possible, we will seek gradual reforms—not sudden intervention.

We must seek partners, not perfection—and to make allies of all who share our goals. . . .

Muslim nations must be willing to take on the burden, if we are going to defeat terrorism and send its wicked ideology into oblivion.

The first task in this joint effort is for your nations to deny all territory to the foot soldiers of evil. Every country in the region has an absolute duty to ensure that terrorists find no sanctuary on their soil.[50]

In Trump's vision of Middle East politics, two states have taken the lead in fighting extremism, one being the United States' perennial ally Israel and the other, somewhat of a latecomer to the fold, Saudi Arabia. As such, both deserve American support in order to be better equipped in their fight against terrorism. In the case of Saudi Arabia, which the president praised for having made huge strides in fighting terrorism, this support comes in the form of massive arms sales.[51]

Trump's effusive praise for Saudi Arabia and other American allies was matched by scorn for Iran:

From Lebanon to Iraq to Yemen, Iran funds, arms, and trains terrorists, militias, and other extremist groups that spread destruction and chaos across the region. For decades, Iran has fueled the fires of sectarian conflict and terror. . . .

Until the Iranian regime is willing to be a partner for peace, all nations of conscience must work together to isolate Iran, deny it funding for terrorism, and pray for the day when the Iranian people have the just and righteous government they deserve.[52]

Principled Realism does not seem to offer anything radically different from what previous American administrations have followed in relation to the Middle East. In line with Donald Trump's "America first" domestic policy, Principled Realism appears to privilege ties with countries whose foreign policies align closely with those of the United States as long as they actively combat terrorism, regardless of their domestic human rights records. In his speech, the U.S. president identified two principal threats to American interests: Daesh and Iran. Countries opposed to these two "forces of evil" will receive American military support; more accurately, they will be allowed to purchase American military equipment. All others will be chastised and castigated.

Iran

Since the 1978–1979 revolution, in light of its conflicts with the United States and tensions with the United States' regional allies, Iran's foreign and security policies in relation to the Persian Gulf have been nearly indistinguishable. In fact, at least when it comes to the Persian Gulf, the security and military dimensions of Iranian foreign policy have often outweighed diplomatic considerations. This securitization of Iran's Persian Gulf policy has been a product of the region's pervasive security dilemma. As will be demonstrated in chapter 4, regional actors are stuck in a vicious cycle in which they feel increasingly threatened by the arms buildup and foreign policy bellicosity around them. In the process of enhancing their own security, they increase the insecurity of others, who then engage in an arms buildup of their own. And the cycle continues. Iran's foreign and security policies have been one of the primary factors in the securitization of the Persian Gulf as a whole and the intractable nature of the region's security dilemma.

Whatever its origins, the Persian Gulf's security dilemma persists to this day. Insofar as the Islamic Republic is concerned, the decades from the 1980s to the 2000s witnessed the development of an American-led and orchestrated "asymmetrical military balance against Iran" in the region that became progressively more pronounced as the years and decades wore on, with the Arab states of the area, especially the UAE and Saudi Arabia, embarking on ever-expansive arms buildups.[53] While the acrimonious rhetoric of Washington and Tehran may have somewhat softened after the signing of the nuclear agreement, serious security issues continued to sow distrust between the two. Even as President Obama sought to find ways of improving relations with Iran over specific issues, he repeatedly reminded Tehran's leaders that for the United States "all options," including the possibility of a military attack on Iran, remained on the table. It was subsequently discovered that these warnings represented more than mere posturing and betrayed the real possibility that Iran might indeed have been attacked by the United States.[54]

This was based on the U.S. military's assessment of the threat Tehran posed to American interests. According to an unclassified 2014 U.S. Defense Department report,

> Iran's covert activities appear to be continuing unabated in countries such as Syria and Iraq. Despite Iran's public denials, for example, other information suggests Iran is increasingly involved, along with Lebanese Hizballah, in the Syria conflict. The Islamic Revolutionary Guard Corps-Qods Force (IRGC-QF) remains a key tool of Iran's foreign policy and power projection, in Syria and beyond. IRGC-QF has continued efforts to improve its access within foreign countries and its ability to conduct terrorist attacks.

Nevertheless, the report asserted that

> Iran's military doctrine is defensive. It is designed to deter an attack, survive an initial strike, retaliate against an aggressor, and force a diplomatic solution to hostilities while avoiding any concessions that challenge its core interests. Of note, Tehran's strategic messaging about its military capabilities through the mass media has been less strident since Ruhani [sic] took office. For example, widespread publicity of major military exercises, previously the norm, has been minimal.[55]

Much of Iran's current military thinking is shaped by the experiences of its war with Iraq, both on and off the battlefield. Iranian military commanders were unable to procure badly needed spare parts and replacements for the American-supplied hardware that had been sold to Iran before the revolution. Throughout the eight-year war, the Saudi and Kuwaiti governments bankrolled Iraq's war chest, to the tune of no less than $55 billion, while the United States supplied Iraq with satellite information on Iranian troop movements.[56] Today, both Iran's military commanders and civilian leaders remember the war with bitter memories of GCC and American support for Iraq. Nor have they forgotten their need to improvise survival strategies and to procure weapons and supplies at exorbitant prices.[57]

Since the end of the war with Iraq, faced with international sanctions and largely unable to purchase advanced fighter jets from international manufacturers, Iran has made a concerted effort to develop an indigenous defense industry, including in ballistic missiles.[58] Having incorporated lessons from the war with Iraq, the Iranian military underwent what one observer has called "the most important transformation in Iranian military doctrine since the inception of the modern military in the late 1920s."[59] Among other innovations, the military command structure was decentralized and field commanders were given the authority to improvise tactics and strategies as called for by evolving circumstances. Iran has also cultivated and maintains ties with a network of strategic allies, both state and nonstate actors, across the Middle East.[60]

The ballistic missile program remains the cornerstone of Iran's national security doctrine, and a source of considerable concern for Iran's southern neighbors in the Persian Gulf. In February 2016, as part of a post-sanctions arrangement with the United States, Iran announced limits on its ballistic missile forces to a range of 2,000–2,300 kilometers.[61] In the words of the director of a government-related strategy think tank in Tehran, "While Iran is committed to developing its deterrent conventional defense capabilities, . . . [its] strategic defense plan currently sees no justification for higher ranges [for the missiles]."[62]

According to a 2015 congressional study, "Iran's armed forces are likely able to fend off any aggression from Iran's neighbors."[63] But to its southern neighbors Iran's abilities are seen less as deterrents and more as threats and aggressive posturing. They remain particularly concerned about Iran's ability to close the Strait of Hormuz, which is of vital importance to GCC economies. Fully 35 percent of all seaborne traded oil and 20 percent of all oil traded worldwide passes through the strait, making it one of the world's most critical choke points. Iran continues to develop "anti-access and area denial" capabilities in order to have the ability to control the strait and its approaches through various means, including expanding its fleet of small attack boats, amassing a large number of anti-ship cruise missiles, and the construction of additional naval bases along the coastline. As a possible signal of its ability to control the strait, in mid-2015 Iran stopped and inspected a number of commercial ships passing through under the pretext of having disagreements with shipping companies.[64]

As far as Tehran is concerned, Iran's strategic depth lies not in its ability to close the Strait of Hormuz, or even in its 2,200-kilometer coastline at the Persian Gulf. Instead, it is the Levant that is seen as an area of Iranian strategic depth. Before the 2011 Arab uprisings, Iran had led the "axis of resistance" to U.S. domination and to Israel. The group had been composed of Iran and its allies the Lebanese Hezbollah, Syria, and Iraq. In reality, this axis serves more as a "corridor of resistance" stretching from Iran to Iraq and on to Syria and Lebanon. This "triple alliance" gives Iran strategic depth. Viewed from this perspective, Tehran sees Syria as a major front in its geostrategic competition with the United States, its cold war with Saudi Arabia, and its fight against Salafism and Daesh.[65]

For Iran, Syria's importance lies in three factors. First, Syria is allied with and empowers the Lebanese Hezbollah, whose deterrence value for Iran against Israel cannot be overemphasized. Second, similar to Iran, Assad's Syria does not give in to pressure from the outside. And third, from Tehran's perspective, forcible regime change in Syria is seen as a prelude to mounting a similar campaign in Iran.[66] Lebanon has also emerged as one of the main battlefields between Iran and Saudi Arabia. In March 2016, Saudi Arabia withheld $3 billion in military assistance to Lebanon because of the country's alleged ties to Iran, and the GCC declared Hezbollah a terrorist organization. Maintaining ties to the Hezbollah is a central aspect of Iran's national security strategy.[67]

The Islamic Republic's strategy to fight anti-Assad militia, meanwhile, has been threefold: preserving existing state structures in Syria and Iraq; providing logistical support, arms, training, and command and control to militias and government forces; and, trying to become indispensable to local combat forces for possible long-term influence.[68] In relation to Syria, Iran has pursued a multifaceted strategy. It has sought to protect Assad through direct military assistance. It has also tried to find a political solution that would protect Assad and his regime. And, at the same time, it has been active in trying to establish a pro-Assad international front and to provide Syria with economic assistance in order to enhance and protect its own interests. It has also fortified its support for the Lebanese Hezbollah and has sought to cultivate new local allies in case of Assad's collapse. Additionally, it has ensured that Hezbollah is directly involved in providing support and assistance to the Assad regime.[69]

For most Gulf leaders, especially the Saudis, Iran's efforts at protecting and preserving its strategic depth in the Levant have turned it into a threatening and hegemonic player in the Arab world. There are widespread assumptions in the region that Iran is using its fight against Daesh and other anti-Assad militia to expand its influence on the ground in Syria.[70] Iranian leaders may harbor bitter memories from the Iraq war, but Gulf leaders point to Iranian actions in Iraq, Syria, and Lebanon as evidence of the Islamic Republic's expansionist and hegemonic aspirations. These strategic moves by Iran only further fuel sectarian sensitivities across the Gulf. Because the Hezbollah is a Shia organization, because of Bashar Assad's Alawite background, and because Iraqi politics since 2003 has been dominated mostly by the country's Shia community, Iran's alliances are seen by Gulf Arabs as driven by sectarian rather than strategic considerations.

These assumptions about Iran persist among most Gulf leaders, as shown in chapter 4, despite what appear to be paradigmatic shifts in Iranian foreign policy since the election of President Hassan Rouhani in June 2013. President Rouhani has called for both a conduct and a discourse of "prudent moderation" in Iranian foreign policy. According to his foreign minister, Mohammad Javad Zarif,

> Prudent moderation is an approach based on realism, self-confidence, realistic idealism, and constructive engagement. Realism requires an understanding of the nature, structure, mechanisms, and power dynamics of the international system and of the potential and limits of its institutions. . . . It demands a deliberate aversion to actions that are insulting, condescending, or self-aggrandizing. It promotes self-confidence based on an understanding of Iran's material and moral resources.

Rouhani has also placed considerable emphasis on "balance" and "moderation" in his foreign policy approach. Zarif maintains that

> Rouhani's approach maintains a delicate balancing act: between national, regional, and global needs, on the one hand, and the available means, instruments, and policies, on the other; between persistence and flexibility in foreign policy; between goals and means; and among various instruments of power in a dynamically changing world.
>
> . . .
>
> The top priority is to diffuse and ultimately defeat the international anti-Iranian campaign, spearheaded by Israel and its American benefactors, who seek to "securitize" Iran—that is, to delegitimize the Islamic Republic by portraying it as a threat to the global order.

According to Zarif, "Rouhani's platform offer[s] a wise critique of the previous administration's conduct of foreign relations."[71] Although this has resulted in some reduction of tensions with the United States, especially over the vexing nuclear issue, Zarif maintains that Iran "will have differences with the United States no matter what. The United States and Iran have different world views. We will not abandon ours. It's a part of our identity, but that identity does not require conflict."[72]

There is a similar stance toward Iran's two most vocal opponents in the Persian Gulf region: Saudi Arabia and the UAE. In an oblique reference to the two countries, Zarif writes:

> A well-orchestrated campaign has promoted Islamophobia, Iranophobia, and Shiite-phobia and depicted Iran as a threat to regional peace and security; extended support to anti-Iran claimants in the region; tarnished Iran's global

image and undermined its stature; armed Iran's regional rivals; actively supported anti-Iran forces, including the Taliban and other extremist groups; and fomented disagreements between Iran and its neighbors.[73]

According to the Iranian foreign minister, the security interests of Iran and Saudi Arabia need not be mutually exclusive, and the two countries can accommodate each other's interests. These common areas of interest could include the free flow of oil and freedom of navigation in the Persian Gulf, as well as technical issues such as nuclear safety. This would require abandoning "a zero-sum perspective" that has been dominant in the region.[74]

This zero-sum perspective is particularly pervasive in relation to alleged Iranian machinations in Yemen. As shown later here and in chapter 4, much of the justification for the Saudi military campaign in Yemen was built around protecting the Arabian Peninsula from actual or potential Iranian expansionism through its alliance with Yemen's Houthi rebels. However, although "the Gulf narrative about the Houthi-Iran connection" may have salience in the GCC, it is not altogether accurate, as shown by the Houthis' disregard of advice by Iran that they not take over Sanaa.[75] According to an April 2015 report, the U.S. intelligence community reportedly did not believe that Iran exerted command and control over the Houthis in Yemen.[76]

There are, no doubt, elements within the Iranian establishment, particularly those close to the paramilitary Islamic Revolutionary Guard Corps (IRGC), who would like to see the country have a strong foothold in Saudi Arabia's backyard in Yemen. But unlike the Levant, Yemen has little or no strategic value for the Islamic Republic, and Iran's purported alliance with the Houthis is more fiction than fact. By the same token, Saudi Arabia's deliberate ratcheting up of tensions with Iran, particularly over Yemen, has less to do with Yemen per se than with Iranian diplomatic and security advances in the Levant and in reducing tensions with the United States and the European Union. So long as U.S.-Iranian relations were tense and antagonistic, it was easy for Saudi Arabia and Israel to sell their strategic value to the United States. But this strategic value is likely to decline if U.S.-Iranian tensions are ever reduced.

A significant step toward reducing U.S.-Iranian tensions was achieved through the landmark nuclear accord between Iran and the P5+1. President Rouhani came to office determined to resolve the nuclear issue and to break the deepening isolation that the previous administration of Mahmoud Ahmadinejad had brought the country. Rouhani's foreign minister, Zarif, maintained that "in Iran's view, the nuclear crisis [was] wholly manufactured and therefore reversible."[77] Zarif's argument against nuclear weapons was echoed by numerous other Iranian policymakers:

> Iran has no interest in nuclear weapons and is convinced that such weapons would not enhance its security. Iran does not have the means to engage in nuclear deterrence—directly or through proxies—against its adversaries. Furthermore, the Iranian government believes that even a perception that Iran is seeking nuclear weapons is detrimental to the country's security and its regional role, since attempts by Iran to gain strategic superiority in the Persian Gulf would inevitably provoke responses that would diminish Iran's conventional military advantage.[78]

The scholar Nader Entessar agrees that a "realistic scenario" in which nuclear weapons would enhance Iran's national security is "inconceivable."[79]

While they had been under way on an intermittent basis for much of the late 2000s, the nuclear negotiations were kicked into high gear shortly after Rouhani assumed office, and they culminated in marathon negotiations in Geneva and Vienna that finally saw an agreement reached in July 2015.[80] According to a veteran observer of the Middle East, Mohammed Ayoob, the nuclear deal has "the potential to become a game changer in the Middle East," and, by leading to a possible rapprochement between Iran and the United States, it could result in "reducing the strategic importance of both Saudi Arabia and Israel."[81] That possibility, of a U.S.-Iranian rapprochement, seems unlikely in the foreseeable future, especially given the much more confrontational positions of the Trump administration toward the Islamic Republic. But if the nuclear negotiations were any indication of a possible future step in that direction, they definitely became a source of worry for the Saudi government and for most of the rest of the GCC.

The GCC

Another key actor in the Persian Gulf's security architecture is the Gulf Cooperation Council. Established in 1981 in the wake of the Iran-Iraq War, the GCC was originally meant to be an organization that encouraged economic and trade cooperation between its members. From the start, however, it was also seen as a mechanism to facilitate diplomatic and security policy coordination over various regional developments. Despite numerous structural weaknesses, and at times intense internal discord, so far the organization has survived and prospered. In fact, in the post-2011 era, largely under Saudi hegemony, the GCC has entered the regional fray by being, among other things, the front organization that sent Saudi and Emirati troops to Bahrain in 2011 to put down that country's uprising and, in 2015, launched the Saudi military campaign in Yemen. For all its internal divisions and structural weaknesses, in the securitized regional environment of the Persian Gulf after 2011, either nominally or substantively as a collective security organization, the GCC has become one of the region's main belligerents.

The 2017 dispute between Saudi Arabia, the UAE, and Bahrain on one side and Qatar on the other presented the GCC with its biggest internal crisis since the organization's inception. The long-term consequences of the crisis on the GCC, and whether the organization can ever withstand an internal shock of this magnitude, is difficult to assess at this point. For now, any examination of the GCC must necessarily take into account three key, interwoven dynamics that have come to define the organization's history and evolution, its functions and efficacy, and its regional positions and profile. First, born out of a crisis, namely, fears of the spillover of the Iran-Iraq War or Iranian belligerence once the war ended, the GCC often comes together and is most effective only at times of region-wide crisis. As a multilateral organization, many of whose young members continue to be in the formative stages of shaping their national identities, the GCC's efforts at greater economic, political, and security integration have often fallen short of the mark. But at crisis points the differences are set aside and the organization has acted with relative unity.

This has had consequences for, and is in turn reinforced by, a second development, which revolves around the basic idea of what the GCC as a multilateral organization is all about. The question of whether the GCC is a collective *security* organization or a multilateral forum for fostering greater economic, commercial, monetary, and diplomatic integration has not yet been quite settled.[82] GCC members appear not to have decided yet whether they want to follow the model of NATO or of the European Union. The default position of wanting to be a little of both, or a lot of each, has confronted the organization with a basic identity crisis. With time, and as dictated by the necessities of circumstance and need, this seeming indecision about the organization's primary purpose will likely be settled one way or another. For now, however, it is the course of events that appears to dictate the organization's overall purpose and functions rather than the other way around.

Third and finally, as a multilateral organization, the GCC is a victim of geography, history, and demography. The organization has six very unequal members in terms of size, history, resources, demography, and regional and global position. Saudi Arabia is a middle power and an aspiring or actual regional hegemon. All the other five members are small states, only one of which, Oman, has a history comparable in scope and age to that of Saudi Arabia. The disparity in size and history has other far-reaching consequences, some of the more important of which include market size, resources, and role perceptions both by the Saudis themselves and by others inside and outside the region. This also translates into the role and influence of Saudi Arabia within the GCC, in particular the extent to which the organization reflects Saudi policies and wishes and priorities if and when they happen to diverge with those of the other members.

In the words of one observer of the GCC, "The six states of the Gulf are as different as they are the same. With the exception of Saudi Arabia and perforce Bahrain, no GCC member is interested in pursuing projects for greater political and military unity. At the root of this disinclination towards unity is fear of Saudi domination and nervousness that unity could foster a Saudi brand of social conservatism that no other Gulf state would welcome."[83] There is, in fact, a "widely shared fear of Saudi dominance" among the states of the Arabian Peninsula.[84]

But it would not be accurate to maintain that the GCC has emerged as a tool of Saudi foreign policy hegemony over the rest of the Arabian Peninsula. Instead, what has developed over time is a bifurcation of the policymaking process within the organization, whereby only those decisions over which there is unanimity are made in its name. As Yusuf bin Alawi, the foreign minister of Oman, explained to me, the GCC was meant to be a collective decision-making body, but not every member agrees with all its decisions. There are critical decisions, such as the Saudi-led invasion of Yemen, with which not every GCC member agrees. Therefore, within the GCC an understanding has emerged that those decisions that may lead to internal divisions and discords can be discussed and decided outside of the GCC framework.[85]

As young states seeking to both assert distinct identities and to place their own mark on regional politics, the competition among the GCC states is often rooted in historical, cultural, economic, and political and personal elements.[86] Some of the historical roots of the competition are not that old, dating as far back as only the early 1970s. For example, it was the Bahraini-Qatari rivalry, and more specifically the sense by Bahraini leaders that the Al-Thanis wanted to dominate the emerging United Arab Emirates, which led to Bahrain's decision not to join the UAE in 1971 and to instead go it alone. Not to be outdone, Qatar followed suit and declared its own independence as well, leaving the rest of the seven emirates to establish the UAE on their own.[87]

The following decade, when the organization was established, saw the simultaneous emergence of several dynamics that impeded meaningful cooperative arrangements in the fields of economy and security. There was, at the regional level, a broader fragmentation of the Arab state system that had started in the 1980s and lasted up until 2003. As part of this general trend, the GCC states also began to diverge greatly. With the 2003 U.S. invasion of Iraq, four new developments were set into motion. First, the GCC was unable to develop a consensus over the Iraq war. Second, as shown above, sectarianism began to affect "state-level perceptions and also to politicise public discourses about 'the other.'"[88] Third, intra-GCC relations evolved in such a way that states became more interested in each other's domestic affairs. This led to widespread suspicion and distrust within the organization. Fourth and finally, benefiting from massive revenue inflows thanks to a second oil boom, each state focused on the accumulation of wealth and capital, thus intensifying competition with neighbors over attracting investments and building infrastructure.

Things came to a head in the aftermath of the Arab Spring, when the regional competition over the spoils of the uprisings, especially between Qatar and Saudi Arabia, led to serious internal rifts within the GCC. As a dramatic sign of displeasure with Qatar's support for the Muslim Brotherhood in Egypt and elsewhere, in March 2014, Saudi Arabia, Bahrain, and the UAE withdrew their ambassadors from Doha. Officially, they claimed to be protesting what they alleged was Doha's interference in the domestic affairs of other GCC states. In a joint statement, the three countries accused Qatar of "a lack of commitment to the principles that ensure non-interference in the internal affairs of any of the GCC countries, either directly or indirectly, including non-support to any organization or party aiming to threaten the security and stability of GCC countries, whether by direct security action, exercising political influence or supporting hostile media."[89]

Despite early and intensive negotiations and a desire to solve the crisis, the withdrawal of the ambassadors demonstrated that "the persistent underlying problem is a deep-rooted lack of confidence" among the member states of the GCC, one unlikely to be overcome soon.[90] The discord ended after eight months and, following a flurry of closed-door negotiations, the three ambassadors returned to Doha the following November. Nevertheless, the episode highlighted the diplomatic power of Saudi Arabia within the GCC and in relation to Bahrain, which in many ways since 2011 has abdicated its foreign and security policies to its much bigger and wealthier cousin. It also brought to light the emergence of a new alliance between Saudi Arabia and the UAE, born out of an emerging convergence of interests. As one observer has noted, the ambassadors' withdrawal was "only a continuation of a series of harmonised policy stances between Saudi Arabia, the UAE and Egypt post-coup."[91] The three countries have also closely collaborated in the military campaign in Yemen and have been almost equally boisterous in their posture toward Iran. Significantly, Saudi Arabia and the UAE have in the past competed with one another, and their post-2011 collaborative efforts were more a marriage of convenience than an indication of a new, lasting alignment within the GCC.[92]

The dispute in 2017 was far more intense and acrimonious than the one in 2014. In the later episode, Saudi Arabia, the UAE, and Bahrain were again joined by Egypt, and once again they accused Qatar of interfering in their domestic affairs. More ominously, however, they imposed a land and air blockade of Qatar, suspended all trade with the country, and launched a global media and public relations campaign to demonize and isolate Qatar. The three other GCC states went so far as to expel all Qataris living on their soil and to demand the immediate return of their own citizens living in Qatar. Two weeks into the crisis, the quartet presented a list of thirteen "demands" to Qatar and a ten-day window for compliance. The demands included the closure of Al Jazeera and all its affiliated media outlets; cutting off ties with Iran and the expulsion of alleged members of the Iranian IRGC operating inside Qatar; and an end to financing and other types of support for terrorist organizations, especially the Muslim Brotherhood and Hamas.

The demands, which Emirati and Egyptian officials repeatedly called "non-negotiable," were designed to be provocative and untenable. The real reasons behind the dispute, of course, went beyond the list of demands and revolved around deeper, more fundamental reasons having to do with Qatar's more independent-minded foreign policy. The Al Jazeera network has been a perennial irritant for Gulf and other Arab dictatorships throughout the Middle East. But even less tolerable has been Qatar's maintenance of open lines of communication with multiple states and nonstate actors, with many of which the Saudis and Emiratis do not get along (discussed more fully below). The 2017 dispute was motivated by nothing less than a desire by Saudi Arabia and the UAE to turn Qatar into another Bahrain—a pleasant vacation destination devoid of fully sovereign foreign and security policies.

There are additional, structural sources of disunity within the GCC that further hamper its intended purpose as a collective security organization. From the very start, the organization felt uncomfortable about forging strong military ties among its members because of vastly different, existing collaborative arrangements some of its members already had in place, principally with the United States. The organization was also eager to project a benign image of itself abroad so as not to be seen as a hostile entity. When in September 1981, at the GCC's first regular foreign ministers' meeting, Oman presented a paper on security cooperation, the other member states refused to approve it. There was, of course, a common assumption among the members that the organization was fundamentally concerned with security. But this security was seen, in the early phases at least, to be best accomplished through their drawing together closer politically rather than militarily.[93]

Frederic Wehrey and Richard Sokolsky point to two further shortcomings. First, they argue, the GCC is "little more than a de facto collective defense alliance directed against Iran." Second, "it provides no multilateral venue for crisis management, conflict resolution, or implementation of measures to strengthen stability." They maintain that the GCC does not provide a meaningful forum "for dialogue on many security challenges or for reducing tensions, managing crises, preventing conflict and improving predictability." There are "a number of structural sources of disunity in the GCC" that "on balance, outweigh the recent signs of unity."[94]

There is also a weak collective-decision-making framework within the GCC, and most member states prefer bilateral to multilateral agreements.[95] Across the GCC, leaders play a critical role in foreign policy formulation; therefore leadership changes could potentially bring with them major shifts in foreign policy behavior.[96] One of the Emirati scholars I interviewed went as far as to claim that "the GCC has little substance in reality. It functions more as a club for leaders, who treat it as if it were one of their private *majalis*. They are fond of summitry, and they engage in showy endeavors that have little traction or little basis in reality."[97] This assessment seems somewhat harsh. It would be more accurate to maintain, as the late Joseph Kostiner did, that "GCC strategic planning is an exercise in disparate security, displaying similar perceptions but particular priorities."[98]

Especially in the 2000s, faced with mounting international tensions and domestic disquiet, the states of the GCC failed to devise comprehensive policies toward Iran, Iraq, and the issue of sectarianism both at home, among their opponents, and among other regional actors. Instead, they relied on the United States' remaining in Iraq and continuing to provide them with security guarantees.[99] The new century's first decade saw mostly intensified economic and commercial competition between the GCC members. At decade's end, the outbreak of the Arab Spring presented the GCC states with one of their biggest crises to date, as they faced internal political agitation and an opening of political opportunities abroad.[100] By far the biggest challenge arose in Bahrain, where initially scattered antigovernment demonstrations soon engulfed much of the small kingdom. Before long, to ensure that the revolt did not spill over their own borders, Saudi Arabia and the UAE dispatched troops to put down the Bahraini uprising.[101]

For the most part, the uprisings were met by pragmatism on the part of the GCC, but also by a fair amount of differences in approach and objectives.[102] To strengthen the alliance, first Morocco and Jordan, and later even Egypt as well, were mentioned as potential additional GCC members.[103] By reaching out to Jordan and Morocco with pledges of $2.5 billion in financial aid to each country, the GCC sought to forge a new identity based not so much on geographic proximity as on political affinity, seeking strength in numbers in order to foster and ensure domestic stability.[104] The proposal to expand the GCC, in the words of one analyst, "smack[ed] of rather empty symbolism" meant to show greater Arab, particularly monarchical, solidarity in the face of growing unrest from restive populations, on the one hand, and ominous regional developments and cross-border tensions, on the other.[105]

In hindsight, the dispatching of Saudi and Emirati troops to Bahrain in 2011 appears to have been the first indication of increasing assertiveness and growing militarism within the GCC. Qatar and the UAE went as far as to introduce military conscription.[106] In many ways, although the Arab Spring gave the GCC states cause for alarm, they soon were able to rely on the significant political and economic capital they had accumulated in the early 2000s to take matters into their own hands and to spearhead a region-wide counterrevolution of sorts.[107] In fact, the foreign policies of the GCC states had changed in tempo as early as the mid-1990s and had become somewhat more proactive. By the start of the 2010s and before the eruption of the Arab revolts, most of the GCC states "were projecting power and influence in virtually every corner of the MENA subsystem."[108] By about 2014–2015, the pattern had been resumed, this time with a strong sectarian tinge.

The American factor figures prominently in GCC calculations. Clearly, the GCC's close security cooperation with the United States has enabled the group "to take foreign policy initiatives more comfortably when pressed."[109] In fact, the United States and the GCC have programs in the works to improve collective defense capabilities, notably in the area of missile defense, maritime cooperation, and cybersecurity. While this military cooperation remains close and multifaceted, the United States has ruled out a formal defense guarantee agreement with the organization.[110] Although the United States has been pushing the concept of a multilateral GCC defense approach, the reality remains that most of the U.S. relationship with regional actors remains essentially bilateral.[111] At the same time, America's (re)discovery of Asia as a strategically important region has resulted in a "systemic shift" in the geopolitical calculations of the GCC states, further strengthening the belief in the need for greater self-reliance and assertiveness.[112] This trend has been reinforced by the rise of new leaders throughout the GCC, especially in the upper and middle echelons of policymaking, who are calling for and devising radically different ways of dealing with the regional challenges facing them.[113] Saudi Arabia has been at the forefront of advocating greater security self-reliance on the part of the GCC. But the extent to which this view is shared across the organization is open to question.[114]

Any discussion of the GCC as a collective security organization must necessarily take into account what for many regional states has become "the Iran factor." Fears and suspicions about Iran run deep among GCC policymakers, who believe it is the Iranian security establishment, especially the IRGC, and not the likes of President Rouhani or Foreign Minister Zarif, who are in charge of Iran's Gulf policy and who are likely to cause trouble for Iran's southern neighbors.[115] Lacking any vision for a reorganized regional security arrangement, the GCC states have persevered in their efforts to maintain the regional order and status quo, refusing to enter into a security arrangement or even a dialogue with Iran.[116] At the same time, however, the GCC's policy toward Iran has been somewhat fragmented as the organization has been unable to formulate a collective approach to the Islamic Republic. Individual Gulf states have therefore managed to have their own bilateral relationships with Iran. Qatar, Kuwait, and Oman, each in its own way and to varying degrees, are trying to balance their relationships with Iran with those of Saudi Arabia.[117] In almost all cases, these bilateral ties with Iran have not gone beyond "ad hoc pragmatic arrangements" and do not extend to such areas as shared strategic interests or common security concerns.[118]

After signing the nuclear deal with Iran, the United States made pledges revolving around enhanced security cooperation with the states of the GCC. The United States sought to reassure its GCC allies of its continued commitment to a "strategic partnership" with them against Daesh and Iran's "malign influence." It therefore strengthened various forms of security cooperation with the GCC, including expedited and more extensive weapons sales.[119] Additionally, it increased U.S.-GCC cooperation on maritime security, cyberspace, and counterterrorism; held joint military exercises with the forces of the GCC states and increased U.S. military training programs; and it renewed its commitment to a Gulf-wide concept of a joint missile defense system.[120] By May 2016, American military personnel were on the ground in Yemen helping Saudi and Emirati troops in their fight against Yemeni rebels.[121]

Up until the 2015 Yemen war, the GCC states had preferred to meet regional challenges and threats with mediation and diplomacy rather than confrontation.[122] In reality, the main threats to the GCC states have been in the form of, not military aggression from other states, but rather sub- or trans-state identity movements.[123] It remains to be seen whether the Yemen war and the coordinated campaign against Qatar are indications of a new modus operandi for the organization, signals that a new militarism is now the norm, or evidence of a zealous campaign by Saudi Arabia and the UAE to which others must adhere, however reluctantly.

Whatever the consequences of the Yemen war, the GCC today is a fact of life, and it has proved its viability and functional efficacy for more than thirty years. The organization has mostly managed to keep the otherwise fractious Gulf states on the same page, and it has been able to bring about a minimum level of coordination and cooperation between their foreign and security policies. There are certain core issues on which all member states agree, regime security chief among them. On Bahrain, for example, the GCC has followed Saudi Arabia's lead and been uniform in its stance that there can be no political role for the country's opposition in the political process.[124] At the same time, at least up until 2017, the GCC gave all of its six members significant autonomy to pursue their own agendas and policy objectives.[125] An extreme example of this relative policy independence is Oman, which has charted an independent foreign policy for itself, especially in relation to Saudi Arabia.[126] Perhaps this mostly unintentional, built-in adaptability is key to the GCC success. As one of my Emirati interlocutors told me in 2016, "Today the GCC is in its best possible shape, even better than the EU, which has problems with its internal policies and (possible) withdrawal of Britain. Comparatively speaking, the GCC is in a much stronger position today than at any other point in its history."[127] This was before the 2017 crisis with Qatar. Only time will tell whether the organization can survive the bitter dispute among four of its six members.

Saudi Arabia

As the discussion of the GCC made evident, by far the most consequential actor in the organization is Saudi Arabia. By virtue of its size, history, and resources, and the self-perceptions of its leaders, Saudi Arabia has emerged as one of the most consequential and significant countries within the Middle East as well as beyond. After a relatively brief initial shock, the 2011 uprisings galvanized the kingdom into action, prompting it to reassert its middle power status as an aspiring regional hegemon. As such, Saudi Arabia came to see itself as the rightful protector of the regional security order, and the articulator, along with its lesser equal partners, of the proper foreign policy orientations and the security architecture of the Persian Gulf and the rest of the Middle East. All this occurred, as argued earlier, under a broad sectarian rubric in which Saudi Sunnism was pitted against the Shiʿism of Iran and its allies in Iraq, Syria, Lebanon, and Yemen.

In this section, I will discuss several aspects of Saudi foreign and security policies, beginning by examining the processes through which these policies are made and what their intended objectives might be. Important in Saudi calculations are other actors such as the United States, which since the 1970s has been by far the kingdom's biggest security guarantor; Iran, long Saudi Arabia's biggest competitor; and other GCC states, with which Saudi Arabia has often sought to establish hegemonic relations. I end the section with a discussion of Saudi relations with and 2015 military campaign in Yemen, the latter a watershed in the kingdom's history of its troubled relations with its poor neighbor to the south.

Saudi Arabia's foreign policy rests on a careful balancing of two distinct pillars, one its close alliance with the United States, the other Saudi Arabia's leadership of the Arab and Muslim worlds—the so-called "Vatican role."[128] Much of the kingdom's attempts at projecting an image of Islamic leadership across the Persian Gulf region, in the larger Middle East, and beyond are motivated by its concern with security on the domestic front and its efforts to placate potential conservative, or even radical, domestic political opponents. This has posed a serious dilemma for Saudi policymakers, as the twin pillars of its foreign policy—US alliance and Islamic leadership—often create inconsistencies and problems. Saudi Arabia's security dilemma, discussed in chapter 4, arises partly out of the very ways in which the kingdom's foreign and security policies are structured.

For the Saudi state, middle power status and self-ascribed assumptions concerning the leadership of the Islamic world have meant frequent spurts of regional diplomatic activism. The 1980s, for example, saw a proliferation of Saudi regional initiatives aimed at balancing its relations with the United States, on the one hand, with stability in the region and at home, on the other.[129] These initiatives culminated in Riyadh's 1992 Arab Peace Plan proposal, designed to resolve the Arab-Israeli conflict. But the kingdom continued to feel threatened both by developments in the region and by many of the nearby states. With the end of Iraq's occupation of Kuwait in 1991 and the disappearance of the Soviet Union, the Saudis concluded that they faced three defined threats from their immediate vicinity: a restoration of Iran's hegemonic ambitions; a competitive and regionally destabilizing Iraq; and Yemen, with its newfound oil, Arab nationalist ideological leanings, and recent unification.

To counter these and other regional threats, the Saudis began pursuing two courses of action. First, stung by their inability to defend or to even stall Iraq's invasion and occupation of Kuwait in August 1990, the kingdom embarked on a massive security and arms buildup to bolster its military defenses.[130] At the same time, it engaged in a careful balancing act between more powerful regional actors such as Egypt, Turkey, and Iran.[131] Never quite trusting any of the region's other middle powers, it nevertheless entered into a détente of sorts with Iran, which led to somewhat reduced regional tensions. For its part, under the presidencies of first Hashemi Rafsanjani and then Mohammad Khatami, Iran was also keen to reduce tensions with its Arab neighbors to the south, in particular Saudi Arabia.

There was a relative lull in Saudi regional activism in the 2000s until the outbreak of the 2011 uprisings, which spurred the kingdom into action on the regional front once again, in Bahrain, then in Syria and Egypt, later in Iraq, and eventually in Yemen. The outbreak of the 2011 uprisings initially caught the Saudis by complete surprise and gave rise to much anxiety in policymaking circles in Riyadh. The seeming political ascendance of Iran, Qatar, and the Muslim Brotherhood after the 2011 uprisings all posed serious challenges to Saudi Arabia's self-ascribed role as the leader of the Muslim world and the dominant hegemon within the GCC.[132] Equally disconcerting for Riyadh was the election of Rouhani to the presidency in Iran in 2013 and his charm offensive designed to end the international isolation that the Ahmadinejad administration had brought the country.

Riyadh's initial sense of panic and policy incoherence was palpable. Writing in 2013, the veteran Saudi observer Thomas Lippman observed that the kingdom's foreign policy had "no strategic vision." Lippman maintained that "it appears the Saudis themselves don't know quite what to make of the various situations in which they find themselves."[133] Throughout 2013 and 2014, Saudi anxiety appears to have reached a high point. In October 2013, in protest against the UN's apparent in-action in Syria, the Saudis refused their newly won seat on the Security Council, a move that many observers "ridiculed as self-defeating."[134] As one observer commented, "The kingdom has no strategic approach to national security, preferring short-term tactical alliances and the comfort of familiar, ill-researched, and exaggerated assumptions about what Iran and its allies are up to—and what they ultimately want. These tactical mo-tivations encourage shifting alliances that can alienate friends and create bigger problems for the kingdom, in Yemen and elsewhere."[135]

In the meanwhile, the kingdom's standing among Middle Eastern pub-lics declined substantially. According to the Pew Research Center, from 2007 to 2011, favorable Arab views concerning the kingdom dropped by nearly 18 percent, from 69.5 percent to 52 percent.[136] Saudi Arabia's involvement in the aftermath of the uprisings, most evidently in Syria, Libya, and Egypt, further eroded its popularity among publics in the Mid-dle East.[137] The 2015 military attack on Yemen and the 2017 campaign against Qatar are unlikely to improve the Saudi image.

Saudi Arabia's initial policy drift into the early years of the Arab Spring appears to have masked, or perhaps been an outgrowth of, serious debates within the kingdom's policy establishment over the proper courses of ac-tion to follow. There were voices within Riyadh's policy and intellectual circles that called for a more active and assertive posture in the kingdom's foreign and security policies. "This is the right moment for KSA [King-dom of Saudi Arabia] to strengthen its defense design," declared one such policy advocacy paper by a Saudi scholar, "and the necessity of an SDD [Saudi Defense Doctrine] only grows with time."

> KSA faces a complex, uncertain, and ever-changing regional landscape. The decline of Western power in the region, the spread of weapons of mass de-struction, the rise of technology and a new cyber-arena, and a series of sec-tarian divisions and extremism will continue to pose profound challenges to regional and international order. . . . KSA is the only Arab nation able to af-ford and sustain large-scale strategic and defense programs as well as sta-bilize regional unrest. As such, KSA faces an obligation to reform itself to

fulfill its responsibility as the indispensable regional leader as well as the ultimate regional defender.[138]

As the course of events were soon to prove, King Salman's ascension to office in 2015 appears to have provided the space for this line of thinking to translate into the kingdom's foreign and security policies.

The king's decision-making powers and authority, meanwhile, are neither limitless nor unchecked, balanced by a number of countervailing norms in the royal household that provide avenues for policy input by other royals, technocrats, and state functionaries. State institutions are also not unimportant and in fact at times wield considerable power and influence, becoming important arenas of policy specialty and authority for well-placed figures in the royal family.[139] Nevertheless, a fair amount of informality continues to permeate the system and the decision-making process. As one observer has noted, "Despite the perceived institutionalization of politics in Saudi Arabia, formal titles mean relatively little. Age, proximity to power, charisma, and the ability to deliver favors all matter much more."[140]

The assumption of power by King Salman in 2015 saw the concomitant rise in political influence and powers of his son Mohammad bin Salman (b. 1985), who was simultaneously appointed as the minister of defense, deputy heir apparent, second deputy prime minister, chief of the royal court, and chairman of the Council of Economic and Development Affairs. In June 2017, shortly after the crisis with Qatar broke, a royal decree removed Crown Prince Mohammed bin Nayef from the position and promoted the king's son to the office of the crown prince instead. In addition to presiding over an ambitious and extensive overhaul of the Saudi economy, Mohammad bin Salman oversaw the increasing securitization of the kingdom's foreign policy, including the launch of its military offensive against Yemen in March 2015. The following December, the defense minister announced the establishment of a thirty-four-nation "Islamic military coalition" designed to fight Daesh and other terrorist groups. Not long after the announcement was made, several members of the supposed coalition—including Pakistan, Indonesia, and Malaysia—declared their unawareness that such a coalition had been formed or that they had agreed to take part in it.[141] By 2016, fully 25 percent of Saudi Arabia's budget was devoted to the military and security services.[142]

The campaign in Yemen was as much an outgrowth of policy paralysis and a tendency toward knee-jerk reactions to regional developments as it was a result of the kingdom's increasing bellicosity. The two, in fact, were intimately connected. As Madawi Al-Rasheed argues, "The [Saudi] regime remains bewildered, erratic and sometimes desperate to fulfil its ambition to become the main arbiter of Arab regional politics."[143] In particular, Saudi Arabia's increasing commitment to the overthrow of the Assad regime in Syria, begun in earnest in 2011, had not borne any fruit and by 2015 was beginning to resemble somewhat of a quagmire.[144] As one observer commented, "How the Saudis propose to win the struggle for Syria is not clear."[145] Before long, observers were characterizing the "Gulf actors' engagement in the Syria crisis as a failure."[146]

Saudi difficulties in Syria were occurring at a time when other regional developments were equally troubling for the kingdom. Saudi Arabia has long viewed the preservation of monarchy in its neighborhood as essential to its own national security. The uprising in Bahrain led the kingdom to point to "Iran and Shiite populations within or near its borders as explicit threats to continued stability."[147] But the Shia were not the kingdom's only source of trouble. As elaborated in chapter 4, the Saudi regime has been particularly vulnerable to ideological crosscurrents from across the Middle East.[148] In June 2012, the Egyptian Muslim Brotherhood assumed the presidency in Egypt with the election of Mohammed Morsi. The Saudis see the Muslim Brotherhood as especially threatening on multiple fronts, as the group occupies a space that the Saudi regime sees as its own preserve.[149] Not surprisingly, when Morsi was overthrown in a military coup in July 2013, King Abdullah was the first to congratulate Egypt's new government and to promise lavish support.[150]

The Egyptian interlude notwithstanding, the Saudi state continues to view the post-2011 Middle East through thick sectarian lenses. The kingdom does not see the current conflicts in the Middle East as between moderates versus violent extremists, but instead between a Sunnism of which it approves and an Iranian Shiʿism it rejects. It actively tries to frame the discourse surrounding the 2011 revolutions in sectarian terms. Before the eruption of the Arab uprisings, Gregory Gause observed that the influence of the religious establishment on foreign policy had waned since the early days of the kingdom.[151] But by about 2012–2013, the country's ostensibly secular policymakers found themselves increasingly closer to the positions once advocated by only the religious establishment.[152]

Before long, Iran had once again emerged as the Saudis' biggest concern. In July 2015 WikiLeaks released confidential Saudi diplomatic cables between Riyadh and its embassies around the world. As the *New York Times* commented, "The documents from Saudi Arabia's Foreign Ministry illustrate a near obsession with Iran, with diplomats in Africa, Asia and Europe monitoring Iranian activities in minute detail and top government agencies plotting moves to limit the spread of Shiite Islam."[153] "The Saudis," wrote another observer, "see localized uprisings as manifestations of a relentless Iranian campaign to dominate the Middle East."[154]

Although far from being the only consequential factor, the question of Iran has figured prominently in Saudi relations with the United States since 2011. The kingdom and the United States have long had a close but often fraught relationship. While U.S. and Saudi strategic interests often converge, historically Saudi Arabia has not always followed the U.S. lead. Despite maintaining very close military and diplomatic relations with the United States under the broader rubric of bandwagoning, the Saudis have long retained significant autonomy from the United States in a number of foreign policy areas. In fact, instead of being viewed as outright dependence on the United States by Saudi Arabia, Saudi-American relations may best be described as "asymmetric interdependence," whereby Saudi resources and wealth have been leveraged to ensure policy independence and autonomy in a whole range of areas, including the exercise of policy independence in the Arab-Israeli conflict and, in 2015, private expressions of dismay and apprehension at U.S.-Iranian nuclear negotiations.[155]

The nuclear negotiations were one of three areas of serious disagreement between the kingdom and the United States after 2011. The other two were the U.S. failure, in Saudi eyes, to rescue its allies, such as Presidents Hosni Mubarak and Zine El Abidine Ben Ali, during the Arab uprisings and Washington's refusal to proactively topple Bashar al-Assad in Syria.[156] These policy disagreements occurred, as described in chapter 4, within a context of Riyadh's growing preoccupation with maintaining preeminence and influence in the Persian Gulf region and the broader Middle East. In addition to competition and tensions with Iran, this preoccupation was fed by fears of abandonment by the United States, on the one hand, and, on the other, the possible emergence of an informal alliance between Turkey, Qatar, and Iran at the expense of the kingdom. That these fears were unfounded did, or has done, little to allay Riyadh's concerns and its drive to be more assertive toward its immediate neighbors, especially Qatar, and to shore up its own alliances across the Middle East.[157] This assertiveness, in fact, dates back to shortly after the eruption of the Arab Spring, when, in addition to continuing to receive support from the United States and the West elsewhere, the Saudis began to "embark on a road to security self-reliance."[158]

Saudi assertiveness has made its presence felt in the kingdom's immediate vicinity, in the Arabian Peninsula. For several decades, establishing hegemony in the Arabian Peninsula—not just in Yemen but also over the smaller oil monarchies of the GCC—has been one of Saudi Arabia's primary foreign policy objectives.[159] By and large, Saudi Arabia's record in asserting its dominance in the Arabian Peninsula has been generally been one of success, notably in times of crisis (over Yemen in 2015, for example). Nevertheless, the kingdom's hegemonic aspirations have not gone unchallenged, in recent years especially by Qatar and the UAE. Oman has also been dogged in pursuing its own, independent policies, although it has assiduously avoided tension and open conflict with Saudi Arabia. Particularly during those stretches when there are no overarching crises facing the region, most GCC states tend to pursue their own agendas and interests, many of which stand in contradistinction to those of the kingdom.[160]

One of the ways in which Saudi Arabia has sought to establish hegemony over the GCC is to play up the Iranian threat. Despite Saudi efforts, the GCC has been far from unanimous in its assessment of Iran.[161] Oman, for example, has long maintained cordial relations with Iran, and Qatar's relations with the Islamic Republic, while not quite as close, have always been much friendlier than Saudi Arabia has preferred. Kuwait has similarly refrained from joining in the vociferous condemnation of Iran on various regional issues in which Saudi Arabia, Bahrain, and the UAE frequently engage.

In the lead-up to and the immediate aftermath of the Arab Spring, it was Qatar's unwillingness to synchronize its foreign and security policies with Saudi Arabia that caused anxiety and consternation for the kingdom. Riyadh saw the Muslim Brotherhood's success in Egypt as a win for Qatar and a setback for the kingdom in the latter's bid for regional hegemony.[162] Saudi Arabia and Qatar also competed in Syria by support-ing rival opposition groups in their efforts to overthrow the Assad regime. Soon, however, with U.S. encouragement, Saudi Arabia replaced Qatar as the principal supporter of Syrian rebels.[163] This only confirmed for the Saudis that Qatar is "the *enfant terrible* of the Gulf monarchies."[164] They therefore used the withdrawal of ambassadors, noted above, as a symbolic gesture to express their displeasure with Doha's actions in Egypt and else-where. More important, the ambassadors' withdrawal was the result of a growing fear in Riyadh that the regional balance of power was tilting against the interests of Saudi Arabia and its partner of convenience, the UAE, and that Qatari support for political Islam, especially for the Mus-lim Brotherhood, was a threat.[165]

Saudi Arabia has viewed Qatar as a frequent irritant since the mid-1990s, when the ambitious Sheikh Hamad bin Khalifa Al-Thani began charting a new foreign policy trajectory designed to pull his small country out of the kingdom's overpowering shadows. But Yemen has been more than just an irritant for Riyadh. In numerous ways Yemen has been an actual threat—its resource-starved economy a source of outward migra-tion, its borders porous and difficult to control, its tribal mosaic complex and subject to frequently shifting alliances, and its political culture divided along multiple conflicting fault lines. Not surprisingly, Saudi-Yemeni ten-sions date back to the beginning of the 1930s and the earliest days of the kingdom's establishment. From the start, Saudi Arabia sought to exert dominance over Yemen, but its success has been at best spotty and spo-radic.[166] The relationship between the two counties, therefore, has been marked by "opportunity and promise interrupted by intermittent conflicts and tension."[167]

Saudi Arabia was particularly troubled by the unification of Yemen in 1990, having tried but failed to prevent it from taking place.[168] In Yemen and even in some Saudi circles, there has long been an assumption that the kingdom prefers two Yemens to its south rather than a united single coun-try.[169] The preference was made explicitly clear in 1994, when Yemen's civil war and secessionist movement, which ultimately failed, was supported by substantial sums of money from Saudi Arabia and the other GCC states. Prompted by the failure, the kingdom shifted tactics, the following year signing an agreement with President Ali Abdullah Saleh that pledged the two countries to settle their disputes through peaceful means.[170]

What followed was an era of "cash diplomacy" by the kingdom toward Yemen.[171] Substantial subsidies flowed to prominent Yemeni personalities in the northern and westernmost regions of the country, meant to ensure their loyalty to Riyadh rather than to Sanaa. The kingdom also paid millions of dollars to Yemeni officials and to the country's major tribal figures in an effort to secure their loyalty. "Those on the Saudi payroll," an observer once noted, "run the gamut of Yemeni politics."[172]

Over the years, however, the Saudis have had few returns on their investments, as most Yemeni tribal leaders on their payroll became "city sheikhs" and lost moral authority among their younger flock. Yemen's political actors and leaders on the Saudi payroll turned out to be even less reliable. Yemen's deeply rooted structural fissures were neglected, and were instead magnified because of Saudi cash inflows. And, ultimately, the cash handouts did not succeed in buying loyalty to Riyadh. Throughout the 1990s, the "longest unsettled frontier in the Middle East," dividing the two countries, witnessed intermittent clashes.[173] When it came to Yemen, "the GCC tactic of divide, bribe and rule [has been] a consistent failure."[174]

As with so many other developments across the region, the 2011 uprisings brought Saudi-Yemeni tensions to a head. Yemen's former president Saleh had once commented that "ruling Yemen is like dancing on the heads of snakes."[175] Wily though he was, Saleh could not withstand the force of the uprisings and was eventually forced out of the presidential office in 2012. He did not leave political life altogether, however, and became a central figure in the country's civil war, supporting Houthi rebels in their march from the north toward Sanaa and their capture of power in 2014. The Houthis happen to belong to an offshoot of Shi'ism, and Saudi Arabia, which at one point supported them, sensed their ascent to power as a sign of growing Iranian influence in its backyard. The Saudi narrative of post-2011 developments in Yemen has revolved around its efforts to defeat Iranian expansionism deep inside the Arabian Peninsula. But factual evidence of Iranian involvement in Yemen has been scarce.[176] Nevertheless, under the pretext of fighting Iranian designs in the Arabian Peninsula, the Saudis launched a spirited military campaign in Yemen beginning in March 2015. They were enthusiastically joined in the effort by the UAE.

The Saudi goal in Yemen has been "to bomb the Houthis into submission" and to restore Saleh's former vice president and successor, Abed

Rabbo Mansour Hadi, as a puppet president in office.[177] More than any-thing else, the war in Yemen is meant to send a message to Saudi Arabia's enemies that the kingdom and its allies will initiate their own "swift and tangible response, instead of waiting for others to step in."[178] In the pro-cess, the kingdom has allied itself with a number of rival Yemeni groups that are united together only in their distaste for the Houthis and Saleh. Especially in the southern parts of the country, many of these rebel groups are often at odds with Saudi Arabia. More important, however, their goals and efforts at ensuring their own autonomy are "making a mockery of Ri-yadh's commitment to one Yemen."[179] Ultimately, apart from getting the Houthis out of power, Saudi military actions in Yemen lack a clear goal and an endgame, and in the long run are likely to worsen the kingdom's security dilemma.[180]

The Saudi campaign in Yemen is likely to create far more difficulties than solutions for the kingdom. As one commentator has noted, "Be-cause of the unfathomable human tragedy unfolding in Yemen, interna-tional pressure will ultimately force Saudi Arabia to end its senseless war. When this happens, many Saudis, some members within the royal family, Yemenis, and other Arabs will hold the king responsible for his poorly thought-out, counterproductive military adventure in Yemen."[181] A more immediate threat is likely to be a resurgent Al Qaeda in the Arabian Pen-insula (AQAP). In fact, the Saudi campaign has allowed AQAP, "a force with a greater proven ability than the Houthis to hurt Saudi Arabia," to gain both strength and territory in Yemen.[182] "Yemen's civil war," one report states, "has secured nearly all of AQAP's immediate military objectives."[183]

Rami Khouri identifies two broad causes of the Yemen war: a rite of passage for both the Saudi Arabia and the UAE, and fear of Iran. "For the Saudis and the Emiratis in particular," he writes, the attack on Yemen "is also about their identity, their place in the region and the world, and their ability to come together when they feel threatened. It is about achieving maturity in the arena of statehood."[184] Whatever the under-lying reasons for the military campaign, it appears to have been poorly thought out and executed, with little appreciation for the multiple pitfalls that awaited such an effort. By early 2016, the Saudi campaign in Yemen could best be described as a dynamic stalemate. For the Saudis, even the slightest appearance of defeat was out of the question, but neither did they exhibit any capacity to meaningfully stabilize the country. The Saudi military performance, meanwhile, was less than exemplary. News reports often described the kingdom's armed forces as "unprepared and prone to mistakes" and unable to make meaningful progress on the ground against Houthi rebels.[185] In fact, the war made Saudi Arabia's long, porous border with Yemen less secure than it had been before.

Yemen itself, the Middle East's poorest country before the war, was plunged into an even deeper abyss. By June 2017, slightly more than two years after the war began, a cholera epidemic had affected more than two hundred thousand and claimed more than thirteen hundred victims. Every day some five thousand more Yemenis were estimated to be infected with the disease.[186] Moreover, according to the World Food Program, by 2017, 60 percent of the country's population, or 17 million people, were food insecure, 6.8 million of them severely so. A total of 3.1 million Yemenis have been internally displaced, and 3.3 million children and pregnant or nursing women are acutely malnourished.[187] Before the war, millions of Yemenis had long found employment in Saudi Arabia as migrant workers, but as the war continued, and as Saudi Arabia's own economic woes worsened, they found fewer opportunities for employment beyond their country's borders. Yemeni workers had always been viewed in Saudi Arabia with a measure of suspicion, and their numbers had gone down from a peak of more than 1.5 million in the late 1980s to an estimated 500,000 in 2000.[188] How Yemen will emerge out of the military campaign, and function as a viable state after its physical devastation by Saudi and Emirati forces, remains an open question.

Yemen—not Iran—represents by far the biggest foreign and security policy challenge that Saudi Arabia faces. In its competition with Iran and to further prolong the Islamic Republic's international isolation, the kingdom has used "dollar diplomacy" to entice its less wealthy friends—for example Sudan, Djibouti, and the Maldives—to cut diplomatic ties with the Islamic Republic.[189] In light of the Rouhani administration's successes in improving Iran's diplomatic and commercial relations with the European Union and with countries such as South Korea, China, and India, Saudi Arabia's foreign policy efforts, to the contrary, appear at best successful only symbolically rather than substantively. The Saudi government has also often pointed to Iran's diverse ethnic mosaic, particularly the Arabs in the southwest and the Baluchis in the southeast, as potential pressure points that can be used to influence Tehran's regional behavior.[190] But the viability of such a threat is open to question. Because of limited institutional capacity, at least in relation to Iran there is little other than financial prowess that the Saudis can use to affect outcomes.[191] The long-term sustainability of buying allies and encouraging enmities is, at best, also questionable.

Within the Arabian Peninsula, which the Saudis regard as their own backyard and where they assume to have a natural leadership responsibility, the kingdom has resorted to diplomatic pressure to ensure that Qatar remains in step with Saudi Arabia's foreign and security policy objectives, and to outright military action to mold Yemen's internal politics to the kingdom's own liking. In the process they have entered into a marriage of convenience of sorts with another rising regional aspirant, the UAE. In the long run, the Yemen campaign is likely to cause more security challenges for the kingdom than the Houthis—even with their much-hyped Iranian connection—could have ever presented.

In the words of one scholar, "The more the Saudi regime wanted to appear hegemonic, the less its actions reflected thoughtful strategies that might have resulted in desirable outcomes."[192] Saudi belligerence in Yemen, its hegemonic aspirations in the Arabian Peninsula, its lead role in the campaign to isolate Qatar, and its intense and relentless competition with Iran have only deepened the kingdom's long-term, multiple security dilemmas. For much of its history, the kingdom has pursued a foreign policy based on its values and identity, but has also been ultimately pragmatic. Insufficient time has elapsed since the 2011 Arab uprisings to determine whether the new policy pursuits represent longer-term paradigmatic shifts in Saudi Arabia's strategic outlook and objectives, or constitute short-term responses by a new leadership to perceived threats. What is clear is that since 2011 Saudi Arabia has become far more assertive than before, and that its foreign and security policies are now hardly distinguishable from one another.

The United Arab Emirates

Unlike Saudi Arabia or Iran, or even Qatar for that matter, the UAE is a relatively new player in regional politics, having for years shown a preference for domestic economic and infrastructural development rather than engagement in international affairs too far from its borders. In the 1950s, the country had a brief military conflict with Saudi Arabia over territory, but in 1992 the UAE's founder and its ruler at the time, Sheikh Zayed bin Sultan Al Nahyan, formally ceded the Zarrarah oil field to Saudi Arabia in exchange for Saudi recognition of Emirati sovereignty over the Buraimi Oasis, which is also claimed by Oman.[193] And since the 1980s, the UAE has become increasingly more vocal in its dispute with Iran over the three Persian Gulf islands of the Greater and Lesser Tunb and Abu Musa. The UAE had been active in the GCC and had joined the military campaign to liberate Kuwait from Iraq. Nevertheless, before the 2000s the UAE was generally neither interested in nor capable of military power projection. Well into the 1990s, in fact, Dubai still had its own military command and a separate military budget. It was only at that point that Dubai integrated its forces with those of the other emirates.[194] It was generally only after 2011 that a new, much more assertive and more security-oriented foreign policy made the UAE one of the militarily active players in civil wars in Syria, Libya, and later Yemen.

The militarization of Emirati foreign policy had actually started a few years before 2011. In 1994, the UAE signed a bilateral defense agreement with the United States, and throughout the 1990s it exponentially increased its military purchases from both the United States and Western Europe. The trend continued into the 2000s, with the Emirates spending an estimated $104 billion from 2007 to 2012 in armaments from the United States alone.[195] The UAE was the only Arab country to have sent a contingent of troops to Afghanistan, and the 250 Emirati troops have been there since 2003. In 2010, the country was reported to have spent $529 million to set up an eight-hundred-member battalion of foreign troops, mostly of Colombian and South African mercenaries. They were being trained by retired soldiers from the United States, Britain, Germany, and the French Foreign Legion.[196] The battalion of foreign mercenaries was entrusted with a number of critical security tasks, including intelligence gathering, urban combat, suppression of possible uprisings inside the country's numerous and sprawling labor camps, the securing of radioactive and nuclear materials, and human missions and special operations "to destroy enemy personnel and equipment."[197] There was even a possibility that the battalion of foreign troops might be used to take over the disputed islands in the Persian Gulf.

The pursuit of the country's more assertive foreign and security policy can be attributed to three primary causes. First, the UAE, not unlike Qatar and Saudi Arabia, has witnessed a generational shift in its leadership, both at the apex of the state and in other layers of the policymaking apparatus. Whereas the older, first generation of Emirati leaders had a more measured and deliberate, consultative method of decision making, the current, younger generation of leaders is more restless and is less reticent to pursue policies that are more aggressive. This younger generation—as in Saudi Arabia—is convinced that it knows the world, is certain of its own expertise, and is generally unwilling to entertain alternative possibilities. This is one of the primary reasons for the more assertive, security-focused, and military-led foreign and security policies in the UAE and elsewhere in the region.[198]

A second factor has to do with the Emirati leadership's greater self-confidence, grounded in the country's resources, agendas, goals, and priorities. Ruling one of the world's wealthiest countries, equipped with some of the most advanced weaponry available anywhere, the Emirati leadership feels confident in its abilities to project power abroad, especially in weak and fragile states like Yemen and Libya. This feeds into a third driving force of a more assertive foreign policy: a sense of concern—concern about the pervasiveness of regional instability as rooted in developments in Yemen, Bahrain, Egypt, Syria, Libya, and Iraq, as well as the rise of Daesh.[199] For Emirati authorities, regional instability was merely a prelude to the spread of political Islam, which they saw as deeply threatening to the UAE's own domestic stability. The authorities became especially alarmed at the increasing number of local Islamists who were attracted to the Muslim Brotherhood and who became politically active in the wake of the 2011 uprisings.[200] The threat from the Muslim Brotherhood was seen not so much in its ability to overthrow the state as in its "potential to disrupt social cohesiveness and stability by challenging the progress made in various aspects of societal development."[201] In December 2011, the authorities clamped down on the local branch of the Muslim Brotherhood, known as Islah. Many of Islah's leaders were arrested and imprisoned and had their passports confiscated, and some had their Emirati citizenship revoked.[202]

Despite its own domestic Islamist threat, the UAE government has long viewed Iran as its most serious security threat based on Iran's alleged ambitions in the Persian Gulf, its ideology and rhetoric, its weapons acquisition program, its purported support for terrorism, and its control over the disputed islands.[203] At times, it seemed possible that the UAE's tensions with Iran over the islands would escalate to unmanageable proportions.[204] There are also approximately four hundred thousand Iranians in Dubai, often seen by the Emirati state as a potential fifth column for the Islamic Republic. Not surprisingly, the UAE, which in the 2000s emerged as a major entrepôt for the transit of goods and services into Iran, has been at the forefront of enforcing U.S.-led trade and banking sanctions against the Islamic Republic. As a result, UAE-Iran trade slowed to approximately $4 billion in 2015 from an estimated $23 billion in 2010.[205]

The UAE's efforts against the Islamic Republic have not gone beyond bandwagoning with the Saudis and the United States and joining forces in implementing diplomatic and economic measures against the country. On other fronts, however, Emirati foreign and security policies have seen steady and more in-depth militarization. In 2011, the UAE sent a total of twelve war jets to Libya to enforce a no-fly zone over the country in the multinational effort to oust Qaddafi from power. At the same time, the UAE emerged as one of the "core members" of the U.S.-led coalition fighting against Daesh in Syria. In May 2011, the UAE signed a $529 million contract with a firm called Reflex Resources, formerly of Blackwater fame, to provide "operational, planning, and training support" to the country's armed forces. A similar contract in November 2013 with another military consulting firm, Knowledge International, was also meant to boost the fighting efficiency of the Emirati military.[206] In 2012, the UAE deployed six F-16 fighter planes to Qandahar Airfield. In August 2014, UAE air force planes, alongside Egyptian fighter planes, took part in bombing the positions of a Libyan militia group with ties to Qatar.[207] And in August 2015, the UAE sent a three-thousand-person armored brigade to Yemen. In September 2015, more than fifty of them were killed in action near Ma'rib. Within the GCC, meanwhile, the UAE has been one of the key states spearheading efforts to establish a coordinated missile defense system, which the United States has been promoting since 2012–2013. With a military base in Eritrea already, in early 2017 the UAE announced plans for a second base in the Horn of Africa, this one in Somaliland.

In 2015, there were approximately five thousand U.S. military forces in the UAE, including thirty-five hundred who worked at the Al Dhafra airbase.[208] While U.S. forces functioned as an additional security guarantee for the Emirates, the country continued to rely heavily on hired mercenaries for training purposes and to carry out operations in Yemen. By 2015, when the UAE joined Saudi Arabia's campaign in Yemen, its battalion of foreign mercenaries had grown to about eighteen hundred troops, each paid between two thousand and three thousand dollars a month. The Emirates reportedly sent 450 Latin American troops to Yemen, many of them from Columbia, Panama, El Salvador, and Chile.[209] For the Yemen campaign, the foreign fighters were handpicked and given ranks in the UAE military, each getting paid fifteen hundred dollars a week for taking part in the war. Before long, Colombian military commanders were complaining of a "gun drain," with many fellow commanders retiring early for the lucrative life of a mercenary.

The need to employ foreign mercenaries gives insight into one of the biggest challenges a country the size of the UAE faces in its efforts at power projection, namely, limits on its human resources capacity. Small states the size of the UAE, and in the Persian Gulf also Qatar, may have aspirations of exerting power and influence beyond their borders. In doing so, they embark on massive and record-breaking arms purchases. But militarily the best they can do is to either engage in quick and surgical strikes, as has been the case in Libya, or perhaps rely on hired foreign fighters. As the Saudis learned in Yemen, money by itself does not win wars. The Saudis are also learning, however, that in foreign policy money does buy allies, a lesson that both the Emiratis and the Qataris are also taking to heart. But there too the success can also be temporary and ephemeral. Friends and allies secured by financial inducements, be they states or nonstate actors, are just as likely to abandon the desired course of action if and when a better offer comes along. At best, money is likely to help one rent friends, but not buy them permanently.

Qatar

Qatari foreign policy differed from that of Saudi Arabia and that of the UAE for much of the 1990s and 2000s, and lasting well after the

Arab Spring. Particularly during the rule of Sheikh Hamad from 1995 to 2013, awash in money and filled with self-confidence, Qatar pursued a foreign policy that often went against expectations and regional norms, which up until that point had meant following Saudi Arabia's lead in international affairs. Whereas Saudi Arabia and the UAE had both adopted bandwagoning as their preferred strategy, synchronizing with and entrusting much of their security to the United States, Qatar opted for hedging, choosing instead to maintain open lines of communication, and comparatively close and cordial relations, with multiple, often opposing actors.[210] To those looking in from the outside, Qatari foreign policy during this time appeared maverick at best and chaotic and incoherent at worst.[211] But there was actually an internal logic and coherence to the policy, which was meant to ensure that the small state had as few enemies and as many friends as possible. At the same time, hedging had steadily helped Qatar secure a place for itself as a critical connector, a mediator, for those who otherwise had no means of communicating with one another.

Hedging was one of four primary tools that Qatar employed in its efforts to carve out a place for itself outside Saudi Arabia's overpowering shadow. The others were an aggressive branding campaign, a robust effort at investing internationally, and continued reliance on the American security umbrella. The combined effects of these foreign policy tools and objectives was the emergence of what elsewhere I have called Qatari "subtle power."[212]

Not surprisingly, Qatar's sense of empowerment, and the brash style of its two chief foreign policy architects—the emir, and Prime Minister Hamad bin Jassim—did not sit well with the Saudis, who had their own hegemonic aspirations in relation to the Arabian Peninsula. The fact that the Qataris maintained ostensibly friendly or even diplomatic relations with many actors that Saudi Arabia did not approve of—the likes of Iran, Hamas, and the Muslim Brotherhood—further aggravated Riyadh. The alleged involvement of Saudi Arabia, along with the UAE, in a plot in 1996 to remove the emir from power and to reinstall his recently overthrown father back in office did little to improve relations between the two states. That same year, 1996, Al Jazeera television started broadcasting out of Doha, giving a new dimension to the public relations battle between the two neighbors.

Tensions between Qatar and Saudi Arabia came to a head shortly after the eruption of the 2011 Arab uprisings. Whereas Riyadh saw the Arab Spring as a threatening moment that could topple the monarchy in Bahrain and spill over into its own Eastern Province, Doha saw it as an opportunity through which it could expand its influence over those states weakened or on the verge of collapse and at the same time to solidify its ties with nonstate actors such as the Muslim Brotherhood, whose fortunes the uprisings appeared to have improved. Saudi Arabia initially resorted to backroom diplomacy in an effort to get Qatar to alter course. In response to open accusations of Qatari interference in the affairs of other states, Qatar's foreign minister at the time, Khaled Al-Attiya, proclaimed that "the independence of Qatar's foreign policy is simply non-negotiable. . . . Qatar is to take decisions, and follow a path, of its own."[213] A month later, Saudi Arabia, Bahrain, and the UAE withdrew their ambassadors from Doha in protest.

If Saudi Arabia wanted to teach Qatar a lesson by publicly expressing its displeasure in 2014, it appeared to have initially succeeded. After the three countries sent their ambassadors back to Doha in November 2014, Qatar began to shift its foreign policy practices and its overall international orientation precipitously. Steadily, the emirate distanced itself from Tehran, with the emir snubbing Rouhani in November 2015 by not accepting his invitation to attend a summit in Tehran along with Russian president Vladimir Putin. When the Saudi embassy in Tehran was attacked in January 2016, Qatar joined the chorus of condemnation and downgraded its diplomatic relations with the Islamic Republic.

Qatari foreign policy changed in other ways as well. Al Jazeera, long a mirror of the country's foreign policy, stopped nearly all coverage of troubling developments in Bahrain and Saudi Arabia and the difficulties of the military campaign in Yemen. The station's Arabic channel also stopped broadcasts by the cleric Sheikh Qaradawi, long considered one of the main spiritual leaders of the Muslim Brotherhood, and instead its programming began to reflect increasingly pro-Saudi tendencies.[214] Further, on September 2014 the Qatari government made a point of publicly distancing itself from the Muslim Brotherhood by asking seven of its leaders living in Doha to leave the country. And, as a show of solidarity with the Saudi campaign in Yemen, Qatar sent one thousand soldiers to aid the war effort in noncombat operations. Qatar also pulled back its ambitions and its operations in both Libya and Syria, because of both strategic set-backs on the ground and its reduced regional competition with Saudi Arabia. As the events of June 2017 were to show, the reorientation of Doha's foreign policy was apparently not enough to assuage Saudi and Emirati concerns. Qatar still retained far too much independent-mindedness in its foreign relations for Riyadh and Abu Dhabi to tolerate.

The reorientation of Qatari foreign policy after 2013–2014 cannot all be explained through the country's changing relationship with Saudi Arabia. The new emir, Sheikh Tamim bin Hamad Al Thani (b. 1985), has a disposition different from his father's and has been far more concerned with domestic rather than international affairs. Soon after taking office, he faced rapidly declining oil and gas prices beginning in June 2014, necessitating further retrenchments from costly international engagements and greater attention to matters closer to home. As far back as the late 2000s, some analysts were warning that the foreign policy successes of Qatar, like that of Saudi Arabia, could prove short-lived because of the institutional limitations of policymaking and follow-up.[215] But the favored panacea for institutional weakness in foreign policy—dollar diplomacy—can be prohibitively expensive, especially if the much bigger and better-resourced Saudi Arabia is already practicing it.

Qatar's foreign policy profile and orientation have therefore clearly changed since the coming to power of its current emir in 2013. In his first few years in power, Sheikh Tamim appears to be following a foreign policy more in line with traditional GCC practices by having allowed Saudi Arabia to play the role of big brother and taking the lead in regional affairs. Such comparatively low-key diplomacy was still apparently not docile enough for Riyadh's ruling elite. Tamim also appears to have abandoned, partly out of temperament and partly out of necessity, his father's ambitions of turning Qatar into one of the most consequential and influential players in the Persian Gulf region, in the greater Middle East, and beyond. Qatari subtle power appears to have receded, and along with it so have, for now at least, Qatar's ambitions of outsizing its geography and demography to become a middle power. "Clearly," one scholar of the region has written, "Qatar is a country in search of a regional role."[216] Whatever that regional role may turn out to be, Tamim, and the circumstances shaping the choices before him, seem to be leaning toward one that is more consistent with those of small states.

The cases of Qatar and the UAE represent those of small states which by dint of circumstance and leadership choices have acted as, or aspired to be, middle powers. In their endeavors, under different circumstances and for different reasons, both countries, Qatar from the mid-1990s until about 2013 and the UAE after 2014 or so, succeeded in traversing limitations of geography and demography and exerted a level of power far beyond that of their status as small states. Unlike traditional middle powers, they were far too small to aspire to become regional hegemons, an aspiration that their bigger neighbors, Iran and Saudi Arabia, could not dispense with. But they did nevertheless seek to become influential in different pockets of territory across the Middle East. In the immediate aftermath of the Arab Spring, most of all in the early months of 2011, Qatar fancied itself as the primary power broker in Libya, Egypt, and Syria. But by 2014 it was becoming glaringly obvious that its carefully calibrated hedging strategy was not bearing any fruit. At the root of *hedging* is a *bet* that those with whom one interacts will one day become trusty and useful allies. But sometimes the bet does not pay off. A bet may be placed on the wrong horse, one, for example, without staying power, as Qatar learned the hard way in relation to the Egyptian Muslim Brotherhood.

Qatar's relative retreat from regional politics—whether tactical or strategic, forced or voluntary—was occurring just as the UAE started entering the scene thanks to its increasingly assertive foreign and security policies. Despite the UAE at times being at odds with Saudi Arabia over territory, trade, and influence within the GCC, the post-2011 period brought the two states much closer together than perhaps at any other time in their modern history. This closeness was built on a common distaste for and competition with Iran, a growing sense of suspicion and fear in both countries over the spread of Islamist tendencies within their populations, and their eagerness to demonstrate to the United States their willingness to take regional matters into their own hands.

In the 1970s and the 1980s, Kuwait played a similarly outsized role across the Persian Gulf and elsewhere in the Middle East. The 1990 Iraqi invasion, and the need to attend to manifold domestic consequences of the ensuing occupation and liberation, put an end to Kuwait's outward focus and its regionally proactive foreign policy. In the 2000s Qatar did the same thing, until the ire of its neighbors prompted the emirate's new leadership to moderate its behavior and shift its foreign policy orientations beginning in 2014. By then the UAE had entered the scene, a new player brimming with confidence and a militarily anchored foreign policy reminiscent of those of the Arab republics of yesteryear in the 1950s and the 1960s. How long the UAE's proactive foreign and security policies remain in place, and how long its ambitions and aspirations will outsize and obscure geographic size and demography, is open to question.

What is certain is that the GCC states in general—and within it especially Qatar, the UAE, and even Saudi Arabia—will continue to remain "security dependent" for some time to come. Discussed in more detail in chapter 4, this security dependence is anchored in the GCC states' small size and demographic limitations, making literally all of them highly dependent on support from more powerful friends and allies outside the region.[217] Ehteshami and Hinnebusch go so far as to maintain that the GCC region continues to be ruled by dependent client elites.[218] In contrast to the case in the immediate decades before and following formal independence in 1971, today in the twenty-first century the ruling elites of the GCC can no longer be considered dependent clients of the Western powers or anyone else. But their security dependence remains unchanged, and their appetite for newer and ever more effective weaponry only perpetuates and deepens their continued dependence on arms manufacturers and civilian decision makers in the West and especially in the United States.

In addition to middle power politics, sectarianism has emerged as a second feature of the foreign policies of the Persian Gulf region in the post-2011 period. Gregory Gause has argued persuasively that this sectarianism has emerged as a useful tool in the Middle East's new cold war between Iran and Saudi Arabia, its rise and spread facilitated by the institutional weaknesses of states such as Lebanon, Syria, and Iraq and their manifold domestic failures.[219] Weak states have become a primary arena of competition between the region's rising powers, and the competition is often fought through appeal to and the employment of nonstate actors within these fragile polities. Societal developments have also been consequential in fueling sectarianism, with social actors increasingly attracted to transnational affinities and forms of identity. When states fail, affinities for one's sect and other more primordial forms of identity assume greater importance. Iran and Saudi Arabia have tapped into the twin and reinforcing developments of state failure and salient sectarian identities.

The outcome has been increasing levels of belligerence across the Middle East, with the Persian Gulf as the epicenter of the raging cold war. And in the process the region's insecurities have increased exponentially. For all the states involved, the resulting security dilemmas they confront have become intractable.

4

The Intractable Security Dilemma

A primary cause of chronic insecurity in the Persian Gulf is the pervasiveness of region-wide security dilemmas for all actors involved. These security dilemmas have resulted in the emergence of a highly competitive, and equally unstable, strategic landscape in the region. The post-2011 era has featured competition between a triad composed of Iran; most of the GCC states, led by Saudi Arabia; and the United States. The pervasive insecurity that has emerged is fed and sustained by deeply ingrained threat perceptions, which in turn serve as key drivers of foreign and security policy behavior and preferences.

This chapter examines the causes of the development and persistence of the security dilemma in the Persian Gulf, the ways and means in which the security dilemma manifests itself, and the measures states tend to take, either in alliance or by "self-binding," to protect themselves from its consequences or to pull out of it. The chapter then analyzes the reasons why a post-2011 strategic landscape emerged in the region, with a focus on the dynamics that in recent decades have deepened multiple and overlaying insecurities. Last, to elucidate the causes and manifestations of the prevailing security dilemma in the Gulf, the chapter explores the threat perceptions of two sets of regional actors: Iran, on the one side, and Saudi Arabia and the United Arab Emirates, on the other.

I argue that a number of developments have combined to make the Persian Gulf's security dilemma intractable and self-sustaining. These are both structural—a product of the larger geostrategic environment in which the region finds itself—and derived from the policy choices of state actors within and outside the region. To begin with, vast geographic discrepancies between much larger, poorer states, alongside "small super-rich mini-states controlling much of the region's oil," have made the Gulf region "an enduring conflict zone."[1] The self-sustaining and self-perpetuating nature of the security dilemma phenomenon has also been highly consequential. Further, at the most fundamental level, the Gulf's security dilemma derives from a basic lack of trust among the actors involved in the region, regardless of whether or not they form alliances over specific issues. Iran does not trust its Arab neighbors on the other side of the Gulf, and the region's Arab states do not trust Iran. Equally pervasive is a lack of trust among the Arab states themselves, even within those belonging to the Gulf Cooperation Council. The GCC has, of course, facilitated better communication and a greater level of coordination among its member states in areas such as commerce and economy, travel and transportation, tourism and migration, and even common defense and security. But, as chapter 3 demonstrated, when it comes to defense and security matters, the GCC has tended to act as a cohesive unit of sorts only in moments of crisis, and its members remain fundamentally deeply mistrustful of each other.

From this pervasive mistrust, and the ensuing insecurity-generating cycles of suspicions and tensions, has emerged a highly volatile strategic landscape in the region. The volatility of this strategic landscape is nothing new and has deep historical roots dating as far back as the 1500s, when the Portuguese first noticed the Persian Gulf's naval and commercial importance and competed with both the Safavids and the Ottomans for greater power and influence over the waterway.[2] The Dutch and then the British followed, the latter holding on until the late 1960s to the resource-rich region whose strategic importance had in the meanwhile grown exponentially. The Americans soon joined in and made themselves an inseparable component of the region's strategic landscape, to this day remaining firmly entrenched in the fabric of its security architecture. They courted, and were in turn courted by, many of the regional actors. As times changed, American policy went from President Richard Nixon's "twin pillars" policy to Bill Clinton's "dual containment," with the Bush and Obama administrations frequently reminding the Iranians that "all options are on the table" and then encouraging Iran and Saudi Arabia to get along and to learn to "share" the region.[3] The Trump administration revived long-standing U.S. animosity toward Iran, and U.S.-Iranian tensions rose again. My focus here is the post-2011 period, when the eruption of popular uprisings in many parts of the Arab world added another layer of interwoven security challenges for the actors involved in the Persian Gulf, including the United States.

President Obama's belated and faint encouragement of a Saudi-Iranian détente notwithstanding, mutual threat perceptions abound and mark multiple layers of mistrust and suspicion among the actors involved in the Persian Gulf. After examining the prevailing strategic landscape, the chapter turns to a more focused discussion of the security dilemma in the Persian Gulf, its causes, how it unfolds, and its consequences. In specific, I examine "bandwagoning" as a preferred policy option for the GCC and explore its consequences both for the regional states adopting it and for the United States and Iran. It has contributed directly to pervasive and seemingly irreconcilable threat perceptions, in turn fueling the region's highly tense and contentious strategic landscape.

Post-2011, the security challenges that the Persian Gulf is facing are forming in a highly charged, sectarian environment. Assumptions about a "Shia crescent" that runs from Iran through Iraq and the oil-rich Eastern Province of Saudi Arabia have gained considerable traction among Gulf political leaders, despite these having little basis in historical reality.[4] As one observer has noted, "The strategic outlook of the elites in the Gulf seems to be determined by three fears: of Persians, Shiites, and populist Islamist movements. Iran is the common denominator of these fears."[5] According to one of my Emirati interlocutors, from a Gulf perspective, "Iran is the first-, second-, and third-biggest threat facing the UAE and the GCC."[6] Other threats, after Iran, include Daesh, extremism, sectarianism, the war in Yemen, and the general state of malaise in the Arab world. Moreover, most leaders of the Gulf monarchies see developments in Iraq through sectarian lenses, viewing Iran as the primary culprit in Iraq's prolonged civil war.[7] These threat perceptions are magnified through the spread of satellite television, the Internet, and social media.[8]

Ultimately, these factors have combined to make the Persian Gulf's security dilemma intractable. The region is stuck in a vicious cycle of multiple and overlapping security dilemmas that reinforce each other and continue to perpetuate dynamics that generate insecurity. This insecurity exists not only at the level of individual states but also at a broader regional level, making the Persian Gulf one of the most contentious and conflict-prone regions in the world.

Dilemmas of Security and Insecurity

Scholars of international relations take as an article of faith the understanding that "the pursuit of security is part and parcel of the production of insecurity."[9] The cycle of security-insecurity thus perpetuated is known as a *security dilemma*: the pursuit of military power can lessen a state's security by prompting other states to follow suit, thereby precipitating an arms race in which the security of all parties deteriorates.[10] "The essence of the dilemma is that the measures a state takes to increase its own security usually decrease the security of other states."[11]

The security dilemma has been called "the *quintessential dilemma* in international politics." It arises from the "existential condition of uncertainty in human affairs." As such, security dilemma involves a two-level strategic predicament, one a dilemma of interpretation—about the motives, intentions, and capabilities of others—and the other a dilemma of response, concerning the most rational way of responding.[12] Uncertainty over the motives of the adversary accounts for much of the self-defeating strategies of competition that states caught in the security dilemma pursue.[13] For those states experiencing it, the security dilemma can have three negative consequences: it can reduce a state's own military capabilities, it can encourage an adversary to engage in expansion, and it can be wasteful of both financial and material resources.[14]

Ken Booth and Nicholas Wheeler use the concept of the "security paradox" to describe the same phenomenon. They define a security paradox as "*a situation in which two or more actors, seeking only to improve their own security, provoke through their words or actions an increase in mutual tension, resulting in less security all around.*" Such a paradox emerges when "leaders resolve their dilemma of response in a manner that creates a spiral of mutual hostility, when neither wanted it."[15] Central to the dilemmas of interpretation and response are accurate threat assessments. The essence of the security dilemma lies in insecurity and private information. The security dilemma can be avoided, therefore, if states provide more information about their intentions.[16]

National security decisions are not made in a contextual vacuum; they are influenced by economic, political, and cultural considerations as well as diplomatic ones.[17] A security dilemma may involve both state and non-state actors and also involves complex interrelationships of the both psychological and material dimensions of security.[18] Along with technology, geography is among the most consequential determinants of whether a security dilemma emerges. More specifically, geographic proximity can heighten or intensify the security dilemma.[19]

Emerging unintentionally and largely as a result of structural factors, a security dilemma is driven by fear and uncertainty over the intentions of others, and as such it can be exacerbated by psychological factors.[20] It arises, in fact, from the "existential condition of unresolvable uncertainty" in the minds of decision makers.[21] In conditions of security dilemma, even conciliatory gestures are likely to be viewed with suspicion and be met with security responses. The intention and capacity to perceive the motives behind and responsiveness toward the intentions of others is called "security dilemma sensibility."[22]

Despite the prevalence of these and other structural factors in the emergence of the security dilemma, nonstructural factors, such as greed or fear, may also play important roles in fostering tensions, an arms race, and security competition.[23] A "strategic challenge" occurs when a security dilemma has been settled, and a state's intentions have been identified as hostile.[24] Not surprisingly, despite having allocated considerable resources to security-producing programs, Arab states are subject to the security dilemma at multiple levels and remain both insecure and vulnerable.[25]

Security dilemma is likely to occur at two levels. Most commonly, it occurs at a *bilateral* level, when efforts by one state to enhance its security increase the insecurity of another actor and a vicious cycle of security-insecurity ensues. A second level at which a security dilemma forms is *regional*, whereby a collection of countries, through either formal or informal multi-lateral means and mechanisms, seek to enhance their own security and as a result increase the insecurity of one or more state actors on the other side. An example of this in the Persian Gulf would be enhanced security and defense efforts by the GCC as a collective organization, viewed as threatening by Iran, which would in turn react by initiating its own security enhancing measures, thus perpetuating a vicious cycle.

Kenneth Waltz has famously argued that the international system is one of anarchy and self-help.[26] Ever since World War II, this anarchy has been kept at bay largely through the efforts of multinational organizations such as the United Nations; the World Trade Organization; and regional organizations like the Organization of American States, the African Union, and even the GCC. When it suits their purposes, states often defy international regimes if they figure that the benefits outweigh the reputational and actual costs of the sanctions imposed on them. Alternatively, as the United States did in the lead-up to its invasion of Iraq in 2003, states can seek to manipulate international regimes in ways that fit their own self-interests. What has transpired as a result is a balance-of-power system in which states strive to ensure their survival.[27]

As Joseph Nye maintains, given changing circumstances and the evolution of new instruments of power, balance of power remains a viable but ultimately limited strategy.[28] At the same time, the pervasiveness of economic and security hierarchies at both global and regional levels cannot be denied; through them varying degrees of authority, regional peace and stability, and international trade prevail.[29] Smaller, weaker states tend to bandwagon with more powerful patrons for protection against potential, often nearby, foes. Some states may voluntarily cede partial authority—in the GCC's case especially in the security arena—in order to enjoy the benefits of a U.S.-dominated hierarchy, while a few others, most notably Iran, must resort to self-help to survive. This closely approximates Hedley Bull's conception of an international arena in which rules and understandings that limit resort to violence and foster respect coexist with anarchy and self-help.[30]

Despite a proliferation of norms and regimes governing the international system, states tend to fear one another and do not trust each other's intentions. In such an atmosphere of mistrust and suspicion, even efforts aimed at increasing one's defensive capabilities are likely to be seen as engaging in offensive build-up, further perpetuating a self-reinforcing vicious cycle.[31] This "fatalist thinking" is premised on the assumption that the adversary simply cannot be trusted, except perhaps by mistake. The primary driving force of policymaking, therefore, is fear, and fear is central to the security dilemma.[32] According to Booth and Wheeler, "*embracing the assumption of uncertainty* must be the basis for building and sustaining trust between peoples." This is where the notion of common security comes into play; common security rests on the premise that security is best guaranteed when based not on mutual fear, but on a reciprocal relationship between states. Cooperation mechanisms should be developed with those states that may be potential or actual threats.[33]

Security dilemma prompts states to form alliances, in turn prompting the establishment of counteralliances.[34] States must choose between building up their own armed forces or placing themselves under the protection of more powerful patrons. To allay or ameliorate their security dilemma, many states form alliances, especially with more powerful states with whom they share strategic objectives.[35] One of the determinants of alliance choice in the security dilemma is the degree of strategic interest that the parties have in depending on each other.[36] There is at best a "modest association between ideology and alignment."[37] What matters instead are common strategic objectives and interests.

The biggest factor in the choice of alliance is, in fact, "the relative *dependence* of the partners on the alliance—how much they need each other's aid—and their perceptions of each other's dependence."[38] The weaker the state, the more likely it is to bandwagon.[39] Smaller, less powerful, and more subordinate states tend to bandwagon with, instead of balance against, more dominant states, especially those states that have credibly committed to restraints on their exercise of power.[40] When bandwagoning, states choose on the basis not so much of power but of assessments of the threats they face.[41] In such alliances, fears of "abandonment" and defection are considerable, as are the risks of entrapment. Entrapment occurs when a state is "being dragged into a conflict over an ally's interests that one does not share."[42] "Firmness toward the adversary increases the risk of entrapment by the ally," as the ally becomes confident of support.[43] The risks of abandonment and entrapment have an inverse relationship—decreasing one can lead to increases in the other.

Given the pervasiveness of the security dilemma, and given that conditions of anarchy prevail in the international arena, the more powerful states work together to strike a balance of power.[44] Thus are born alliances, which are essentially security institutions meant to deal with threats from nonmembers. Some alliances are better at dealing with conflict among members, as they have institutional mechanisms for internal dispute resolution. Highly institutionalized alliances are more likely to persist.[45] More complex security alliances are more likely to be able to adapt to the ending of the threat that led to its formation.

Since states tend to bandwagon with a powerful ally against another threat, perceptions of power and status are important determinants of attracting potential bandwagoners. Status drives from "collective beliefs about a given state's ranking on valued attributes," such as wealth, coercive capabilities, culture, demographic position, sociopolitical organization, and diplomatic clout. To win allies and attract bandwagoners, *"states signal their status claims through rhetoric, diplomatic activity, and acquisition of status symbols."*[46]

As we have seen, security dilemmas can cause self-reinforcing vicious cycles. They can therefore have unintended and self-defeating consequences resembling a spiral.[47] Just as there is an intimate link between a security dilemma and insecurity, there is a similar link between securitization and insecuritization.[48] Strong commitment and support reduces one's bargaining leverage over an ally, which, assured of the support being given, can become "less influenceable." At the same time, strong support for an ally can also increase an adversary's perceptions of threats to it.[49]

Another way out of a security dilemma is "self-binding," whereby a state engages in "unilateral initiatives, with no expectation of specific reciprocity." The challenge is to make the gesture seem credible by "imposing visible sacrifices on oneself." "As a precondition for self-binding it may be necessary for a state to revise downward, on its own, its estimate of the threats its [sic] faces."[50] Self-binding as a strategy will not succeed in the long run if other international actors do not reciprocate, and its eventual success depends on the emergence of shared norms of self-restraint.

By and large, self-binding has not yet occurred in the Persian Gulf, or elsewhere in the Middle East for that matter, and the region's multiple security dilemmas have only become more acute over time. Regional and global developments have amplified pervasive feelings of insecurity and the prevalence of threat perceptions. Balancing, bandwagoning, omnibalancing, and even hedging (by Qatar) continue to be employed in the constant search to enhance security and to address or at least ameliorate perceived threats.[51] But alliances remain impermanent, suspicion underpins interstate relations, and the region's strategic landscape continues to remain unpredictable and volatile.

The Prevailing Strategic Landscape

The Middle East's persistent security dilemma has resulted in the emergence of an unstable strategic environment, at times making the use of force the least damaging choice among the menu of options available.[52] Up until the 1980s and the early 1990s, Arab states were subject to the security dilemma in dealing with Israel, with one another, and with outside powers.[53] Today, the strategic competition with Israel has subsided and been settled, in Israel's favor, and has been replaced with a new security dilemma, this one involving Iran. This new strategic competition is only one in a whole array of challenges facing state leaders in the Gulf region and beyond.

Middle Eastern policymakers are "quintessential realists" motivated by regime survival, sovereignty, territorial integrity, international acceptance, and internal and external threats.[54] Faced with pressures from a global hierarchy, regional competitors, and domestic sources, leaders in the Middle East's status quo regimes generally tend to omnibalance with global patrons to contain trans-state threats. In the Persian Gulf region, these status quo regimes have historically included the oil monarchies, which, as close allies of the West, have perceived of themselves as supportive actors in helping sustain the regional security architecture crafted by the West, mostly the United States. Meanwhile, revisionist regimes, such as Iraq between 1990 and 2003 and Iran after the 1978 revolution, engage in reverse omnibalancing in order to mobilize regime alliances against Western global powers and their regional allies.[55]

In the Middle East, states have long tried to address their security dilemma through power balancing, by engaging in arms buildup on the one hand and alliance formation on the other.[56] For the most part, however, they have been poor balancers and weak hegemons because of several notable factors, among them persistent rivalries, an absence of stable and durable hierarchies between states, the presence of powerful identities that overlap and are even discordant with the existing state system, and the conflicting influences of external actors.[57]

Mention was made in chapter 1 of the intimate connection, in the Middle East in general and in the Persian Gulf in particular, between domestic politics—more specifically the imperative of domestic legitimacy and stability—and foreign policy. As Gregory Gause has observed, Persian Gulf leaders often assume the domestic-destabilization threat to be more serious and immediate than the classic power-capabilities threat. And the greater importance accorded to a domestic-destabilization threat is one of the key drivers of foreign policy and regional-alliance decisions.[58] Over time, this has resulted in the emergence of close alliances with outside patrons, first with the British and then with the Americans. These alliances have in turn been facilitated through the Middle East being a "penetrated" system, subject to exceptional levels of external—that is, Western—intervention and control.[59] The fragmentation of the Arab order in the early 1980s further allowed external penetration by the United States. At the same time, cracks in the region-wide alliance enabled local actors to pursue their own goals and agendas without much concern about such region-wide issues as the Palestinian cause or Arab unity.[60]

The 2011 Arab uprisings gave impetus to a new regional power struggle, this time between the United States and Iran through their respective proxies.[61] More ominously, the uprisings also manifested the ongoing conflicts between rival, coexisting identities. As the consequences of the uprisings spilled over into civil wars and heightened interstate tensions, identity-based conflicts intensified.[62] This only magnified the dramatic appeal of Muslim transnationalist tendencies across the Middle East, especially among nonstate actors.[63] There was already a highly unstable environment in the Middle East and especially in the Persian Gulf region because of the prevalence of paranoia.[64] The 2011 uprisings, and their nightmarish consequences in places like Libya and Syria, only made Persian Gulf policymakers more jittery and insecure in their hold on power.

The United States has played a decisive and integral role in Persian Gulf security, part of a broader history of in-depth political, diplomatic, and military engagement in the region. But the United States has been unable to translate its direct and extensive military presence in the Persian Gulf into corresponding political gains.[65] To the contrary, its presence in the region has directly led to both heightened anti-Americanism and to deepening of regional tensions. This engagement has caused "a series of political conundrums for the United States" but has changed neither the extent nor the nature of the U.S. security commitment to the Middle East and the Persian Gulf.[66]

There have never really been any serious challenges to U.S. hegemony in the Middle East, and yet the United States views the region as most threatening to its national security.[67] Raymond Hinnebusch distinguishes two phases of American hegemony in the Middle East. First, as an off-shore balancer in the 1990s, the United States sought to ensure its hegemony through three means: the "dual containment" policy, pushing for Arab-Israeli peace, and strengthening its alliance with the Persian Gulf monarchies. A second phase of U.S. hegemony began in the 2000s, this one far more direct and driven by military means, through the invasions of first Afghanistan and then Iraq.[68] As Mohammed Ayoob has observed, the U.S. invasion of Iraq was "the culmination of a directly intrusive military policy in the region."[69]

In the 2000s, the United States found itself involved in a quagmire in Iraq. To this was added an intense strategic competition with Iran, not just in Iraq and the Persian Gulf waterway but also in areas as distant as Africa and South America. Despite a surge in the number of its combat troops in 2007, the United States was unable to provide Iraq with security and stability, and the American occupation officially ended in 2011 under a dark cloud of an Iraq in turmoil. The American withdrawal did little to lessen U.S.-Iranian tensions. In fact, it was partly, if not largely, a product of expanding Iranian political and military influence in Iraq and its deepening strategic competition with the United States and its regional allies. Among the key non-Arab actors in the Middle East, Iran gained the most leverage in the post-2003 period.[70] Not surprisingly, throughout the 2000s, a zero-sum game emerged between Iran and the United States that resembled a security dialogue of the deaf. Neither Iran nor the United States saw any validity to the security concerns of the other, and each sought to curtail, contain, and undermine the other and its allies whenever and by almost whatever means possible.

Within this context, tensions across the Persian Gulf continued to deepen throughout the 2000s and the 2010s. These tensions were fanned by the rise of transnational loyalties and identity-centered movements. There are, in fact, two kinds of perceived threats in the Persian Gulf, one revolving around the military capabilities of neighbors and the military threat they pose, the other the appeal of neighbors to domestic populations. Persian Gulf governments have been particularly paranoid about the meddling of neighbors in their domestic affairs. In 2017, for example, although no evidence was produced, one of the demands presented to Qatar by the UAE, Saudi Arabia, and Bahrain was that it stop interfering in their domestic politics. As Gause has observed, "Perceptions of threat to regime stability, originating domestically but abetted by foreign actors," play a key role in the foreign policy decisions of Gulf leaders.[71] These fears are magnified because of a number of cross-border links and common identities, including ethnic, sectarian, tribal, and ideological linkages between and within peoples across the Gulf region and between peoples and leaders across borders. By the end of the new millennium's first decade, the Persian Gulf's security dilemma had become so deeply entrenched that escape from it seems all but impossible.

Across the Middle East, as elsewhere, foreign policymaking is driven by a combination of perceived and actual threats, both domestic and international, and also by regional rivalries. In fractured polities like Iraq, foreign policy is influenced by regime-society relations and by intra-regime struggles.[72] But, as we shall see shortly in the case of Iran, a state need not necessarily suffer from the same level of institutional paralysis and fragmentation as Iraq (or post-2011 Libya and Syria) for foreign policymaking to be influenced by intrastate factionalism or countervailing social dynamics. Specific policy responses can vary according to type and extent of dependency on the United States, levels of democratization, and the priorities and decisions of policymakers.[73] Despite an intense arms race and the procurement of increasingly more sophisticated weaponry, the states of the Persian Gulf are today less secure and indeed are much more vulnerable than ever before. Much of the weaponry being sold is actually offensive and not defensive in nature, which makes the regional security dilemma much more intense and dangerous. The potential for the outbreak of a military conflict in the region is therefore high and keeps rising. It is no accident that the contemporary Gulf exhibits features of the classic security dilemma, with none of the regional state actors quite able to resist devoting significant resources to arms buildup.

The sources of the security dilemma do not always reside outside a state's borders. In the Gulf's Arab monarchies, for example, challenges to domestic stability are seen as one of the most serious threats a state can face.[74] The security dilemma has therefore not been limited to the strategic competition between the GCC and Iran but has fueled an arms race within the alliance itself.[75] Bahrain's arms acquisitions following the eruption of antistate protests in 2011 is a case in point. British arms sales to the small kingdom increased dramatically beginning in 2011. Whereas from 2007 to 2010, Britain sold 6 million pounds worth of military equipment to Bahrain, the volume shot up to 45 million pounds in the five years following the uprisings.[76]

The Bahrain example typifies the multiple dimensions and consequences of the security dilemma, both regionally and domestically. These variations have prompted scholars like Fred Lawson to divide the security dilemma into different categories. Lawson argues that in addition to what he calls the "classic security dilemma," the Persian Gulf region is faced with an alliance dilemma, whereby regimes need to craft relations between allies and adversaries alike. There is also a stability dilemma, revolving around the choice of reliance on outside patrons and the need to placate domestic opposition to such a dependent relationship. Finally, regional actors need to forge strategic partnerships with external patrons while trying to keep themselves and the region insulated from global rivalries and disputes.[77]

At the core of all of these security dilemmas lie perceptions of threats by regional actors. These perceptions, which may or may not have a basis in reality, are dependent as much on interpretations of moves by allies and adversaries as on their actual intended consequences. It is to the examination of these regional threat perceptions, especially after the 2011 Arab uprisings, that the chapter turns next.

Regional Threat Perceptions

One of the main drivers of foreign policy are responses to real or potential threats, both as these threats are perceived to exist and as they are likely to emerge. Seldom is foreign policy only reactive, at times capitalizing on emerging opportunities or even fostering opportunities on which the state can capitalize. But threat perceptions are also key in shaping foreign policy behavior and priorities, especially in a region like the Gulf, where both local and extraregional state actors assume threats to their interests to be pervasive.

These threat perceptions are dynamic. They change and evolve depending on shifting alliances; power transitions; the rise or decline of certain nonstate actors; and other national, regional, and global developments. Across the Persian Gulf region, the 2011 Arab uprisings introduced a host of new threat perceptions and heightened some of the existing ones, prompting local actors to initiate specific foreign and security policies in response. Within the region, the threat perceptions of state actors in Iran, Saudi Arabia, and the UAE were particularly instrumental in influencing regional security dynamics, especially in the wake of several key developments with region-wide repercussions, not the least of which included the rise of Daesh in Syria and Iraq, continued state fragility and civil war in Yemen, the nuclear agreement between Iran and the P5+1, and, slightly farther afield, developments in the Levant and North Africa. These regional threat perceptions—by Iran, Saudi Arabia, and the UAE—are greatly influenced by the overall security arrangement, or, more accurately, by the pervasiveness of insecurity in the immediate Gulf region. While such threat perceptions feed off and are part of the broader strategic calculus of each of the actors, the ensuing discussion focuses on the threat perceptions of each state only in relation to the Persian Gulf security complex.

Since the 2011 Arab uprisings, threat perceptions in most of the GCC states have drawn close to each other. I have highlighted threat perception in Saudi Arabia and the UAE, the two GCC states that have opted for more assertive foreign and security policies in the aftermath of the Arab Spring. As demonstrated in chapter 3, not only have Saudi and Emirati foreign policies undergone a qualitative change, the two states represent more pronounced and robust manifestations of threat perceptions among the remaining GCC states. Invariably, these threat perceptions include, first and foremost, Iran; particularly the specter of Iranian expansionism and its export of revolutionary militancy. Related to this is the threat of sectarianism, of both the Shia and Sunni varieties, and the religious militancy and radicalism they entail. Again, especially in the post-2011 period, Iranian Shia sectarianism looms large in the Arab psyche (more on which below). Another perceived threat is seen to revolve around the consequences of American foreign policy, either from a broader structural perspective—centered on what the intentions and actions of the world's only superpower mean for the region—or the more specific ramifications of the foreign and security policies pursued by the Obama administration in such critical areas as the Arab Spring, the nuclear negotiations with Iran, and U.S. relations with the states of the GCC and Saudi Arabia in particular.

Before discussing threat perceptions in Iran, Saudi Arabia, and the UAE, I will briefly examine the case of Oman, which in many respects serves as a regional outlier. Oman's relative poverty compared with its neighbors, and its lack of burning sectarian divisions, have enabled, or rather required, the country's leaders to seek good relations with both regional and international powers. Through diplomacy, Oman has succeeded in simultaneously developing positive relations with actors who are not always on good terms with one another.[78] Especially within the rubric of the GCC, this has manifested itself in a certain level of independence, as exemplified by Oman's notable absence from the military campaign against the Houthis in Yemen beginning in 2015, or its consistently cordial relations with Iran even when GCC-Iran tensions have been at their highest.

Not surprisingly, Oman's threat perceptions tend to be somewhat different from those of most other actors in the region. In rhetoric at least, but also in reality, Omani concerns appear markedly different from those of other regional actors. According to Yusuf bin Alawi bin Abdullah, who has served as the sultanate's foreign minister since 1982, the biggest security challenge that Oman faces is not necessarily Iran or sectarianism but rather the possibility of radicalization of the youth, both inside the country and elsewhere.[79] The essence of many of the problems that Oman and other regional states confront are internal, not international, and these are the issues that each of the regional states needs to address individually. There are indeed a number of regional and international threats, but their root causes, and therefore the remedies they demand, are all too often to be found in the domestic arena. Oman, the foreign minister maintains, is part of the region and cannot afford to have conflicts with its neighbors. To avoid or at least minimize the potential for conflicts, Oman must search for win-win scenarios that are in the region's larger interests and not solely in Oman's interests.[80]

Even as empty rhetoric, this sort of reflective explanation of threat perceptions is unlikely to come from the foreign ministers of other GCC states or Iran. Oman has remained loyal to the broader organizing principles of the GCC and has been largely supportive of the group's security and military initiatives. The sultanate has, for example, consistently sided with the rest of the GCC in calling on Iran to resolve the islands' dispute with the UAE in favor of the latter. But at the same time it has also engaged in its own subtle, quiet diplomacy, often lending its good offices, away from the limelight, to the United States and Iran to talk through contentious issues, seeking to foster diplomatic dialogue rather than exacerbate further tensions. Its centralized decision-making apparatus, with foreign policy being largely decided by Sultan Qaboos bin Said al Said and the foreign minister, has minimized the possibilities of internal frictions and policy disagreements. However, how long this quiet, mature diplomacy outlasts the ailing and aging sultan, who has been in power since 1970, is an open question.

Iran

Iran's post-2011 threat perceptions in relation to the Persian Gulf are animated by three factors: real or potential threats posed by the United States, the collective actions of the GCC states, and, more recently, Daesh. Iran has sought to counter these threats in an atmosphere of heightened tensions with the United States and Saudi Arabia.

According to Behzad Khoshandam, a specialist in Iranian national security strategy, given the prevailing, U.S.-engineered security architecture of the region, Iran has pursued two complementary strategic objectives that may be summed up as "active neutrality," on the one hand, and "constructive intervention," on the other.[81] The Islamic Republic, Khoshandam maintains, has followed a policy of active neutrality in relation to the U.S. invasions of Afghanistan and Iraq, and also in relation to intra-regional tensions in Central Asia and the South Caucasus.[82] In many of these regional conflicts, although Iran has *actively* made its preferences known, it has ultimately remained *neutral* and has abstained from formally siding with one party or the other. When the United States invaded Iraq in 2003, for example, Iran insisted that the United States respect Iraq's territorial sovereignty. But it did not formally enter the conflict on the side of Iraq. As later revealed by Zalmay Khalilzad—who at the time of the invasion served as the U.S. ambassador to the UN and later to Afghanistan and Iraq—before the operation got under way, the United

States and Iran had actually held talks concerning some of the operational aspects of the U.S. invasion.[83] Iran's diplomatic rhetoric, in other words, did not match its pragmatic, neutral approach to the consequences of the U.S. invasion.

Alongside Iran's active neutrality is its strategy of constructive intervention, in which the Islamic Republic has brought its resources to bear in fractured polities toward the construction of an order supportive of its own national interests.[84] State fragmentation in Iraq and Syria, as well as the ongoing political paralysis in Lebanon, have created opportunities for outside regional actors to forge alliances with their own client actors in each country, and by doing so further blurring the lines between domestic, regional, and international arenas of policymaking.[85] This has created not just opportunities but indeed obligations for Iran to work with its state and nonstate allies in nearby, fragmented polities in order to ensure that the right type of political system, one that is consistent with its strategic interests, emerges there. In practice, in both Iraq and Afghanistan, constructive intervention has resulted in a seemingly contradictory policy of supporting nonstate actors while also seeking to strengthen the central government. In particular relation to Iraq, Iran has supported and sustained the Shia militia force known as the Mahdi Army while at the same time supporting the central government in Baghdad, especially during the tenure of Prime Minister Nouri al-Maliki from 2006 to 2014.[86]

Both active neutrality and constructive intervention were devised in direct response to U.S. strategies and military presence in the Persian Gulf region in general and in Iraq and Afghanistan in particular. Iranian threat perceptions in the Persian Gulf have historically revolved around great power politics, especially the designs and machinations of the United States since the early 1970s, when that country replaced Great Britain as the region's dominant external power. In Iranian strategic thinking, since the Islamic Revolution of 1978–1979, the primary threat the country has faced in the Persian Gulf is the presence in the region and the strategic objectives of the United States and its local proxies.[87] It is for this reason that Iran has advocated the withdrawal of foreign military forces from the region and the establishment of a new security architecture involving only the littoral states of the Persian Gulf plus Yemen.[88]

For the past decade or so, Iran's advocacy of U.S. withdrawal from the Persian Gulf has assumed more of a rhetorical character and has lost some of the urgency with which it was expressed during the revolution's earlier decades. In fact, in recent years, a growing number of individuals in policy circles have expressed hopes for a win-win scenario between Iranian and U.S. interests in the Persian Gulf.[89] As a senior Iranian policy analyst explained to me, one of the biggest threats that Iran faces in the Persian Gulf is the possibility of disruptions to the flow of oil. No other regional country is as dependent on the Strait of Hormuz as Iran is for its energy exports. Not surprisingly, while Iran opposes the presence of extraregional forces in the Persian Gulf as a matter of political principle, it also sees them as indirect guarantors of its energy security. Since Iran's energy security is actually enhanced by the presence of foreign forces in the Gulf, in practice it does not actively oppose or impede their work.[90]

Searching for win-win scenarios, and even resolving differences over the seemingly intractable nuclear issue, does not necessarily mean that Iran conceives of the United States in friendly terms. As was argued in chapter 3, Iran sees itself as a global middle power with regional great power aspirations. Even the Rouhani administration's principal figures, including Foreign Minister Zarif and the president himself, have repeatedly stated that despite the nuclear agreement, fundamental differences continue to separate Iran and the United States on a whole range of key global issues.[91] The even more uncompromising statements of the Supreme Leader, Ali Khamenei, are echoed by equally vitriolic and hawkish declarations about Iran by influential Washington insiders.[92] A win-win scenario in the Persian Gulf may be an optimal outcome for both Iran and the United States, but so far no one in the United States has openly entertained the thought of one, and the Iranians discussing its possibility do so mostly in academic circles and journal articles.

Integral to the tensions between Iran and the United States have been the six states of the Gulf Cooperation Council. Similar to the United States, Iran and its Arab neighbors have never tried to view the region's strategic landscape from a win-win perspective in which both sides would benefit. Instead, all too often they have approached strategic competition with each other as a zero-sum game.[93] Regional developments have exponentially accentuated threat perceptions between Iran and its Arab neighbors. These developments include the Iran-Iraq War; the 2003 invasion of Iraq and its aftermath; and the 2011 Arab uprisings and the increasing instability that ensued in the region, especially in Yemen and Bahrain.[94] For Iran, the most serious threat was posed by Iraq's Saddam Hussein, who sought to capitalize on the country's military weakness following the revolution. Although the war ended some thirty years ago, the support of the Arab states for Iraq during the Iran-Iraq War has left an indelible impression on the minds of Iranians, and the aftermath of the war similarly left a lasting impression on the minds of Iran's Arab neighbors.[95] It is worth quoting Mohammad Javad Zarif, President Rouhani's foreign minister, at length as he explained the psychological effects of the war with Iraq to a Western audience:

> In 1980, in the aftermath of the Islamic Revolution, Iraq's Saddam Hussein launched a war against Iran fully supported financially and militarily by almost all of our Arab neighbors and by the West. Unable to secure a quick victory, Hussein used chemical weapons against our soldiers and civilians. The West not only did nothing to prevent this, but it also armed Hussein with sophisticated weapons, while actively preventing Iran from getting access to the most rudimentary defensive necessities. And during the eight long years that this war continued, the U.N. Security Council did not issue a single condemnation of the aggression, the deliberate targeting of civilians or the use of chemical weapons.
>
> This may have been forgotten by most in the West, but it is not forgotten by our people. They remember the missiles raining down, the horrific images of men, women and children murdered with chemical weapons and, above all, the lack of a modern means of defense.
>
> On top of this, having listened to the outdated U.S. mantra of "all options are on the table" for 37 years, our people understand that we need to be prepared to prevent that illegal and absurd threat from ever becoming a reality.
>
> The words "never again" resonate with Iranians, too.[96]

Iran does not see any single one of the GCC states as a direct threat. There are different facets to the bilateral relationships between Iran and each of the GCC states, and none on its own poses a security challenge or a threat of any sort to Iran. This is even the case with Saudi Arabia. However, when they are united, and when they cooperate with and act as a superpower's proxy, they can pose a serious threat to Iran.[97] Along similar lines, Iranian policymakers see the GCC as a potentially serious threat because of its collective positions in regard to Iran in various international forums. This is evident in the positions that the GCC has adopted toward the ownership of the three disputed islands in the Persian Gulf, its manifold relationships with nonstate actors and with other networks opposed to Iran and with organizations such as NATO and the EU, its close military cooperation with the United States on a variety of fronts, and its increasingly strict enforcement of various sanctions against Iran as spearheaded by the United States. In its initial formative years in the 1980s, the GCC was not seen by Tehran as much of a threat. Today, however, the challenges that emanate from GCC actions, and the group's role in fostering anti-Iranian feelings and hostilities, are seen by Tehran as serious challenges to Iranian interests.[98]

Policymakers in Tehran believe that Iran is the only country in the Persian Gulf region that is "security independent," able to defend itself against regional adversaries as well as global great powers. This has bestowed on it a certain sense of confidence especially in relation to its neighbors. By contrast, the security dependence of the GCC states, so starkly evident in their deep reliance on the United States for military protection, is a fundamental source of insecurity for them.[99] There is, therefore, an asymmetrical power relationship between Iran and the GCC states, simply by virtue of the Islamic Republic's size, demography, and geographic location.[100] From Tehran's perspective, the GCC states see Iran as having hegemonic ambitions in the region, not necessarily because of Iranian actions and strategic pursuits but simply because of its size, its security independence, and its strategic depth. Because of their small size and their own security dependence, and the natural vulnerabilities that ensue, the GCC states see Iran as a major threat and have an outsized fear of Iranian ambitions.[101]

As far as the GCC states are concerned, the collapse first of the Soviet Union, then the Taliban, and finally Saddam Hussein has opened up strategic space for Iran. Combined with the consequences of the Arab Spring and the supposed "Asia pivot" by the United States, these developments have increased GCC threat perceptions about Iran.[102] Saudi Arabia in particular sees Iran as a rising regional power and the United States as a declining global power, and this has significantly added to Saudi fears and psychological anxieties about Iran. During his tenure as the kingdom's ambassador to Washington, DC, Adel al-Jubeir reportedly commented that "Iran is the new great power of the Middle East, and the U.S. is the old."[103] Tehran is aware of this sense of fear, which it then sees as translating into bellicose and belligerent policies and actions by Saudi Arabia.[104]

Although not necessarily located in the Persian Gulf region, a final regional threat with presence in Iraq and parts of the Arabian Peninsula has been the rise of Daesh in recent years. In June 2017, for the first time, Daesh carried out simultaneous attacks in Tehran, resulting in a number of deaths and injuries. For Iran, the threat posed by Daesh is no longer extraterritorial. This is a threat to which Iran has actually devoted resources and combat operations, having in the process lost a number of senior military commanders assigned to the Syrian and Iraqi militaries as "advisers." There have also been reports of Iran recruiting and sending Shia civilians from Afghanistan to Syria to fight Daesh.[105] As seen through regional eyes, the primary purpose of Iran's fight against Daesh is to strengthen the country's strategic position in the Middle East.[106] In countries such as Syria and Iraq, Iran is perceived as wanting to only weaken, rather than destroy, Daesh, as the former would allow it the opportunity to continue having leverage over its allies in these countries.[107]

Iran's strategy in fighting Daesh has been threefold. First, its has sought to ensure that existing state structures in Iraq and Syria are preserved and that central authority in each country remains intact. This is designed to prevent the two countries from slipping into complete chaos and lawlessness. Second, in an effort to boost each of the two states, Iran has provided logistical support, arms, training, and command and control to nongovernmental militias and to government forces fighting Daesh. Finally, through its own efforts and those of its proxies, Iran has sought to become indispensable to political actors and local combat forces. This is meant to ensure that the Islamic Republic maintains long-term influence in both Iraq and Syria.[108]

Daesh, of course, is far from only an Iranian problem. And it is highly doubtful whether on its own Iran can successfully mend the broken polities of either Iraq or Syria, much less of both. A small example from Iraq illustrates the magnitude of the difficulties involved in reconstituting the Iraqi state. At the time of the withdrawal of U.S. forces from Iraq in 2011, Iraqi security forces (ISF) reportedly numbered approximately 800,000, of which some 300,000 were in the army. But an Iraqi investigation in 2014 following the army's collapse in the north revealed that many army personnel were "ghosts" or "no-shows," leaving the regular army with perhaps no more than 50,000 troops.[109]

This depleted military capacity on the part of the central government in Baghdad is likely to result in the continued presence in Iraq of Daesh and of Iranian and perhaps American military forces. Iraq's former prime minister, Nouri al-Maliki, perceived the "neo-Ottomanism" pursued by Turkey and supported by Qatar and Saudi Arabia as a major threat to the domestic stability and regional position of Iraq. Not receiving the support he had anticipated from the United States, al-Maliki turned to Iran and Russia, seeking domestic political support from Iran and military and diplomatic assistance from Russia. By the end of his tenure in office (May 2006–August 2014), he had become almost completely dependent on Iranian support for staying in power.[110] For their part, Iranian leaders failed to see how the strident sectarian policies advocated by their allies in Iraq, and at times by themselves, contributed to the rise of Daesh, viewing the terrorist group's rise as another American ploy.[111] As long as Tehran's blind spot to the sectarian consequences of its own actions persists, social strife in Iraq and Iran's own tensions with Saudi Arabia are also likely to continue.

Saudi Arabia

Since regime security is the primary objective of Saudi domestic and foreign policies, Saudi Arabia's foreign policy is highly securitized. According to the Stockholm International Peace Research Institute (SIPRI), in 2013 and 2014, Saudi Arabia had the world's fourth-highest military expenditure, at $80.8 billion, behind the United States, China, and Russia. SIPRI figures also indicate a jump of 112 percent in Saudi Arabia's military expenditure from 2014 to 2015.[112] In 2014, fully 26 percent of the national budget was spent on the military.[113] Competitive tensions with Iran, the rise of Daesh and other related developments in Iraq and Syria, and the Saudi military campaign in Yemen (started in March 2015) have reinforced the securitization of Saudi foreign policy and the kingdom's reliance on the military as a mainstay of its regional foreign policy.

Saudi Arabia's perceived threats fall into four broad, interrelated categories. They are (1) a series of structural vulnerabilities inherent in the kingdom's domestic institutional makeup and its regional position,

(2) Saudi security dependence on the United States, (3) competition with, and the threat posed by, Iran, and (4) the Al Qaeda phenomenon and the more recent appearance of Daesh. Each of these threat perceptions has a symbiotic, mutually reinforcing relationship with one another, which accentuates the kingdom's deep sense of vulnerability to threats emanating from within and from outside its borders.

In critical ways, the Saudi system appears structurally ill-equipped to deal with some of the domestic and international challenges facing the country. In his pioneering study of ruling families in the Arabian Peninsula, Michael Herb outlines several dynamics that underlie the continued resilience of dynastic rule in the region. These include the monopoly of state power and the difficulties of coup making, the choice of successors and comparatively high-quality leadership, relatively smooth transitions of power, the accountability of the ruler to the dynasty, and the function of the dynasty itself as an important information network.[114] These sources of strength notwithstanding, the historical pathways along which Saudi and other Peninsula monarchies have evolved have left them largely unable to adapt structurally to changing domestic and global circumstances.

Comparisons with other Middle Eastern monarchies are instructive. In Morocco and Jordan, kings rule as individuals, while in the GCC it is the ruling family that governs. The institutional framework of dynastic monarchies in Jordan and Morocco better lend themselves to democratization, whereby the king can, at least in theory, cede some power to the parliament. In the GCC, however, having entire families relegate some of their power is much more difficult. Since the monarchies of the GCC have less institutional leeway for coping with pressures from below, they instead often rely on a combination of strengthened patronage ties with their constituents, on the one hand, and reinvigorated authoritarianism, on the other. Coalitions, both of domestic clients and foreign allies, are central to the political health and longevity of monarchies. But, as the Shah of Iran learned the hard way, outside allies cannot by themselves save a monarch.[115]

The institutional inelasticity of monarchies in the Gulf, notably in Saudi Arabia, leaves them especially sensitive to perceived challenges and threats in the international arena. It is little wonder that the Iranian Revolution of 1978–1979—that mass-based, religiously inspired social movement that replaced a monarchy claiming to have a 2,500-year-old genealogy with an Islamic Republic—was seen as such an existential threat to the House of Saud.[116] Equally threatening were the 2011 Arab uprisings—which inspired a planned Day of Rage in the kingdom that was prevented by a heavy deployment of security forces—as well as a number of royal petitions demanding constitutionalism, separation of powers, an independent judiciary, freedom of expression, human rights, and political entitlement.[117] Such petitions have a rich history in Saudi Arabia. Between 1990 and 1994, for example, a series of petitions demanding similar reforms were presented to the royal court.[118]

The Gulf Arab monarchies managed to survive the 2011 uprisings through two means: deploying ample hydrocarbon wealth to blunt popular demands for reform and maintaining powerful coalitions of supporting domestic clients and foreign patrons to bolster regime security and stability.[119] Saudi Arabia was able to stave off the contagion effects of the Arab Spring through its help in suppressing the uprising in Bahrain, the existence of few external pressures for reform, the adroit leadership of King Abdullah, and the royal family's continued control of key state institutions and levers of power. At the same time, Saudi rivals such as Iran and Al Qaeda were unable to exploit the consequences of the uprisings to their advantage and to the detriment of the Saudi state.[120]

But the regional consequences of the uprisings, and the changing alignments that followed, were somewhat more difficult to manage. What followed was a Saudi-led counterrevolution, with the kingdom and the UAE "actively seeking to delegitimize the political effects of the Arab Spring revolutions." Soon, the military coup in Egypt in July 2013 drew "a clear, dividing line" across the Middle East, with Saudi Arabia and the UAE supporting Cairo's new military regime and Qatar and Turkey opposing it.[121] The ensuing tensions between Qatar and Saudi Arabia exposed the institutional fragility of the GCC. With the kingdom's blessing and encouragement, Bahrain and the UAE joined Saudi Arabia in recalling their ambassadors from Doha in March 2014, citing Qatar's support for the Muslim Brotherhood as evidence of its interference in the affairs of neighboring Arab countries.[122] The spat finally ended the following November, after six senior members of the Muslim Brotherhood residing in Qatar left the country and Qatar's young emir, Sheikh Tamim bin Hamad Al Thani, paid two unannounced visits to the kingdom for "consultations" with King Abdullah.[123]

The Saudi-led withdrawal of ambassadors from Qatar was the first of three interrelated manifestations of Saudi threat perceptions arising from the consequences of the Arab Spring. The second was the Saudi military intervention in Yemen beginning in March 2015, and the third an unprecedented, deliberate ratcheting up of tensions with Iran following the storming of the Saudi embassy by a mob in Tehran in January 2016.[124] Saudi Arabia's intervention in Yemen was justified by Riyadh on the grounds that Iran's Houthi allies were unlawfully taking over the country and seeking the overthrow of the official government in Sanaa. And the Saudi diplomatic campaign against Iran—which resulted in Saudi Arabia's rallying a number of its allies to either cut or downgrade their diplomatic relations with Iran shortly after the Tehran embassy attack—was geared at, in the words of the Saudi foreign minister, "resisting Iranian expansion and responding forcefully to Iran's acts of aggression."[125] Through resort to "checkbook diplomacy," a number of poorer countries once close to Iran, such as Sudan, were lured away from the Islamic Republic and into the kingdom's orbit. Those states that refused, or were slow to respond, as in the case of Lebanon, were financially punished.[126] These and other similar Saudi actions were motivated by a deep sense of unease and insecurity rather than a newfound self-confidence.

This insecurity—at least as manifested in rising Saudi-Iranian tensions as Iran's negotiations with the U.S. and the European Union over its nuclear program were reaching their climax in late 2015 and early 2016—bespeaks a basic sense of vulnerability in the kingdom. As elaborated in chapter 3, Saudi Arabia has long sought to maintain a position of hegemonic leadership within the Arabian Peninsula. Qatar's balking at Saudi leadership was finally settled in early 2015 when the country's young emir disavowed patronage of the Muslim Brotherhood and reoriented the policy of hedging that his father had pursued in favor of bandwagoning with the kingdom and with the United States. But for Riyadh there is room in the region for only one rising power, and any indication that Iran may be emerging out of its long isolation, or that it may finally be changing its self-destructive foreign policies, is seen as a threat. Not surprisingly, the kingdom has spent inordinate sums of money with U.S.-based public relations firms to put "a positive spin on Saudi Arabia's own image . . . [and attack] its political rival Iran."[127]

For Riyadh, the nature of Saudi Arabia's relationship with the United States, and the extent of the security dependence that the kingdom has developed vis-à-vis the United States, is seen as another source of threat. Saudi Arabia represents a classic case of the alliance dilemmas of entrapment or abandonment in its relations with the United States.[128] The Saudi military dependence on the United States is deep and structural, to the point that the day-to-day bombing operations of the Saudi Air Force in Yemen would not be possible without help from American trainers and maintenance experts.[129] According to a report prepared for the U.S. Congress, American advisers on the payroll of the Saudi government are "embedded in industrial, energy, maritime and cybersecurity offices within the Saudi government."[130]

During the administration of George W. Bush, when the possibilities of a military conflict between Iran and the United States appeared high, Saudi Arabia, along with other GCC states, feared being caught in between the two warring states, in which case their territories, resources, and infrastructure would have been used for and targeted in the ensuing hostilities. When the Obama administration and the Islamic Republic began negotiating in earnest over Iran's nuclear program, those GCC states bandwagoning with the United States, especially Saudi Arabia, started to worry about the possibility of being abandoned by an ally on whom they had become deeply reliant for security and military needs.

Since the Iranian Revolution, in fact, U.S.-Saudi relations have evolved to encompass more than Saudi security dependence on the United States. With Iran as a perennial regional and global pariah state, Saudi Arabia and its regional allies emerged as pro-Western bastions of peace and stability. The Saudis capitalized on Iran's isolation and supposed destabilizing policies in order to spend ever-greater sums on arms and other investments with few questions asked. The Iranian bogeyman enabled Saudi Arabia to help the world forget that fifteen of the nineteen 9/11 terrorists hailed from the kingdom (of the remaining four, two were from the UAE, one from Egypt, and another from Lebanon). At a time when many Daesh fighters were either from Saudi Arabia or were inspired by its strict, Wahhabi interpretation of Islam, the last thing Saudi leaders wanted was a thawing of relations between Saudi Arabia's rival Iran and the West, in particular the United States. Hence the repeated Saudi warnings in 2015 and 2016, either directly or through the public relations firms the kingdom had hired, that Iran "cannot be trusted" and that it "remains dangerous."[131]

It was this resulting deep insecurity that prompted Saudi leaders to take matters into their own hands and to employ more assertive foreign and military policies not just in relation to Iran but also across the region in Bahrain, Qatar, Yemen, Syria, Iraq, Lebanon, and elsewhere.[132] To allay Saudi misapprehensions about abandonment by the United States, American officials have been streaming into the kingdom to reassure Saudi leaders of their continued support and friendship. To further reassure the Saudis, the United States has also consistently agreed to sell Saudi Arabia ever-greater sums of sophisticated American weaponry, in the process deepening Saudi security dependence on the United States.[133] Saudi Arabia may see its dependent military relationship vis-à-vis the United States as a security threat. But it appears incapable, or unwilling, to break out of it.

Another major Saudi threat perception concerns Iran. For policymakers in Riyadh, in fact, Iran represents one of the biggest threats to the kingdom. The Saudi fixation with "the Iranian threat" dates back to 2003 and even before, ever since the kingdom began perceiving the rise of Iranian power in the Middle East as a threat both in terms of balance of power and as a transnational ideological threat.[134] According to the Saudi foreign minister, "Iran is the single-most-belligerent-actor in the region, and its actions display both a commitment to regional hegemony and a deeply held view that conciliatory gestures signal weakness either on Iran's part or on the part of its adversaries."[135] As far as Saudi Arabia is concerned, Iran has sought to deal with the Persian Gulf region very differently after the revolution than it did before 1979. The regime of the shah was interested in security and stability in the Gulf region. After the revolution, Iran has tried to export both Shiʿism and its revolution, and its leaders cultivated close ties with terrorist organizations such as Hezbollah, Hamas, and the Muslim Brotherhood. In this sense, for both Saudi Arabia and the smaller states of the region, the GCC is a necessity so that Iranian-originated threats can be more effectively countered.[136]

A common sentiment in Saudi Arabia, as expressed by a Saudi journalist, is that "Iran is an aggressor." The Islamic Republic is seen as having "ambitions and plans that it is implementing in the region, and it is using force, not diplomacy."[137] Iran's activities in Iraq and U.S. inaction there are seen in Riyadh as a major threat to the Gulf states. This was the start of the Iranian penetration first of the Levant, in Lebanon and Syria, and then Yemen.[138] The Iranian nuclear program was also seen as a real security challenge, much more as an environmental threat than as anything else, especially since the Fukushima disaster in Japan showed that nuclear technology can be insecure and therefore dangerous.[139] From Riyadh's perspective, Iran is seen as a real and serious threat. In 2008, King Abdullah was reported to have gone as far as to urge the United States to take military action against Iran in order "to cut off the head of the snake."[140]

Since 2003, Riyadh and Tehran have sought to become the Gulf's dominant local powers. This jockeying is no longer limited to their immediate neighborhood and has assumed a pan-regional dimension. In fact, as Saudi foreign ministry documents released by WikiLeaks reveal, Saudi threat perceptions toward Iran border on obsession, with Saudi diplomats monitoring in minute detail even the most mundane efforts by their Iranian counterparts.[141] These concerns extend far beyond the immediate Persian Gulf region and include efforts to counter potential or real Iranian influence in far-flung areas in Africa, Europe, Central Asia, South Asia, China, and elsewhere.[142]

Personalities are important in setting the tone of diplomacy, and although Iranian-Saudi relationships improved somewhat during the presidencies of Rafsanjani and Khatami, Ahmadinejad's personality and his rhetoric made it difficult for Saudi Arabia to maintain close and friendly relations with Iran.[143] There are, nevertheless, deeper structural chasms that divide the two sides, as argued in chapter 3, and even brief periods of Saudi-Iranian détente have had their fair share of tensions and disputes.[144] These deep-seated chasms are reinforced by misperceptions on both sides that often feed off one another. All too frequently, Saudi and Iranian diplomats fail to grasp the motivations and true intentions of the other side, their misunderstanding compounded by the opacity of institutional and policymaking mechanisms in each of their states. These misunderstandings and negative assumptions are formed in an atmosphere of extensive U.S. presence in the region and hypersensitivity to potential moves by Iran or others that could undermine American or Saudi interests. Pressure from the United States on the Saudi leadership, and Iranian efforts to read the "true" meaning of U.S. actions and preferences, further complicate Iranian-Saudi relations and mutual threat perceptions.[145]

A final source of threat to Saudi Arabia is what may be called the Al Qaeda phenomenon. Over the past two to three decades, many states, both in the Middle East and elsewhere, have faced the threat of militant Islamic radicalism and the violence that it has wrought in its wake. And, over the years, Saudi Arabia has experienced its share of violent attacks by religious extremists.[146] But for Saudi Arabia the problem of religious extremism goes beyond implementing effective counterterrorism measures. For some time now, Saudi society has been fertile breeding ground for the recruitment of radical militants.[147] The very structure of Saudi society—in particular, the educational and religious establishments—coupled with the Wahhabi ideology of the state, has been among the biggest contributors to the rise of religious radicalism in the Middle East region and beyond. U.S. foreign policy in recent decades, especially the country's aggressive tone during the administration of George W. Bush, also helped mobilize reactionary forces in Saudi society.[148] More recently, under state sanction, the Saudi media is helping foment heightened anti-Persian and anti-Shiite sectarianism, in turn enhancing the popular currency of Daesh extremism.[149] In the meanwhile, with demands for substantive change falling on deaf ears, or worse yet actively suppressed by the state, radicalization has spread.

Al Qaeda and its more recent—and more violent—iteration in the form of Daesh claim to be the true heirs and standard-bearers of Wahhabism. Daesh sees itself, not the Saudi state, as the true guardian of Wahhabism, and therefore competes with the Saudi state not just materially but also ideologically. Daesh often claims that its actions find sanction in the official teachings of Wahhabism. In fact, "Islamic State supporters online frequently quote official Saudi scholars to justify anti-Shia attacks." Not surprisingly, the Saudi religious establishment has not engaged in a serious intellectual rebuttal of Daesh. "There is no bold reexamination of the Wahhabi heritage, only self-vindication." In reality, in addition to having a sizeable following among Saudi Arabia's estimated four thousand jihadi Salafist prisoners, Daesh appears to have considerable support among the kingdom's clerical class.[150]

This is not to imply that the Saudi state does not see Daesh as a major threat. To the contrary, because of its largely indigenous roots, the threat posed by Daesh is seen as a more fundamental, existential one. Daesh itself sees the Saudi state as the "head of the snake" that needs to be decapitated. And ideologically it departs from the Wahhabi tradition in four critical respects: its rejection of dynastic alliances, its advocacy of the caliphate system of government, its continued employment of extreme violence, and its apocalyptic fervor. Nevertheless, for the foreseeable future, Daesh's primary theater of operation is likely to be outside Saudi Arabia, especially in such fragile polities as Iraq, Syria, and Yemen, rather than inside the kingdom itself. Because of their relative wealth, the religious character of the state, and effective counterterrorism measures by the state, Saudi jihadists appear to prefer jihad abroad to jihad at home.[151] Daesh, and the broader phenomenon of religious extremism that it represents, is likely to continue to threaten the Saudi establishment. Although most of its violent attacks may take place outside the kingdom, Daesh will remain one of the main sources of threat to the Saudi state and its interests for many years to come.

United Arab Emirates

Emirati threat perceptions closely parallel those of Saudi Arabia, varying only in degree, rather than in nature. Similar to those of Saudi Arabia, these threat perceptions are connected to Iran and its regional ambitions, the interrelated phenomena of religious extremism and sectarianism, and the consequences of U.S. policies and actions in the Persian Gulf and elsewhere. What difference there is lies in the extent to which each of these perceived threats is seen as more pressing by one as compared with the other. The Iranian threat, for example, is much more palpable for Emirati policymakers than for Saudi leaders, largely because of the UAE's geographic proximity to Iran; its territorial dispute over the ownership of three islands in the Persian Gulf; and the presence of hundreds of thousands of Iranian residents, tourists, and merchants in Dubai and other Emirati cities.[152] At the same time, given the relative small size of its citizen population compared with the large and more diverse communities of expatriates living in the country, religious militancy and sectarianism are not as threatening in the UAE as they are in Saudi Arabia. The same applies to the consequences of U.S. policies and actions, on which the UAE's military and security dependence has been historically less direct and overt than has been the case with Saudi Arabia.

In this context, Emirati policymakers consider Iran to pose by far the biggest threat to their country as well as to the rest of the GCC. The danger that Iran poses, they believe, simply cannot be overstated.

This danger is real and not imagined, and neither is it a danger that is played up for domestic political purposes. Iran has always been a difficult state since the 1978–1979 revolution. But today, following the nuclear deal with the United States, it is assumed to have become even more dangerous than in the days of Ahmadinejad. The "moderate" administration of Rouhani is perceived to be even more dangerous than Ahmadinejad's belligerent tenure in office, since real decision making in Iran is seen to lie outside the presidency and rests with the office of the Supreme Leader and the IRGC (Islamic Revolutionary Guards Corps). With sanctions having been partially lifted and with more money coming into government coffers, and with the European Union eager to invest in the country and the United States no longer at their heels, the Iranians have a newfound sense of self-confidence that makes them more threatening today than at any point in the past.[153]

For the countries of the Arabian Peninsula, "the Iranian model" is inherently destabilizing, as it inspires Shia activism in places such as Bahrain, Saudi Arabia, and even Kuwait.[154] More alarmingly, as far as the Gulf states are concerned, Iran has practically occupied Iraq and has assumed the role of an occupying force in an Arab country.[155] GCC leaders seem convinced, without much evidence, that with the coming to power of the Rouhani administration and the signing of the nuclear deal, Iran today is looking "more arrogant and expansionist" than at any other point in its postrevolutionary history.[156] The partial deescalation of tensions between the United States and Iran demonstrates that the Islamic Republic will be a power in the region. It will not be the dominant power or a hegemon, but it will be a power that can no longer be ignored, marginalized, or taken for granted.[157] This emergence of Iran out of its international and economic isolation presents a vexing problem for the Emirati leadership.

One of the challenges posed by Iran is the related threat of sectarianism. In the calculations of the Emirati leadership, Iran has become increasingly more sectarian in its policies in recent years, especially since the rise of the new Shia political elite in Iraq beginning in 2003. From an Emirati perspective, sectarianism is one of the tools propagated and frequently used by Iranian policymakers and is central to their thinking and their worldview. Even the 2016 elections for the Majlis and the Assembly of Experts, which resulted in ostensibly "moderate" candidates to both bodies, showed that the Iranian polity remains fundamentally highly sectarian.[158]

Related to sectarianism is religious extremism and the broader issue of political Islam. Shortly after the eruption of the Arab Spring, political Islam reared its head in the UAE in the form of the Muslim Brotherhood. But that threat, although it has not completely gone away, has now receded.[159] Religious militancy, and the sectarianism that comes with it, are not the pressing threat in the UAE that they are in Saudi Arabia and Bahrain. As one of my Emirati interlocutors explained, given the rich mosaic of different communities that live in the UAE—as many as 200 different nationalities, more than the 193 member states of the UN—the UAE cannot afford to fan the flames of sectarianism. Instead, it proactively tries to deemphasize them and to ensure that social harmony prevails. "The creation of a ministerial portfolio devoted to encouraging social tolerance in the UAE demonstrates that the state is concerned about social harmony and lack of communal tensions and therefore it tries to preemptively ensure that tensions do not break out in society."[160]

Last, there is the perception in the UAE that the United States might be pulling away from the region and that perhaps it is instead shifting its security and strategic interests toward Asia. The "old days of the U.S. being a guarantor of Gulf security are over," goes the Emirati thinking.[161] This a product of the Obama administration's foreign policy, which was a major concern until Trump's victory.[162] Nevertheless, to counter ever greater threats, such as Iran or the regional tensions and instabilities that continue to proliferate across the Middle East, a U.S.-oriented security arrangement cannot be abandoned. With Trump's victory, these concerns were largely laid to rest, and Abu Dhabi once again saw itself very close to Washington's strategic thinking. "The war in Yemen shows to the U.S. that the UAE and Saudi Arabia are its allies" and that they will do their best to protect their own interests as well as the interests of the United States.[163]

Threat perceptions, strategies states use to contain and undermine each other, the pursuit of zero-sum policies and objectives, and the widespread inability or unwillingness to devise win-win scenarios have made the Persian Gulf one of the most contentious and insecure regions in the world. In the post-2011 era, this chronic insecurity is fueled by three complementary, reinforcing dynamics. The first development has to do with Iranian strategic objectives and pursuits in the Persian Gulf region and beyond.

Particularly under the administration of President Hassan Rouhani, in office since June 2013 and reelected in 2017, Iran has sought to break out of its international isolation, maintain whatever strategic leverage it has so far acquired in Syria and Lebanon, and preserve and expand its influence Iraq. In the earlier years of his tenure in office, Rouhani's foreign policy was focused on reducing Iran's long-simmering tensions with the West, especially with the European Union and the United States. But this appears to have occurred at the expense of Iran's relations with its Arab neighbors, who remain deeply mistrustful—fearful, in fact—of Iranian intentions and designs across the Persian Gulf region. Neither does Iran trust its Arab neighbors to the south, many of whom have colluded with Iran's adversaries, especially the United States.

This mistrust touches on a second dynamic, the role of the states of the Gulf Cooperation Council, especially those that follow Saudi Arabia's foreign policy lead, namely, the UAE and Bahrain. Throughout the GCC, with the exception of Oman, mistrust and fear of Iran runs deep. What Iran claims to be its security needs are seen by Saudi Arabia, the UAE, and Bahrain as a mask for expansionist efforts, guided not by realpolitik but by the revolutionary state's impulse to spread Shia militancy across the Middle East and beyond. Iran, they reason, must therefore be contained and isolated, and there should be no room for Iran in any regional security architecture.

Iranian foreign policy may indeed be informed by the theocracy's Shia doctrinal underpinnings and worldview. But GCC and especially Saudi foreign policies are no less sectarian. The critical difference is that for Saudi Arabia and its post-2011 allies, notably the UAE, sectarianism has emerged as a double-edged sword. On the one hand, the emphasis on Sunni identity and the need to contain and counter "the Shia threat" has helped rally allies throughout the GCC—especially Bahrain, Kuwait, and even Qatar, with whom Saudi Arabia often had tense relations from the mid-1990s to the 2000s. At the same time, however, state-fanned sectarianism has helped galvanize and further popularize militancy of the Daesh and Al Qaeda varieties, only to further facilitate their radicalism and violence at home and abroad.

The third dynamic is represented by the United States, in its role as a remote balancer in the region. As long as the Persian Gulf dominates the political economy of the Middle East region, the presence of outside actors such as the United States and the European Union will continue unabated. And U.S. military hegemony in the Persian Gulf and its role as an offshore balancer are certain to provoke counterhegemonic tendencies, thus further complicating regional security and stability.[164] Balance-of-power arrangements remotely controlled by the United States are likely to fail or to at least result in continued instability.[165] Belatedly, late in the Obama administration, the United States appeared to have come to the realization that continued neglect of Iranian security needs is not only untenable and not viable but itself a source of insecurity. But changing course has not been easy, made all the more difficult, both in process and in outcome, by the deeply entrenched dynamics and history of bandwagoning. Even the slightest indications of a shift in U.S. policy were perceived as signs of indecisiveness at best or abandonment at worst. The GCC, and especially Saudi Arabia, often privately complained about being left to fend for themselves against Iranian machinations and expansionist plots. Having to take matters into their own hands has meant pursuing more assertive, bellicose, and militaristic policies. In the process, the regional security dilemma has been further exacerbated. President Trump's assumption of office in the United States may have allayed fears of abandonment among some Gulf leaders. But his rhetoric and bluster have only magnified the region's multiple insecurities.

No policy or strategy is immutable, and the architects of the zero-sum strategies that have perpetuated the Gulf's chronic insecurity will invariably leave office sooner or later. Even the Saudis' King Salman and the Iranian leader Ali Khamanei, who effectively have lifetime tenure in office, have finite life spans. But personality changes, or rotations in office of different elected administrations, are not sufficient on their own. What needs to change are strategic perspectives, zero-sum assumptions, deeply embedded mistrust, and the worldviews and mechanisms that sustain them. For now, such possibilities appear highly remote and very unlikely. At least for the foreseeable future, therefore, the Persian Gulf's strategic landscape is likely to remain highly contentious and filled with intra-regional tensions. The security dilemmas characterizing the region will also continue to be deeply entrenched and intractable.

5

INSECURITY IN THE PERSIAN GULF

Since the early years of the twentieth century, when oil was first discovered in southwestern Iran, and even before that, the Persian Gulf has been viewed as a strategically vital waterway, both for the global economy in general and for the continued prosperity of advanced economies in particular. In the process, the region has become an arena for the emergence of multiple and often overlapping security challenges, many of them indigenous to the area and many imported from abroad. Up until the 2011 Arab uprisings, most of these security challenges revolved around territorial, political, and military competitions and conflicts within and between actors from the region itself and from the outside. While threats and challenges to human security were also present, they were often overshadowed by more immediate and more tangible threats to territorial sovereignty and those posed by various forms of political and military competition between state actors.

The 2011 uprisings added a new dimension to the menu of security threats and challenges prevalent in the Persian Gulf region and the larger

Middle East, this time from the consequences of the rise of identity politics. More specifically, the rise and spread of sectarianism introduced a new element in the societies and cultures of the region in which large swaths of the population felt threatened because of their very core identity and belief systems. In its latest iteration, sectarianism initially started as a politically salient tool used by regional states for purposes of deflecting blame and enhancing faltering legitimacies. But its instrumentalist use occurred in receptive social and cultural milieus in which it was readily adopted and internalized by influential nonstate actors and nongovernmental organizations, with religious clerics, mosques, and the traditional and social media chief among them. The cross-border conflicts and civil wars that predominate the Middle East, and the Iranian-Saudi competition in and around their immediate neighborhood, only reinforce the salience of sectarian beliefs among peoples of the region. In the contemporary era, threats to human and hard security have converged in the Persian Gulf and assumed a mutually reinforcing relationship with one another.

In this context, this book has identified a series of interlocking and reinforcing challenges that continue to perpetuate pervasive insecurity across the Persian Gulf. The sources of this insecurity can be divided into four broad, overlapping categories. First, the security architecture that has emerged in the region is itself a source of insecurity. As was demonstrated in chapter 2, until now this security architecture has largely rested on the exclusion of Iran and the continued and extensive efforts of an external balancer and its footprints, namely, the United States. U.S. and Gulf Cooperation Council security and strategic thinking was long premised on the assumption that Iran does not have any legitimate security concerns of its own. The flawed nature of the assumption prompted the administration of Barack Obama to rethink and revise its thinking on Iran, largely through ensuring that the long-running nuclear negotiations with the Islamic Republic came to a successful fruition in 2015. Despite considerable consternation among Saudi and Israeli leaders, the Obama administration stayed the course. But its successor, Donald Trump's administration, reversed course and U.S.-Iranian tensions once again increased with Obama's departure from office.

A second reason for pervasive insecurity in the Persian Gulf is the widespread neglect of security threats that are not strictly military in nature.

More specifically, the rise of identity politics and sectarianism has created considerable tension between communities across the region and also within them. Sectarianism has added force and potency to the rhetoric of state and nonstate actors who have sought to advance their own agendas, and to also compensate for their own shortcomings, by claiming to be defenders of supposedly threatened identities and communities.

This has been fed and reinforced by a third cause of insecurity in the Persian Gulf: the belligerence of the actors involved. Agency matters. At its core, politics and international relations are products of actions by individual policymakers and reflect their preferences. As outlined in chapter 3, aspirations of regional hegemony, and ambitions of power projections and of the attainment of middle power status, have propelled regional state actors to compete with and undermine one another. These ambitions, combined with the force of sectarianism, on the one hand, and the proliferation of weak and fragile polities in the Middle East, on the other, have made the region particularly volatile.

Foreign and security policy belligerence has had a fourth consequence, the ironic production of insecurity. In chapter 4, the causes and consequences of the Persian Gulf's intractable security dilemma were examined. Security-enhancing measures by one state increase the insecurity of its adversary, whose own measures at strengthening its security make its adversary insecure. The vicious cycle of security-insecurity that the security dilemma represents continues to undermine the prospects of regional peace and stability in the Persian Gulf.

The result has been the emergence of a highly volatile and tense regional security complex characterized by chronic tensions, diplomatic disputes, highly charged and tense emotions, deep-seated anxieties and animosities, and, more recently, open military conflict and warfare. In the current global context, the Gulf's instability is not occurring in isolation and is fed by, and is in turn feeding, instability in other places near and far. In fact, it can be argued that the flows of instability from Yemen to Somalia are tying together one regional security complex with another.[1] Since 2011, we have witnessed uncharacteristic diplomatic and military assertiveness, often bordering on bellicosity, from the likes of Saudi Arabia and the United Arab Emirates. And the proliferation of weak and fragile polities has afforded them, and also Iran, the opportunity to try to expand their respective spheres of influence to places as far flung as Yemen, Iraq, Syria,

Lebanon, and Libya. Ruling elites across the Persian Gulf have histori-cally demonstrated pragmatism in pursuit of political survival strategies.[2] Whether their new pursuits, meant not so much to ensure their survival as to enable them to project power, will end up confronting them with new security challenges is as yet unclear.

Looking Ahead

Not surprisingly, for some time now the question of "what is to be done?" when it comes to fostering security in the Persian Gulf has attracted the attention of numerous analysts, diplomats and policy practitioners, and academics.[3] Here I do not intend to recount such possible scenarios or to offer new ones. Instead, I will briefly highlight three critical indepen-dent variables whose change in one direction or another is likely to greatly affect the overall security architecture and stability of the region. These are the role of the region's natural resources, oil and gas, in shaping ongo-ing domestic and international politics; perceptions toward and the direc-tion of Iranian foreign policy and the Islamic Republic's evolving strategic role and position in the region; and the shape and direction of U.S. foreign and security policies as they relate to the Persian Gulf. These, I believe, are the great unknowns as we look ahead to the evolution of security dynam-ics in the Gulf.

Natural resources have played the role of a double-edged sword for the Persian Gulf. On the one hand, they have brought the region a "resource curse" on the domestic front and the unwanted intrusion and attention of the West. On the other hand, natural resources have turned what were desert outposts and dusty fishing villages not that long ago into global cities and regional powerhouses today.[4] Given their oil reserves and wealth-driven foreign policies, many GCC states have in fact emerged as "strategic and commercial pivots" around which shifts in the global bal-ance of power are taking place.[5] And oil and gas reserves will no doubt continue to keep global interests in the region high for the foreseeable future.[6]

But given the centrality of oil to the evolution of the region's contempo-rary political economies, and its continued role in enabling politically unac-countable regimes to stay in power, the nature and shape of the post-oil era remains a big question mark. By most accounts, the "second oil boom" of the early 2000s has now come to an end. The petroleum bubble has burst, with prices going from more than a $100 a barrel in 2014–2015 to between $30 to $40 in 2015 and early 2016. By mid- to late 2017, they had crawled up to the mid-$40 range.[7] No oil-dependent country can withstand this kind of a decline in revenues without facing a crisis.[8] International investments, along with serious moves across the GCC to prepare the domestic economy for the post-oil era are likely to go some way toward alleviating some of the potential pains of transitioning to a new political economy. But exactly what that new era will look like, and how domestic populations and international and other regional actors will react, remain unknown.

Most observers agree that the post-oil era will be one of increasing domestic conflicts and threats to human security in the Persian Gulf.[9] What is unclear is the extent to which current moves toward fostering a knowledge-based instead of a resource-dependent economy are substantive and appropriate enough in addressing potential future needs. Also unknown are the intra-regional and international ramifications, if there are any, of the arrival of the post-oil era. Will the Persian Gulf still remain geopolitically important in global strategic calculations? As small, security-dependent states, will the GCC countries still be able to attract offshore balancers and especially the United States? And will new and as yet unforeseen sources of tension and competition emerge and become points of contention within and between states?

A second unknown is Iran's evolving role in the Persian Gulf. More specifically, there are two questions concerning Iran and the rest of the Persian Gulf. First, what direction, if any, will domestic Iranian politics take as the country continues to decide on the precise terms on which it wants to engage the rest of the world? Although labels such as *hardliners*, *moderates*, and *conservatives* are notoriously inaccurate indicators of who governs the country at any given point and how they perceive of Iran's role in the region and beyond, factional alignments in Iran do continue to change, often quite unpredictably, and such changes often alter the country's foreign policy and its international relations in significant ways. If there is a constant in Iranian politics it is its fluid and unpredictable nature.

As described in chapter 2, one of the primary, structural causes of tension in the Persian Gulf is the deliberate exclusion of Iran so far from the prevailing regional security arrangement. As the United States and its regional allies have sought to isolate and marginalize Iran in the Persian Gulf and elsewhere, the Islamic Republic has cultivated ties with militias and other nonstate actors across the Middle East. These include not just the Lebanese Hezbollah or the Iraqi Al-Muqawama Al-Islamiya (the Islamic Resistance), but also even the Afghan Taliban.[10] The outcome has all too often been a zero-sum game in which strategic competition between Iran and its southern Gulf neighbors has only heightened regional and intra-national tensions and instability. Mohammed Ayoob warns that "isolating Iran and building a security structure to contain it rather than include it is bound to fail." He likens such a scenario to building a South Asian secu-rity structure without India's participation.[11] Integration of Iran into a regional security framework, Ayoob and others agree, will no doubt result in a lowering of Arab-Iranian tensions.[12]

The third and final independent variable affecting Persian Gulf secu-rity in the coming years is the United States. The United States has been one of the central constitutive elements of the regional security arrange-ment in the region for a number of decades. As recently as the early 2000s, experts were confidently stating that "the sine qua non of any future Gulf security system will be a U.S. military umbrella."[13] Today, more than a decade later, however, it is no longer clear whether the his-toric raison d'être of American military presence in the Persian Gulf still holds. For decades, both before and after the Cold War, America's strategic interests in the region boiled down to oil. In his 1987 state-ment to the U.S. Congress, Secretary of Defense Caspar Weinberger was clear in outlining American strategic objectives in the Persian Gulf. For over four decades, he said, America's "vital national interests [were] at stake in the Gulf" and required the United States to be "present, vigilant, and resolute in the Gulf." These national interests included "denying Soviet access/influence in the region which would threaten free world access to regional oil resources; stability and security of the Gulf states which is critical to insure Free World access to oil; and access to Gulf oil resources, the disruption of which would seriously affect the Free World oil market."[14]

In the second decade of the 2000s, imported oil in general and Persian Gulf oil in particular do not have the same significance vis-à-vis the U.S. economic engine that they had in the 1980s. Beginning with President Obama's second term, a new strategic perception seemed to be emerging in which the U.S. military presence in the Gulf was no longer strictly necessary.[15] Moreover, the Obama administration's notion of "leading from behind," coming on the heels of George W. Bush's hegemonic interventionism, appeared to be signaling "US acknowledgement of the end of its regional hegemony."[16] But actual signs of a lessening of U.S. military commitment to and presence in the Gulf were few and far between. In fact, there is no reason to believe that Obama's evolving views about U.S. security commitments in the Gulf, especially near the end of his tenure, were shared by the Trump administration or, for that matter, within the larger U.S. foreign policy establishment.[17]

What has been clear for some time is that unilateral U.S. attempts at imposing liberal democracy, and a return to old-fashioned balance-of-power approach, reminiscent most recently of George W. Bush's foreign policy toward the Persian Gulf, is no longer a viable option.[18] Also problematic have been U.S. attempts to act as an external balancer via unsteady or unreliable regional allies.[19] Despite the failure of such approaches to produce desired results so far, the Trump administration has declared its pursuit to be integral to its policies toward the region. Ideally, U.S. engagement in and commitment to the Persian Gulf should move in a nonmilitary direction.[20] If oil supplies are generally safe, and a modus vivendi is reached between Iran, on the one side, and the U.S. and its allies, on the other, then the American military presence in the Gulf can be substantially reduced.[21] This would not resolve all regional tensions, but it would go some way toward reducing them. This could then pave the way for gradually replacing the current balance-of-power system with one that takes into account a "balance of interests."[22] As Frederic Wehrey and Richard Sokolsky argue, "A new regional security forum should be an integral element of the United States' vision of a rules-based and more stable security order in the Gulf."[23]

These are only *ideal* scenarios that could potentially turn the United States from one of the region's most powerful belligerents into a primary catalyst for reduced tensions and increasing stability. Academics often excel at laying out such scenarios, but seldom do politicians and policymakers think they are viable or even realistic. These types of scenarios have been around for some time, but none so far has come to pass. More than a decade ago, for example, Michael Kraig called for a "principled multilateralism" in which "security is sought with other states, rather than against them." He argued that "domestic developments in the Gulf will follow a more beneficial course if all states are gradually intertwined in a web of military and economic agreements that create strong interdependence."[24] Today, Iran and Saudi Arabia are locked in an intense and conflict-prone competition, there are proxy wars raging in Syria and Iraq, Libya is in tatters and has become a new arena of power projection for the UAE, and a Saudi-led military coalition is unable to fully extricate itself from Yemen without having the country swirl completely into chaos and disorder. And neither the Saudis nor the Iranians appear capable of or are willing to contain the destructive sectarianism that their policies keep fanning. Persian Gulf security today remains as elusive as ever.

NOTES

Introduction

1. I explored this issue in an earlier publication. See Mehran Kamrava, "Preserving Non-Democracies: Leaders and State Institutions in the Middle East," *Middle Eastern Studies*, Vol. 46, No. 2 (March 2010), pp. 231–250.

2. *Securitization* will be defined and analyzed in greater detail in Chapter 1. Here I adopt the widely accepted definition of the concept offered by Buzan, Waever, and de Wilde, which refers to a process whereby state actors view one or more issues as matters of security even if in reality they may not necessarily pose security challenges to the state. Barry Buzan, Ole Waever, and Jaap de Wilde, *Security: A New Framework for Analysis* (Boulder, CO: Lynne Rienner, 1998), p. 33.

Chapter 1. The Trouble with the Persian Gulf

1. Jimmy Carter, State of the Union address to the U.S. Congress, January 23, 1980, http://www.presidency.ucsb.edu/ws/?pid=33079.

2. The term "axis of evil" was used by President George W. Bush in his 2002 State of the Union address to the U.S. Congress. See "President Delivers State of the Union Address," January 29, 2002, https://georgewbush-whitehouse.archives.gov/news/releases/2002/01/2002 0129-11.html.

3. One of Secretary Tillerson's earliest, comprehensive statements on Iran, delivered on April 19, 2017, is available at https://www.c-span.org/video/?427259-1/secretary-state-tiller son-says-us-must-assess-threats-posed-iran. See also Gardiner Harris, "Tillerson Toughens Tone on Iran Nuclear Agreement," *The New York Times*, April 20, 2017, p. 9.

4. Raymond Hinnebusch, "Foreign Policy in the Middle East," in *The Foreign Policies of Middle East States*, 2nd ed., Raymond Hinnebusch and Anoushiravan Ehteshami, eds. (Boulder, CO: Lynne Rienner, 2014), pp. 22–27.

5. Anoushiravan Ehteshami, "Making Foreign Policy in the Midst of Turmoil," in *The Foreign Policies of Middle East States*, 2nd ed., Raymond Hinnebusch and Anoushiravan Ehteshami, eds. (Boulder, CO: Lynne Rienner, 2014), p. 340.

6. Tareq Y. Ismael, *International Relations of the Contemporary Middle East: A Study in World Politics* (Syracuse, NY: Syracuse University Press, 1986), pp. 51–65.

7. Ehteshami, "Making Foreign Policy in the Midst of Turmoil," p. 340.

8. F. Gregory Gause, *The International Relations of the Persian Gulf* (Cambridge, UK: Cambridge University Press, 2010), p. 86.

9. Kristian Coates Ulrichsen, *Insecure Gulf: The End of Certainty and the Transition to the Post-oil Era* (New York: Columbia University Press, 2011), p. 26.

10. Anoushiravan Ehteshami, *Dynamics of Change in the Persian Gulf: Political Economy, War, and Revolution* (London: Routledge, 2013), p. 216.

11. Ismael, *International Relations of the Contemporary Middle East*, p. 37.

12. Bahgat Korany, "The Middle East since the Cold War: Initiating the Fifth Wave of Democratization," in *International Relations of the Middle East*, 3rd ed., Louise Fawcett, ed. (Oxford: Oxford University Press, 2013), p. 81.

13. Anoushiravan Ehteshami, "GCC Foreign Policy: From the Iran-Iraq War to the Arab Awakening," *The New Politics of Intervention of Gulf Arab States*, LSE Middle East Center, Vol. 1 (April 2015), p. 15.

14. Kristian Coates Ulrichsen, "Internal and External Security in the Arab Gulf States," *Middle East Policy*, Vol. 16, No. 2 (Summer 2009), p. 40.

15. Besides the sources cited here by the likes of Ehteshami, Fawcett, Gause, and Hinnebusch, a very small sampling of important theoretical contributions to the study of the region include Michael N. Barnett, *Dialogues in Arab Politics: Negotiations in Regional Order* (New York: Columbia University Press, 1998); Fred Halliday, *The Middle East in International Relations: Power, Politics, and Ideology* (Cambridge, UK: Cambridge University Press, 2005); and Fred H. Lawson, *Constructing International Relations in the Arab World* (Stanford, CA: Stanford University Press, 2006).

16. Louise Fawcett, "Alliances, Cooperation, and Regionalism in the Middle East," in *International Relations of the Middle East*, 2nd ed., Louise Fawcett, ed. (Oxford: Oxford University Press, 2009), p. 193; Janice Gross Stein, "War and Security in the Middle East," in *International Relations of the Middle East*, 2nd ed., Louise Fawcett, ed. (Oxford: Oxford University Press, 2009), p. 208.

17. Anoushiravan Ehteshami, "Security and Strategic Trends in the Middle East," in *The Transformation of the Gulf: Politics, Economics, and the Global Order*, David Held and Kristian Coates Ulrichsen, eds. (London: Routledge, 2011), p. 274.

18. Ismael, *International Relations of the Contemporary Middle East*, p. 37.

19. Louise Fawcett, "Alliances and Regionalism in the Middle East," in *International Relations of the Middle East*, 3rd ed., Louise Fawcett, ed. (Oxford: Oxford University Press, 2013), p. 189.

20. I have elaborated on this line of argument in Mehran Kamrava, "Preserving Non-Democracies: Leaders and State Institutions in the Middle East," *Middle Eastern Studies*, Vol. 46, No. 2 (March 2010), pp. 231–250.

21. F. Gregory Gause, "Systemic Approaches to Middle East International Relations," *International Studies Review*, Vol. 1, No. 1 (Spring 1999), pp. 26–27.

22. Ehteshami and Hinnebusch call this "complex realism." See Anoushiravan Ehteshami and Raymond Hinnebusch, "Foreign Policymaking in the Middle East: Complex Realism,"

in *International Relations of the Middle East*, 3rd ed., Louise Fawcett, ed. (Oxford: Oxford University Press, 2013), p. 225.

23. Gerd Nonneman, "Determinants and Patterns of Saudi Foreign Policy: 'Omni-balancing' and 'Relative Autonomy' in Multiple Environments," in *Saudi Arabia in the Balance: Political Economy, Society, Foreign Affairs*, Paul Aarts and Gerd Nonneman, eds. (London: Hurst, 2005), pp. 317–318.

24. Edward Burke and Sara Bazoobandi, "The Gulf Takes Charge of the MENA Region," *FRIDE Working Paper*, No. 97 (April 2010), p. 1.

25. Gause, "Systemic Approaches to Middle East International Relations," p. 28.

26. David Held and Kristian Ulrichsen, "The Transformation of the Gulf," in *The Transformation of the Gulf: Politics, Economics, and the Global Order*, David Held and Kristian Ulrichsen, eds. (London: Routledge, 2012), pp. 8–10.

27. See Mehran Kamrava, *Qatar: Small State, Big Politics* (Ithaca, NY: Cornell University Press, 2015), p. 66.

28. Ben Hubbard, "Saudi King Changes Line of Succession," *The New York Times*, April 29, 2015, p. 8.

29. David D. Kirkpatrick, "Surprising Observers, a Young Saudi Rises as a Prince among Princes," *The New York Times*, June 7, 2015, p. 10.

30. Emily B. Hager and Mark Mazzetti, "Emirates Deploy Colombians in Yemen; Hundreds of Mercenaries Join Complex Proxy War, Highlighting Global Trend," *International New York Times*, November 26, 2015, p. 7.

31. Burke and Bazoobandi, "The Gulf Takes Charge of the MENA Region," p. 11.

32. Hussein Sirriyeh, "A New Version of Pan-Arabism?" *International Relations*, Vol. 15, No. 3 (December 2000), pp. 58.

33. Mehran Kamrava, "The Arab Spring and the Saudi-Led Counterrevolution," *Orbis*, Vol. 56, No. 1 (Winter 2012), pp. 96–104.

34. As Justin Gengler has observed, "Beyond the utter undoing of Bahrain's social fabric, this sectarian stratagem has had the equally disastrous effect of exporting the country's internal political conflict abroad. The swift labeling of the February 14 uprising as an Iranian-backed coup attempt, followed by a decisive military intervention by Saudi Arabia to end mass protests, transformed a fundamentally domestic event into a new regional cold war." Justin Gengler, "How Bahrain's Crushed Uprising Spawned the Middle East's Sectarianism," *The Washington Post*, February 13, 2016, https://www.washingtonpost.com/news/monkey-cage/wp/2016/02/13/how-bahrains-crushed-uprising-spawned-the-middle-easts-sectarianism/.

35. Sirriyeh, "A New Version of Pan-Arabism?" pp. 61–63.

36. Kristian Coates Ulrichsen, "The GCC States and the Shifting Balance of Global Power," *CIRS Occasional Paper*, No. 6 (Doha: Center for International and Regional Studies, 2010), p. 20.

37. Gause, *The International Relations of the Persian Gulf*, p. 180.

38. Ulrichsen, "Internal and External Security in the Arab Gulf States," pp. 42–43.

39. After concluding an arms deal worth upward of $110 billion during his 2017 trip to Riyadh, President Trump boasted about the Gulf states' "purchase of lots of beautiful military equipment." Quoted in Karen DeYoung, Kareem Fahim, and Sudarsan Raghavan, "Trump Jumps into Dispute between Qatar and Arab Bloc," *The Washington Post*, June 7, 2017, p. 1.

40. Barry Buzan, Ole Waever, and Jaap de Wilde, *Security: A New Framework for Analysis* (Boulder, CO: Lynne Rienner, 1998), p. 21; Columba Peoples and Nick Vaughan-Williams, *Critical Security Studies: An Introduction* (London: Routledge, 2010), p. 76.

41. Steve Smith, "The Contested Concept of Security," in *Critical Security Studies and World Politics*, Ken Booth, ed. (Boulder, CO: Lynne Rienner, 2005), p. 41; Roger Tooze,

"The Missing Link: Security, Critical International Political Economy, and Community," in *Critical Security Studies and World Politics*, Ken Booth, ed. (Boulder, CO: Lynne Rienner, 2005), p. 133.

42. Peter Hough, *Understanding Global Security*, 3rd ed. (London: Routledge, 2013), p. 10.

43. Ibid. p. 8. Buzan, Waever, and de Wilde maintain that for threats to be considered as such, they will "have to be staged as existential threats to a referent object by a securitizing actor who thereby generates endorsement of emergency measures beyond rules that would otherwise bind." Buzan, Waever, and de Wilde, *Security*, p. 5.

44. Peoples and Vaughan-Williams, *Critical Security Studies*, p. 17.

45. Ken Booth, "Emancipation," in *Critical Security Studies and World Politics*, Ken Booth, ed. (Boulder, CO: Lynne Rienner, 2005), p. 181.

46. Barry Buzan and Lene Hansen, *The Evolution of International Security Studies* (Cambridge: Cambridge University Press, 2009), p. 37.

47. Booth, "Emancipation," p. 182.

48. Andrew Linklater, "Political Community and Human Security," in *Critical Security Studies and World Politics*, Ken Booth, ed. (Boulder, CO: Lynne Rienner, 2005), p. 113.

49. Ibid. p. 127.

50. Hayward Alker, "Emancipation in the Critical Security Studies Project," in *Critical Security Studies and World Politics*, Ken Booth, ed. (Boulder, CO: Lynne Rienner, 2005), p. 208.

51. The relationship between rentierism and democracy is a topic of much research and debate. For a sample of this literature, see Timothy Mitchell, *Carbon Democracy: Political Power in the Age of Oil* (London: Verso, 2011); Michael Ross, "Does Oil Hinder Democracy?" *World Politics*, Vol. 53 (April 2001), pp. 325–361; Michael Ross, *The Oil Curse: How Petroleum Wealth Shapes the Development of Nations* (Princeton, NJ: Princeton University Press, 2012); and Robert Springborg, "GCC Countries as 'Rentier States' Revisited," *Middle East Journal*, Vol. 67, No. 2 (Spring 2013), pp. 301–309.

52. Hough, *Understanding Global Security*, pp. 161–165.

53. Buzan, Waever, and de Wilde, *Security*, p. 74.

54. Iran had laid mines in the Persian Gulf earlier in the war as well, on at least one previous occasion eliciting a military response from the United States. See Patrick E. Tyle, "Gulf Rules of Engagement a Dilemma for U.S." *The Washington Post*, July 4, 1988, p. 1.

55. Stephen Walt, "The Renaissance of Security Studies," *International Studies Quarterly*, Vol. 35, No. 2 (1991), p. 212.

56. John J. Mearsheimer, *The Tragedy of Great Power Politics* (New York: W.W. Norton, 2001), p. 3.

57. Graeme Cheeseman, "Military Force(s) and In/security," in *Critical Security Studies and World Politics*, Ken Booth, ed. (Boulder, CO: Lynne Rienner, 2005), p. 65.

58. Mearsheimer, *The Tragedy of Great Power Politics*, pp. 32–34.

59. Cheeseman, "Military Force(s) and In/security," p. 77.

60. Ibid. p. 79.

61. Peoples and Vaughan-Williams, *Critical Security Studies*, p. 126.

62. Buzan and Hansen, *The Evolution of International Security Studies*, p. 36. See also Smith, "The Contested Concept of Security," p. 52.

63. Hough, *Understanding Global Security*, p. 92.

64. Ibid. pp. 10, 20.

65. Roland Paris, "Human Security: Paradigm Shift or Hot Air?" in *New Global Dangers: Changing Dimensions of International Security*, Michael Brown, Owen Cote, Jr., Sean M. Lynn-Jones, and Steven Miller, eds. (Cambridge, MA: MIT Press, 2004), p. 258.

66. Smith, "The Contested Concept of Security," p. 52.

67. Myron Weiner, "Security, Stability, and International Migration," in *New Global Dangers: Changing Dimensions of International Security*, Michael Brown, Owen Cote Jr., Sean M. Lynn-Jones, and Steven Miller, eds. (Cambridge, MA: MIT Press, 2004), pp. 313–314.

68. Ibid. pp. 324, 313.

69. Jan Jindy Pettman, "Questions of Identity: Australia and Asia," Ken Booth, ed. *Critical Security Studies and World Politics* (Boulder, CO: Lynne Rienner, 2005), p. 160.

70. Ibid., p. 174.

71. See, for example, K. M. Fierke, *Critical Approaches to International Security* (London: Polity, 2007), pp. 75–98.

72. Buzan, Waever, and de Wilde, *Security*, p. 119.

73. Ibid. p. 120.

74. Ibid. p. 123. Original emphasis.

75. Ibid. p. 119.

76. Hough, *Understanding Global Security*, pp. 117–121.

77. Sean Foley, *The Arab Gulf States: Beyond Oil and Islam* (Boulder, CO: Lynne Rienner, 2010), p. 153.

78. Ibid., p. 152.

79. Michael Herb, *Wages of Oil: Parliaments and Economic Development in Kuwait and the UAE* (Ithaca, NY: Cornell University Press, 2014), p. 120.

80. Ibid., p. 115.

81. Quoted in ibid., p. 4.

82. Quoted in ibid., p. 122.

83. Abdullah Ghanem Alhinali Mohannadi, "'Christmas' and Happy New Year," *Al-Watan* (Doha), May 21, 2016.

84. Hough, *Understanding Global Security*, pp. 177, 243.

85. Security challenges arising out of state weakness are discussed more fully in the coming chapters. For a collection of essays on the topic, see also Mehran Kamrava, ed. *Fragile Politics: Weak States in the Greater Middle East* (New York: Oxford University Press, 2016).

86. Hough, *Understanding Global Security*, p. 256.

87. Buzan, Waever, and de Wilde, *Security*, p. 22.

88. Ibid. pp. 22–23.

89. Ibid. p. 25.

90. Peoples and Vaughan-Williams. *Critical Security Studies*, p. 77.

91. Buzan, Waever, and de Wilde, *Security*, p. 33.

92. Ibid. p. 190.

93. Ibid. p. 12.

94. Barry Buzan and Ole Waever, *Regions and Powers: The Structure of International Security* (Cambridge, UK: Cambridge University Press, 2003), pp. 47–48.

95. Ulrichsen, *Insecure Gulf*, p. 41.

96. Gause, *The International Relations of the Persian Gulf*, p. 181.

97. David Held and Kristian Ulrichsen, "The Transformation of the Gulf," p. 14.

98. Gary Sick, "A Plague of Black Swans in the Middle East," February 24, 2016, http://lobelog.com/a-plague-of-black-swans-in-the-middle-east/.

Chapter 2. The Persian Gulf Security Architecture

1. Anoushiravan Ehteshami, *Dynamics of Change in the Persian Gulf: Political Economy, War, and Revolution* (London: Routledge, 2013), p. 24.

2. F. Gregory Gause, *The International Relations of the Persian Gulf* (Cambridge, UK: Cambridge University Press, 2010), p. 3; Ehteshami, *Dynamics of Change in the Persian Gulf*, p. 243.

3. Gause, *The International Relations of the Persian Gulf*, p. 246.

4. Ehteshami, *Dynamics of Change in the Persian Gulf*, p. 65.

5. Kristian Coates Ulrichsen, *Insecure Gulf: The End of Certainty and the Transition to the Post-oil Era* (New York: Columbia University Press, 2011), p. 69. Mehran Kamrava, *Qatar: Small State, Big Politics* (Ithaca, NY: Cornell University Press, 2013).

6. Ulrichsen, *Insecure Gulf*, p. 63.

7. See Mehran Kamrava, *The Modern Middle East: A Political History since the First World War*, 3rd ed. (Berkeley, CA: University of California Press, 2013), pp. 25–67.

8. Louise Fawcett, "Alliances, Cooperation, and Regionalism in the Middle East," in *International Relations of the Middle East*, 2nd ed., Louise Fawcett, ed. (Oxford: Oxford University Press, 2009), p. 190.

9. Michael C. Hudson, "The United States in the Middle East," in *International Relations of the Middle East*, 2nd ed., Louise Fawcett, ed. (Oxford: Oxford University Press, 2009), pp. 308–309.

10. Ulrichsen, *Insecure Gulf*, p. 16.

11. Tareq Y. Ismael, *International Relations of the Contemporary Middle East: A Study in World Politics* (Syracuse, NY: Syracuse University Press, 1986), pp. 37–38.

12. Robert E. Hunter, *Building Security in the Persian Gulf* (Santa Monica, CA: Rand, 2010), p. 14.

13. The doctrine was enunciated during the president's State of the Union address to the U.S. Congress in January 1980. Full text of the speech is available at http://www.presidency.ucsb.edu/ws/?pid=33079.

14. Gause, *The International Relations of the Persian Gulf*, p. 7.

15. Ehteshami, *Dynamics of Change in the Persian Gulf*, p. 34.

16. F. Gregory Gause, "The International Politics of the Gulf," *International Relations of the Middle East*, 2nd ed., Louise Fawcett, ed. (Oxford: Oxford University Press, 2009), p. 274.

17. Fawcett, "Alliances, Cooperation, and Regionalism in the Middle East," p. 204.

18. Ibid., p. 205.

19. Ismael, *International Relations of the Contemporary Middle East*, p. 41.

20. "Foundations and Objectives," The Cooperation Council for the Arab States of the Gulf, http://www.gcc-sg.org/en-us/AboutGCC/Pages/StartingPointsAndGoals.aspx.

21. Ulrichsen, *Insecure Gulf*, p. 23, 25.

22. F. Gregory Gause, "The Illogic of Dual Containment," *Foreign Affairs*, Vol. 73, No. 2 (March–April 1994), p. 57.

23. Gause, *The International Relations of the Persian Gulf*, p. 6.

24. Ibid., p. 183.

25. Ehteshami, *Dynamics of Change in the Persian Gulf*, p. 37; Gause, *The International Relations of the Persian Gulf*, p. 7.

26. While arms race in the Persian Gulf is nothing new, the scale and magnitude of arms purchases by regional actors, especially Saudi Arabia and the UAE, is indeed historically unprecedented.

27. Anoushiravan Ehteshami, "Security and Strategic Trends in the Middle East," David Held and Kristian Ulrichsen, eds., *The Transformation of the Gulf: Politics, Economics, and the Global Order* (London: Routledge, 2012), p. 264.

28. Ehteshami, *Dynamics of Change in the Persian Gulf*, p. 6.

29. Qatar's hedging, of course, did not take it away from the Western security umbrella, with the country housing two of the United States' largest forward bases in the world. It simply increased the country's diplomatic connections with multiple actors which were often at odds with one another. See, Kamrava, *Qatar*, pp. 72–88.

30. Ehteshami, *Dynamics of Change in the Persian Gulf*, pp. 37–38.

31. Ulrichsen, *Insecure Gulf*, p. 9.

32. Ibid., p. 61.

33. Michael Ryan Kraig, "Forging a New Security Order for the Persian Gulf," *Policy Analysis Brief*, The Stanley Foundation, January 2006, p. 3.

34. Ibid., p. 4.

35. Joshua Rovner and Caitlin Talmadge, "Less Is More: The Future of the U.S. Military in the Persian Gulf," *The Washington Quarterly*, Vol. 37, No. 3 (Fall 2014), p. 47. Soon after assuming office, the Trump administration decided not to disclose U.S. troop numbers in Syria and Iraq because of tactical considerations. See W. J. Hennigan, "U.S. Military Escalation, Off the Radar," *The Los Angeles Times*, March 30, 2017, p. 1.

36. Gause, *The International Relations of the Persian Gulf*, p. 14.

37. Ehteshami, *Dynamics of Change in the Persian Gulf*, p. 211.

38. Ibid., p. 218.

39. Quoted in Robert E. Hunter, "Securing the Persian Gulf: Diplomacy, Not Arms," December 18, 2013, www.lobelog.com.

40. U.S. Department of Defense, *Sustaining U.S. Global Leadership: Priorities for 21st Century Defense* (Washington, DC: U.S. Department of Defense, 2012), p. 2. Original emphasis.

41. Kraig, "Forging a New Security Order for the Persian Gulf," p. 4.

42. Rovner and Talmadge, "Less Is More," p. 48.

43. Robert H. Johnson, "The Persian Gulf in U.S. Strategy: A Skeptical View," *International Security*, Vol. 14, No. 1 (Summer 1989), p. 160.

44. Andrew Rathmell, Theodore Karasik, and David Gompert, "A New Persian Gulf Security System," *Rand Issue Paper*, 2003, p. 1.

45. Johnson, "The Persian Gulf in U.S. Strategy," p. 122.

46. Kraig, "Forging a New Security Order for the Persian Gulf," p. 2.

47. Ibid., p. 6.

48. Rathmell, Karasik, and Gompert, "A New Persian Gulf Security System," p. 4.

49. Barry Posen, "Command of the Commons: The Military Foundation of U.S. Hegemony," in *New Global Dangers: Changing Dimensions of International Security*, Michael Brown, Owen Cote Jr., Sean M. Lynn-Jones, and Steven Miller, eds. (Cambridge, MA: MIT Press, 2004), pp. 5, 20–21.

50. Ibid., p. 21.

51. Ulrichsen, *Insecure Gulf*, p. 45.

52. Rathmell, Karasik, and Gompert, "A New Persian Gulf Security System," p. 2.

53. Ibid., p. 4.

54. R. K. Ramazani, "Security in the Persian Gulf," *Foreign Affairs*, Vol. 57, No. 4 (Spring 1979), p. 833.

55. Ehteshami, *Dynamics of Change in the Persian Gulf*, p. 6.

56. Mehran Kamrava, "The Political Economy of Rentierism in the Persian Gulf," in *The Political Economy of the Persian Gulf*, Mehran Kamrava, ed. (New York: Oxford University Press, 2012), pp. 64–65.

57. Ramazani, "Security in the Persian Gulf," p. 826.

58. Gause, "The International Politics of the Gulf," pp. 273–274.

59. Ulrichsen, *Insecure Gulf*, p. 30–32.

60. Kraig, "Forging a New Security Order for the Persian Gulf," p. 7.

61. Kristian Coates Ulrichsen, "Internal and External Security in the Arab Gulf States," *Middle East Policy*, Vol. 16, No. 2 (Summer 2009), p. 46.

62. Ulrichsen, *Insecure Gulf*, p. 8.

63. Ethan Bueno de Mesquita, "Correlates of Public Support for Terrorism in the Muslim World," *United States Institute of Peace Working Paper*, May 17, 2007, pp. 41, 19, 8, 20.

64. Ulrichsen, *Insecure Gulf*, p. 181.

65. According to Ulrichsen, these measure are likely to "merely postpone the eventual reckoning." Ibid., p. 127.

66. Ehteshami, *Dynamics of Change in the Persian Gulf*, p. 22.

67. Laurie A. Brand, *Official Stories: Politics and National Narratives in Egypt and Algeria* (Stanford, CA: Stanford University Press, 2014).

68. Ulrichsen, "Internal and External Security in the Arab Gulf States," p. 45.

69. de Mesquita, "Correlates of Public Support for Terrorism in the Muslim World," p. 7.

70. Ehteshami, *Dynamics of Change in the Persian Gulf*, p. 22.

71. Ulrichsen, *Insecure Gulf*, p. 40.

72. Raymond Hinnebusch, "The Politics of Identity in Middle Eastern International Relations," *International Relations of the Middle East*, 2nd ed., Louise Fawcett, ed. (Oxford: Oxford University Press, 2009), p. 149.

73. Justin Gengler, "How Bahrain's Crushed Uprising Spawned the Middle East's Sectarianism," *The Washington Post*, February 13, 2016, https://www.washingtonpost.com/news/monkey-cage/wp/2016/02/13/how-bahrains-crushed-uprising-spawned-the-middle-easts-sectarianism/.

74. Gause, *The International Relations of the Persian Gulf*, p. 241.

75. Toby Matthiesen, *Sectarian Gulf: Bahrain, Saudi Arabia, and the Arab Spring That Wasn't* (Stanford, CA: Stanford University Press, 2013), p. ix.

76. Data from "Energy Use (Kg of Oil Equivalent per Capita)," http://data.worldbank.org/indicator/EG.USE.PCAP.KG.OE/countries/.

77. Joseph Varghese, "Daily Water Consumption: 500 Liters," *The Gulf Times* (Doha), November 26, 2013, p. 1.

78. Strategy&, "Achieving a Sustainable Water Sector in the GCC: Managing Supply and Demand, Building Institutions," Beirut, 2014, pp. 5–6.

79. Ibid., p. 7.

80. Strategy&, "Achieving a Sustainable Water Sector in the GCC," p. 4.

81. James A. Russell, "Environmental Security and Regional Stability in the Persian Gulf," *Middle East Policy*, Vol. 16, No. 4 (Winter 2009), p. 91.

82. Ibid., p. 92.

83. Nadim Khouri, "Food Security Strategies in the GCC Region," UN-ESCWA and IFPRI, 2012, p. 5.

84. Ibid., p. 11.

85. Rob Bailey and Robin Willoughby, "Edible Oil: Food Security in the Gulf," *Chatham House Briefing Paper*, November 2013, p. 6.

86. Khouri, "Food Security Strategies in the GCC Region," p. 12.

87. On segregated urban spaces, see Jane Bristol-Rhys, "Socio-spatial Boundaries in Abu Dhabi," in *Migrant Labor in the Persian Gulf*, Mehran Kamrava and Zahra Babar, eds. (New York: Columbia University, 2011), pp. 59–84.

88. Ali Khalifa Al Kuwari, "Qataris for Reform," http://dr-alkuwari.net/sites/akak/files/qatarisforreform-translation.pdf.

89. Abdulkhaleq Abdullah, "UAE's Demographic Imbalance," *The Gulf News* (Dubai), April 14, 2007.

90. See, for example, Marc Valeri, "Summering Unrest and Succession Challenges in Oman," Carnegie Endowment for International Peace, January 2015, pp. 8–9; Human Rights Watch, "Bahrain: Drop Twitter Charges against Rights Advocate," January 16, 2015, http://www.hrw.org/news/2015/01/16/bahrain-drop-twitter-charges-against-rights-advocate.

Chapter 3. The Belligerents

1. Frederic M. Wehrey, *Sectarian Politics in the Gulf: From the Iraq War to the Arab Uprisings* (New York: Columbia University Press, 2014), p. 207.

2. Aslı Ü. Bâli, "A Turkish Model for the Arab Spring?" *Middle East Law and Governance*, Vol. 3 (2011), pp. 24–42.

3. Mehran Kamrava, *Qatar: Small State, Big Politics* (Ithaca, NY: Cornell University Press, 2015), pp. 99–100.

4. Kevin Downs, "A Theoretical Analysis of the Saudi-Iranian Rivalry in Bahrain," *Journal of Politics and International Studies*, Vol. 8 (Winter 2012/13), pp. 229–231.

5. See, for example, the collection of essays in Lawrence G. Potter, ed. *Sectarianism in the Persian Gulf* (New York: Oxford University Press, 2014); Toby Matthiesen, *Sectarian Gulf: Bahrain, Saudi Arabia, and the Arab Spring That Wasn't* (Stanford, CA: Stanford University Press, 2013); and Wehrey, *Sectarian Politics in the Gulf*. Also, brief mention of the phenomenon is made above, in chapter 2.

6. Helle Malvig, "Power, Identity, and Securitization in Middle East: Regional Order after the Arab Uprisings," *Mediterranean Politics*, Vol. 19, No. 1 (2014), p. 146.

7. Ibid., p. 147.

8. Ibid., pp. 146–147.

9. Barry Buzan and Ole Waever, *Regions and Powers: The Structure of International Security* (Cambridge, UK: Cambridge University Press, 2003), pp. 34, 35, 37.

10. Robert Olson, *Turkey-Iran Relations, 1979–2004: Revolution, Ideology, War, Coups, and Geopolitics* (Costa Mesa, CA: Mazda, 2005), pp. xxvii–xxviii.

11. Hongying Wang and Erik French, "Middle Range Powers in Global Governance," *Third World Politics*, Vol. 34, No. 6 (2013), p. 985.

12. Ronald L. Tammen et al. *Power Transitions: Strategies for the 21st Century* (New York: Seven Bridges, 2000), p. 65.

13. See, for example, Miles Kahler, "Rising Powers and Global Governance: Negotiating Change in a Resilient Status Quo," *International Affairs*, Vol. 89, No. 3 (2013), pp. 711–729; and Kevin Gray and Craig N. Murphy, "Introduction: Rising Powers and the Future of Global Governance," *Third World Politics*, Vol. 34, No. 6 (2013), pp. 183–193. Canada and Australia, for example, are often cited as middle powers or "secondary states." Both have limited military and economic assets compared with the major powers but nonetheless attempt to play an active international role through reliance on their diplomatic and technical skills. See Andrew Cooper, Richard A. Higgot, and Kim Richard Nossal, *Relocating Middle Powers: Australia and Canada in a Changing World Order* (Vancouver: University of British Columbia Press, 1993).

14. Andrew Cooper and Daniel Flemes, "Foreign Policy Strategies of Emerging Powers in a Multipolar World: An Introductory Review," *Third World Politics*, Vol. 34, No. 6 (2013), p. 948.

15. Ian S. Lustick, "The Absence of Middle Eastern Great Powers: Political 'Backwardness' in Historical Perspective," *International Organization*, Vol. 51, No. 4 (Autumn 1997), p. 656.

16. Ibid., p. 657. Original emphasis.

17. For more on institutions curse, see Victor Menaldo, *The Institutions Curse: Natural Resources, Politics, and Development* (Cambridge, UK: Cambridge University Press, 2016).

18. Mohammed Ayoob, "American Policy toward the Persian Gulf: Strategies, Effectiveness, and Consequences," in *The International Politics of the Persian Gulf*, Mehran Kamrava, ed. (Syracuse, NY: Syracuse University Press, 2011), pp. 124–25.

19. For more on offshore balancing, see Christopher Laney, "From Preponderance to Offshore Balancing: America's Future Grand Strategy," *International Security*, Vol. 22, No. 1 (Summer 1997), pp. 86–124.

20. Frederic Wehrey and Richard Sokolsky, *Imagining a New Security Order in the Persian Gulf* (Washington, DC: Carnegie Endowment for International Peace, 2015), p. 3.

21. Thomas W. Lippman, "The U.S. Dilemma in Bahrain," *POMED Policy Brief*, September 22, 2011, p. 2. Another defense cooperation agreement was signed in 2016, but its terms have not been publicly revealed as of this writing.

22. For a concise list of U.S. sanctions on Iran, see Kenneth Katzman, "Iran, Gulf Security, and U.S. Policy," Congressional Research Service, 7-5700 (May 19, 2015), p. 46.

23. Ibid., p. 41.

24. U.S. Department of Defense, *Sustaining U.S. Global Leadership: Priorities for 21st Century Defense* (Washington, DC: Department of Defense, 2012), p. 2. Original emphasis.

25. Ibid., 3. Original emphasis.

26. Jeffrey Goldberg, "The Obama Doctrine," *The Atlantic*, April 2016, p. 72.

27. Marc Lynch, "Obama and the Middle East: Rightsizing the U.S. Role," *Foreign Affairs*, Vol. 94, No. 5 (September/October 2015), p. 19.

28. Goldberg, "The Obama Doctrine," p. 73.

29. Ibid., p. 77.

30. F. Gregory Gause, "The Illogic of Dual Containment," *Foreign Affairs*, Vol. 73, No. 2 (March–April 1994), p. 62.

31. Lynch, "Obama and the Middle East," p. 23.

32. Ibid., p. 21.

33. Quoted in Goldberg, "The Obama Doctrine," p. 79.

34. Gary Sick, "US Persian Gulf Policy in Obama's Second Term," http://garysick.tumblr.com.

35. Ibid.

36. Obama, in fact, was very reticent about the large-scale use of U.S. military power. Nevertheless, he was the one U.S. president most eager to use U.S. drones for targeted killings of U.S. adversaries. Goldberg, "The Obama Doctrine," p. 79. For more on "Obama's drone war," see the collection of essays in Peter Bergen and Daniel Rothenberg, eds., *Drone Wars: Transforming Conflict, Law, and Policy* (Cambridge, UK: Cambridge University Press, 2014).

37. Goldberg, "The Obama Doctrine," p. 84.

38. James Traub, "America Has Abdicated Its Guiding Role in the Middle East to a Sectarian Arab Military Force," *FP* April 10, 2015, http://foreignpolicy.com/2015/04/10/america-has-abdicated-its-guiding-role-in-the-middle-east-to-a-sectarian-arab-military-force/?wp_login_redirect=0.

39. Goldberg, "The Obama Doctrine," p. 79.

40. Ibid., p. 78.

41. Katzman, "Iran, Gulf Security, and U.S. Policy," p. 43. U.S. Senate, Committee on Armed Services, "Department of Defense Authorization of Appropriations for Fiscal Year 2014 and the Future Years Defense Program," March 5, 2013, pp. 12–13.

42. Stephen Hadley, President George W. Bush's national security adviser, quoted by David Ignatius, "A Reluctant Warrior's Fight," *The Washington Post*, September 12, 2014, p. 23.

43. In the words of one critic, "The notion that the United States can lead from behind is pitiful, the sorry concoction of an Obama administration that mistakes dulcet passivity for a foreign policy." Richard Cohen, "The Failure of Leading from Behind," *The Washington Post*, September 18, 2012, p. 19.

44. Lynch, "Obama and the Middle East," p. 27.

45. Ibid.

46. Nawaf Obeid, "The Salman Doctrine: The Saudi Reply to Obama's Weakness," *The National Interest*, March 30, 2016, http://nationalinterest.org/feature/the-salman-doctrine-the-saudi-reply-obamas-weakness-15623.

47. United States Joint Chiefs of Staff, *The National Military Strategy of the United States of America, 2015* (Washington, DC: Department of Defense, 2015), p. 9.

48. Quoted in Elizabeth Dickinson, "His Excellency, Sheikh Donald of the House of Trump: Why the President-Elect Is Already a Big Hit in the Persian Gulf," foreignpolicy.com, December 16, 2016, http://foreignpolicy.com/2016/12/16/his-excellency-sheikh-donald-of-the-house-of-trump/.

49. "Saudi Adviser: Deputy Crown Prince, Trump Meeting . . . a 'Turning Point,'" *Riyadh Daily*, March 15, 2017, p. 1.

50. "President Trump's Speech to the Arab Islamic American Summit," The White House, May 21, 2017, https://www.whitehouse.gov/briefings-statements/president-trumps-speech-arab-islamic-american-summit/.

51. It is not precisely clear why the U.S. president sees Saudi Arabia as a principal U.S. ally in fighting religious extremism and Daesh, given the pervasiveness of organic connections, discussed in chapter 4, between the kingdom and religious extremism. Donald Trump does have extensive business interests in both Saudi Arabia and the UAE. During those states' 2017 dispute with Qatar, Trump rebuked his secretary of state and the U.S. ambassador to Qatar by expressing support for Saudi Arabia and the UAE and criticizing Qatar, where he does not have any business interests. See David D. Kirkpatrick, "Trump's Persian Gulf Ties," *The International New York Times*, July 19, 2017, p. 3.

52. "President Trump's Speech to the Arab Islamic American Summit."

53. Nader Entessar, "Iran's Security Challenges," *The Muslim World*, Vol. 94, No. 4 (October 2004), p. 538.

54. Katzman, "Iran, Gulf Security, and U.S. Policy," p. 39.

55. U.S. Department of Defense, unclassified executive summary, "Annual Report on Military Power of Iran," p. 1.

56. Mehran Kamrava, *The Modern Middle East: A Political History since the First World War*, 3rd ed. (Berkeley, CA: University of California Press, 2013), pp. 181–182.

57. Personal interview with Kazem Sajjadpour, director of the School of International Relations, Tehran, June 17, 2014. Also, for Iranian efforts to secure spare parts from arch enemy Israel, see Trita Parsi, *Treacherous Alliance: The Secret Dealings of Israel, Iran, and the U.S.* (New Haven, CT: Yale University Press, 2007), p. 112.

58. For a snapshot of some of Iran's major ballistic missiles, see Katzman, "Iran, Gulf Security, and U.S. Policy," p. 28. For a similar snapshot of Iran's conventional armaments, see p. 31. A useful summary of the Islamic Revolutionary Guards Corp (IRGC) can be found on p. 32 of the same report.

59. Entessar, "Iran's Security Challenges," p. 540.

60. Behnam Ben Taleblu, "Enemy of Convenience: Iran's Fight against Daesh," *FRIDE Policy Brief*, No. 2013 (December 2015), p. 2.

61. While Riyadh, Tel Aviv, and even Ankara remained within the range of Iranian missiles, much of NATO forces in Europe fell outside it.

62. Abbas Qadiri, "President Hassan Rouhani's Defense Policy," Atlantic Council, February 11, 2016, http://www.atlanticcouncil.org/blogs/new-atlanticist/president-hassan-rouhani-s-defense-policy.

63. Katzman, "Iran, Gulf Security, and U.S. Policy," p. 26.

64. Kenneth Katzman, "Iran, Gulf Security, and U.S. Policy," Congressional Research Service, 7-5700 (March 30, 2016), p. 28.

65. Mohsen Milani, "Why Tehran Won't Abandon Assad(ism)," *The Washington Quarterly*, Vol. 36, No. 4 (Fall 2013), pp. 83, 88.

66. Ibid., p. 85.

67. Shahram Akbarzadeh, "Why Does Iran Need Hizbollah?" *The Muslim World*, Vol. 106 (January 2016), p. 136.

68. Taleblu, "Enemy of Convenience," p. 1.

69. Milani, "Why Tehran Won't Abandon Assad(ism)," pp. 85–88.

70. Taleblu, "Enemy of Convenience," p. 3.

71. Mohammad Javad Zarif, "What Iran Really Wants: Iranian Foreign Policy in the Rouhani Era," *Foreign Affairs*, Vol. 93, No. 3 (May/June 2014), pp. 56, 57, 54.

72. Christiane Hoffmann, "Interview with Iranian Foreign Minister," *Speigel Online*, May 16, 2015, http://www.spiegel.de/international/world/interview-with-iranian-foreign-minister-mohammad-javad-zarif-a-1033966.html.

73. Zarif, "What Iran Really Wants," p. 55.

74. Mohammad Javad Zarif, "Overcoming Regional Challenges in the Middle East: An Iranian Perspective," Chatham House, February 4, 2016, p. 3.

75. Ali Watkins, Ryan Grim, and Akbar Shahid Ahmed, "Iran Warned Houthis against Yemen Takeover," *The Huffington Post*, April 20, 2015, http://www.huffingtonpost.com/2015/04/20/iran-houthis-yemen_n_7101456.html.

76. Ibid.

77. Zarif, "What Iran Really Wants," p. 51.

78. Ibid., p. 58.

79. Entessar, "Iran's Security Challenges," p. 545.

80. Much has been written on the process, and the stakes, of the nuclear negotiations between Iran and the five permanent members of the UN Security Council and Germany, the so-called P5+1. For a small sample, see Mark Fitzpatrick, "Iran Nuclear Framework Is a Win for All Sides," International Institute for Strategic Studies, April 3, 2015, www.iiss.org; Jessica Mathews, "The New Deal," *The New York Review of Books*, Vol. 62, No. 8 (May 7, 2015), p. 4; and Richard Nephew, "The Grand Bargain: What Iran Conceded in the Nuclear Talks," *Brookings Markaz: Middle East Politics & Policy*, April 18, 2015, pp. 1–11.

81. Mohammed Ayoob, "The Iranian Nuclear Deal: Long-Term Implications for the Middle East," *Insight Turkey*, Vol. 17, No. 3 (Summer 2015), p. 45.

82. For a sample discussion on some of the obstacles to greater GCC monetary integration, see Alexis Antoniades, "The Gulf Cooperation Council Monetary Union," in *The Political Economy of the Persian Gulf*, Mehran Kamrava, ed. (London: Hurst, 2012), pp. 173–191.

83. Richard LeBaron, "The Jordan-Morocco Solution for GCC Defense Masks Bigger Issues," Atlantic Council, April 18, 2014, p. 2.

84. Richard LeBaron, "Hagel's Meeting with GCC Defense Ministers: How to Measure Results," Atlantic Council, May 14, 2014, p. 3.

85. Personal interview with Yusuf bin Alawi Bin Abdullah, minister of foreign affairs of Oman, Muscat, April 6, 2015.

86. Brandon Friedman, "The Arab Gulf States: Balancing Regional Security and Domestic Political Changes," *Bustan: The Middle East Book Review*, Vol. 4 (2013), pp. 43–56.

87. Ibid., p. 48.

88. Anoushiravan Ehteshami, "GCC Foreign Policy: From the Iran-Iraq War to the Arab Awakening," *The New Politics of Intervention of Gulf Arab States*, LSE Middle East Center, Vol. 1 (April 2015), p. 19.

89. Quoted in Jamal Abdullah, "Motives and Consequences of Ambassador Withdrawals from Doha," Aljazeera Centre for Studies, 10 April 2014, p. 4.

90. Ibid., p. 1.

91. Ibid., p. 3.

92. Anthony C. Cordesman, *Saudi Arabia: National Security in a Troubled Region* (Washington, DC: Center for Strategic and International Studies, 2009), p. 36.

93. Joseph Wright Twinam, *The Gulf, Cooperation, and the Council* (Washington, DC: Middle East Policy Council, 1992), pp. 12–13.

94. Wehrey and Sokolsky, *Imagining a New Security Order in the Persian Gulf*, pp. 4, 1, 19.

95. Kristian Coates Ulrichsen, *Insecure Gulf: The End of Certainty and the Transition to the Post-oil Era* (New York: Columbia University Press, 2011), p. 79.

96. Ehteshami, "GCC Foreign Policy," p. 16.

97. Personal interview with Jamal Sanad Al-Suwaidi, director General of the Emirates Center for Strategic Studies and Research, Abu Dhabi, March 12, 2016.

98. Joseph Kostiner, "GCC Perceptions of Collective Security in the Post-Saddam Era," in *The International Politics of the Persian Gulf*, Mehran Kamrava, ed. (Syracuse, NY: Syracuse University Press, 2011), p. 117.

99. Ibid., pp. 101–103.

100. Silvia Colombo, "The GCC and the Arab Spring: A Tale of Double Standards," *The International Spectator*, Vol. 47, No. 4 (December 2012), p. 110.

101. See Ethan Bronner and Michael Slackman, "As Protests Mount, Saudi and U.A.E. Troops Enter Bahrain," *The International Herald Tribune*, March 16, 2011, p. 3.

102. Colombo, "The GCC and the Arab Spring," p. 123.

103. Matteo Legrenzi and Marina Calculli, "Middle East Security: Continuity amid Change," in *International Relations of the Middle East*, 3rd ed., Louise Fawcett, ed. (Oxford: Oxford University Press, 2013), p. 214.

104. Colombo, "The GCC and the Arab Spring," p. 121.

105. LeBaron, "The Jordan-Morocco Solution for GCC Defense Masks Bigger Issues," p. 2.

106. Rami Khouri, "The War in Yemen as a Rite of Passage," September 16, 2015, http://america.aljazeera.com/opinions/2015/9/the-war-in-yemen-as-a-rite-of-passage.html.

107. Mehran Kamrava, "The Arab Spring and the Saudi-Led Counterrevolution," *Orbis*, Vol. 56, No. 1 (Winter 2012), pp. 96–104.

108. Ehteshami, "GCC Foreign Policy," p. 20.

109. Ibid., p. 14.

110. Wehrey and Sokolsky, *Imagining a New Security Order in the Persian Gulf*, p. 10.

111. LeBaron, "Hagel's Meeting with GCC Defense Ministers," p. 2.

112. Ehteshami, "GCC Foreign Policy," p. 18.

113. Rami Khouri, "Threats and Responses in the GCC's New Militancy," Agence Global, April 22, 2015, http://www.belfercenter.org/publication/threats-and-responses-new-gcc-militancy.

114. Friedman, "The Arab Gulf States," p. 51.

115. Wehrey and Sokolsky, *Imagining a New Security Order in the Persian Gulf*, p. 17.

116. Kostiner "GCC Perceptions of Collective Security in the Post-Saddam Era," p. 112.

117. Fatima Ayub, "Introduction," in *Post-Nuclear: The Future for Iran and Its Neighbourhood*, European Council on Foreign Relations, ed. (London: ECFR, 2014), p. 3.

118. Colombo, "The GCC and the Arab Spring," p. 122.

119. Katzman, "Iran, Gulf Security, and U.S. Policy," pp. 40–41.

120. Kenneth Katzman, "The United Arab Emirates (UAE): Issues for U.S. Policy," Congressional Research Service, 7-5700 (September 14, 2015), p. 16.

121. Thomas Gibbons-Neff and Missy Ryan, "U.S. Advisers on the Ground in Yemen, Pentagon Says," *The Washington Post*, May 8, 2016, p. 9.

122. Kostiner "GCC Perceptions of Collective Security in the Post-Saddam Era," p. 108.

123. Anoushiravan Ehteshami and Raymond Hinnebusch, "Foreign Policymaking in the Middle East: Complex Realism," in *International Relations of the Middle East*, 3rd ed., Louise Fawcett, ed. (Oxford: Oxford University Press, 2013), p. 243.

124. Bernard Haykel, "Saudi Arabia and Qatar in a Time of Revolution," Gulf Analysis Paper, Center for Strategic and International Studies, February 19, 2013, p. 4.

125. Personal interview with Abdulkhaleq Abdulla, chairman of the Arab Council for the Social Sciences, Dubai, March 28, 2016.

126. Dana El Baltaji, "Oman Fights Saudi Bid for Gulf Hegemony with Iran Pipe Plan," Bloomberg, April 21, 2014, http://www.bloomberg.com/news/articles/2014-04-21/oman-fights-saudi-bid-for-gulf-hegemony-with-iran-pipeline-plan.

127. Personal interview with Abdulkhaleq Abdulla.

128. Alan Munro, "The Dilemma for Saudi Foreign Policy," *RUSI Journal*, Vol. 147, No. 5 (October 2002), p. 46.

129. Ibid., p. 47.

130. Joseph Kechichian, "Trends in Saudi National Security," *The Middle East Journal*, Vol. 53, No. 2 (Spring 1999), p. 233.

131. F. Gregory Gause, "The Foreign Policy of Saudi Arabia," in *The Foreign Policies of Middle East States*, 2nd ed., Raymond Hinnebusch and Anoushiravan Ehteshami, eds. (Boulder, CO: Lynne Rienner, 2014), p. 186.

132. Crystal A. Ennis and Bessma Momani, "Shaping the Middle East in the Midst of the Arab Uprisings: Turkish and Saudi Foreign Policy Strategies," *Third World Quarterly*, Vol. 34, No. 6 (July 2013), p. 1141.

133. Thomas Lippman, "Saudi Arabia's Ad Hoc Foreign Policy," Inter Press Service, December 20, 2013, http://www.ipsnews.net/2013/12/saudi-arabias-ad-hoc-foreign-policy/.

134. Robert Worth, "U.S. and Saudis in Growing Rift as Power Shifts," *The New York Times*, November 25, 2013, p. 10.

135. Neil Partrick, "Saudi Arabia's Yemen Gambit," *Sada Journal*, Carnegie Endowment for International Peace, p. 1, http://carnegieendowment.org/sada/?fa=61475.

136. Pew Research Center, "Saudi Arabia's Image Falters among Middle East Neighbors," Pew Research Center, Washington, DC, 2013, p. 1.

137. Ibid.

138. Nawaf Obaid, "A Saudi Arabian Defense Doctrine: Mapping the Expanded Force Structure the Kingdom Needs to Lead the Arab World, Stabilize the Region, and Meet its Global Responsibilities," Belfer Center for Science and International Affairs, Harvard Kennedy School, May 2014, pp. 4–5.

139. Fahad M. Alsultan, "The Saudi King: Power and Limitations in the Saudi Arabian Foreign Policy Making," *International Journal of Social Science and Humanity*, Vol. 3, No. 5 (September 2013), p. 457.

140. Nathan Hodson, "Not a Saudi Succession Crisis," *Sada Journal*, Carnegie Endowment for International Peace, June 20, 2015, p. 1.

141. Scott Lucas, "Saudi Arabia's 'Coalition' is a Brazen Challenge to Syria, Iran, and the US," The Conversation, December 17, 2015, http://theconversation.com/saudi-arabias-coalition-is-a-brazen-challenge-to-syria-iran-and-the-us-52455.

142. Reuters, "Saudi Security Spending Rises $5.3 Bln in 2015—Minister," www.zawya.com, December 28, 2015.

143. Madawi Al-Rasheed, "Saudi Arabia's Foreign Policy: Loss without Gain?" *The New Politics of Intervention of Gulf Arab States*, LSE Middle East Center, Vol. 1 (April 2015), p. 40.

144. Haykel, "Saudi Arabia and Qatar in a Time of Revolution," p. 5.

145. Worth, "U.S. and Saudis in Growing Rift as Power Shifts," p. 10.

146. Christopher Phillips, "Gulf Actors and the Syrian Crisis," *The New Politics of Intervention of Gulf Arab States*, LSE Middle East Center, Vol. 1 (April 2015), p. 49.

147. Ennis and Momani, "Shaping the Middle East in the Midst of the Arab Uprisings," p. 1128.

148. See also F. Gregory Gause, "Saudi Arabia's Regional Security Strategy," in *The International Politics of the Persian Gulf*, Mehran Kamrava, ed. (Syracuse, NY: Syracuse University Press, 2011), p. 170.

149. Haykel, "Saudi Arabia and Qatar in a Time of Revolution," p. 6.

150. Al-Rasheed, "Saudi Arabia's Foreign Policy," p. 37.

151. Gause, "The Foreign Policy of Saudi Arabia," p. 201.

152. In the words of Ennis and Momani, "The awful stench of sectarianism and divisive politics across much of the Gulf has been fuelled, in large part, by Saudi Arabia and its religious establishment." Ennis and Momani, "Shaping the Middle East in the Midst of the Arab Uprisings," p. 1135.

153. Ben Hubbard and Mayy El Sheikh, "Saudi Obsession with Iran Revealed," *The International New York Times*, July 18, 2015, p. 6.

154. Traub, "America Has Abdicated Its Guiding Role in the Middle East to a Sectarian Arab Military Force."

155. Gause, "The Foreign Policy of Saudi Arabia," pp. 187–88.

156. Al-Rasheed, "Saudi Arabia's Foreign Policy," p. 38.

157. Fatima Ayub, "Introduction," p. 2.

158. Friedman, "The Arab Gulf States," p. 50.

159. Gause, "The Foreign Policy of Saudi Arabia," p. 186.

160. Ibid., p. 193.

161. Al-Rasheed, "Saudi Arabia's Foreign Policy," p. 38.

162. Ibid., p. 36.

163. Chris Zambelis, "Royal Rivalry in the Levant: Saudi Arabia and Qatar Duel over Syria," *Terrorism Monitor*, Vol. 11, No. 16 (August 9, 2013), p. 10.

164. Al-Rasheed, "Saudi Arabia's Foreign Policy," p. 39.

165. Kirk H. Sowell, "Saudi Arabia and Iran: Rouhani Fades as Riyadh Focuses on Containment," in *Post-Nuclear: The Future for Iran and its Neighbourhood*, European Council on Foreign Relations, ed. (London: ECFR, 2014), p. 5.

166. Gause, "Saudi Arabia's Regional Security Strategy," p. 174.

167. John Duke Anthony, "Saudi Arabian-Yemeni Relations: Implications for U.S. Policy," *Middle East Policy*, Vol. 7, No. 3 (June 2000), p. 78.

168. Kechichian, "Trends in Saudi National Security," 245.

169. Anthony, "Saudi Arabian-Yemeni Relations," p. 79.

170. Ibid., 84.

171. Haykel, "Saudi Arabia and Qatar in a Time of Revolution," p. 4.

172. James Spencer, "The GCC Needs a Successful Strategy for Yemen, Not Failed Tactics," Middle East Research and Information Project, September 11, 2015, http://www.merip.org/gcc-needs-successful-strategy-yemen-not-failed-tactics.

173. Anthony, "Saudi Arabian-Yemeni Relations," p. 78.

174. Spencer, "The GCC Needs a Successful Strategy for Yemen, Not Failed Tactics."

175. Victoria Clark, *Yemen: Dancing on the Heads of Snakes* (New Haven, CT: Yale University Press, 2010), p. xi.

176. Thomas Juneau makes the following observation: "The Houthis . . . are not Iranian proxies; Tehran's influence in Yemen is marginal. The civil war in Yemen is driven first and foremost by local and political factors, and is neither an international proxy war nor a sectarian confrontation. It is primarily a domestic conflict, driven by local grievances and local competition for power and resources." Thomas Juneau, "Iran's Policy Towards the Houthis in Yemen: A Limited Return on a Modest Investment," *International Affairs*, Vol. 92, No. 3 (May 2016), p. 647.

177. Traub, "America Has Abdicated Its Guiding Role in the Middle East to a Sectarian Arab Military Force."

178. Khouri, "Threats and Responses in the GCC's New Militancy."

179. Neil Partrick, "Saudi Arabia's Problematic Allies against the Houthis," *Sada Journal*, Carnegie Endowment for International Peace, February 12, 2016, p. 1.

180. Partrick, "Saudi Arabia's Yemen Gambit," p. 1.

181. Emile Nakleh, "Political Earthquake Hits Saudi Arabia?" May 4, 2015, http://lobelog.com/political-earthquake-hits-saudi-arabia/.

182. Partrick, "Saudi Arabia's Yemen Gambit."

183. Katherine Zimmerman, "AQAP: A Resurgent Threat," *CTC Sentinel*, Vol. 8, No. 9 (September 2015), p. 19.

184. Khouri, "The War in Yemen as a Rite of Passage."

185. Angus McDowell, Phil Stewart, and David Rohde, "Yemen's Guerrilla War Tests Military Ambitions of Big-Spending Saudis," Reuters, April 19, 2016, http://www.reuters.com/investigates/special-report/saudi-military/. The report goes on to argue that "even with more weaponry, the Saudi-led coalition has struggled in Yemen. That's apparent in its bombing campaign from the start."

186. "Statement from UNICEF Executive Director Anthony Lake and WHO Director-General Margaret Chan on the Cholera Outbreak in Yemen as Suspected Cases Exceed 200,000," World Health Organization, June 8, 2017, http://www.who.int/mediacentre/news/releases/2017/suspected-cholera-yemen/en/.

187. "Yemen," World Food Program, http://www1.wfp.org/countries/yemen.

188. Anthony, "Saudi Arabian-Yemeni Relations," pp. 82, 85.

189. See below, chapter 4, especially note 139.

190. Obaid, "A Saudi Arabian Defense Doctrine," p. 14. The threat to exploit the grievances of Iran's Arab and Sunni minorities was also conveyed to me by Prince Turki. M. Saud al-Kabeer, at the time deputy minister for multilateral affairs in the Saudi Ministry of Foreign Affairs, in Riyadh, on September 11, 2014. There is no evidence to date that the Saudis have made good on the threat, aware, perhaps, that Iran could engage in similar action in the kingdom's Shia-populated and restive Eastern Province.

191. Neil Partrick, "Discreet Persuasion," July 2008, Chatham House, p. 21, www.theworldtoday.org.

192. Al-Rasheed, "Saudi Arabia's Foreign Policy," p. 39.

193. Sean Foley, "The UAE: Political Issues and Security Dilemmas," *Middle East Review of International Affairs*, Vol. 3, No. 1 (March 1999), p. 32.

194. Ibid., p. 27.

195. Katzman, "The United Arab Emirates (UAE)," pp. 17, 19.

196. Mark Mazzetti and Emily B. Hager, "Secret Desert Force Set Up by Blackwater's Founder," *The New York Times*, May 15, 2011, p. 1.

197. Ibid., p. 1.

198. Personal interview with Jamal Sanad Al-Suwaidi, director general of the Emirates Center for Strategic Studies and Research, Abu Dhabi, March 12, 2016.

199. Personal interview with Abdulkhaleq Abdulla, chairman of the Arab Council for the Social Sciences, Dubai, March 28, 2016.

200. Ingo Forstenlechner, Emilie Rutledge, and Rashed Salem Alnuaimi, "The UAE, the 'Arab Spring,' and the Different Types of Dissent," *Middle East Policy*, Vol. 29, No. 4 (Winter 2012), p. 55.

201. Ibid.

202. Ibid., p. 59.

203. William A. Rugh, "The Foreign Policy of the United Arab Emirates," *Middle East Journal*, Vol. 50, No. 1 (Winter 1996), pp. 57–70.

204. Christopher M. Davidson, "Dubai and the United Arab Emirates: Security Threats," *British Journal of Middle Eastern Studies*, Vol. 36, No. 3 (2009), p. 439.

205. Katzman, "The United Arab Emirates (UAE)," p. 12.

206. Ibid., p. 17.

207. Ibid., p. 13.

208. Ibid., p. 17.

209. Emily B. Hager and Mark Mazzetti, "Emirates Secretly Sending Mercenaries to Yemen Fight," *The New York Times*, November 25, 2015, p. 1.

210. Hedging and bandwagoning by the Gulf states are both discussed in greater depth in chapter 4.

211. Andrew F. Cooper and Bessma Momani, "Qatar and Expanded Contours of Small State Diplomacy," *The International Spectator*, Vol. 46, No. 3 (September 2011), pp. 113–114.

212. Kamrava, *Qatar*, pp. 65–68. Specifically, I define *subtle power* as "the ability to exert influence from behind the scenes. It revolves around the ability to influence outcomes to one's advantage through a combination of bringing resources to bear, enjoying international prestige derived from and commensurate with norm-entrepreneurship, and being positioned in a such a way as to manipulate circumstances and the weaknesses of others to one's advantage." Pp. 60–61.

213. Quoted in Amena Bakr, "Defying Allies, Qatar Unlikely to Abandon Favored Syria Rebels," www.reuters.com, March, 20, 2014.

214. Mohamed Zayani, "Al Jazeera's Complex Legacy: Thresholds for an Unconventional Media Player from the Global South," *International Journal of Communication*, Vol. 10 (2016), pp. 3562–3563.

215. Partrick, "Discreet Persuasion," p. 20.

216. Haykel, "Saudi Arabia and Qatar in a Time of Revolution," p. 2.

217. Ehteshami, "GCC Foreign Policy," p. 15.

218. Ehteshami and Hinnebusch, "Foreign Policymaking in the Middle East," p. 243.

219. F. Gregory Gause, "Beyond Sectarianism: The New Middle East Cold War," *Brookings Doha Center Analysis Paper*, No. 11 (July 2014), p. 1.

Chapter 4. The Intractable Security Dilemma

1. Raymond Hinnebusch, "Order and Change in the Middle East: A Neo-Gramscian Twist on the International Society Approach," in *International Society and the Middle East: English School Theory at the Regional Level*, Barry Buzan and Ana Gonzalez-Pelaez, eds. (New York: Palgrave Macmillan, 2009), p. 203.

2. Salih Ozbaran, "The Ottoman Turks and the Portuguese in the Persian Gulf, 1534–1581," *Journal of Asian History*, Vol. 6, No. 1 (1972), pp. 45–87.

3. U.S. policy toward the Persian Gulf is discussed in chapter 3. For a slight apparent change in President Obama's policy toward the region, see Jeffrey Goldberg, "The Obama Doctrine," *The Atlantic,* April 2016, pp. 70–90.

4. Kristian Coates Ulrichsen, *Insecure Gulf: The End of Certainty and the Transition to the Post-oil Era* (New York: Columbia University Press, 2011), p. 40.

5. Eldar Mamedov, "The Triple Fear of Gulf Elites," April 23, 2015, http://lobelog.com/the-triple-fear-of-gulf-elites/.

6. Personal interview with Abdulkhaleq Abdulla, chairman of the Arab Council for the Social Sciences, Dubai, March 28, 2016.

7. Ulrichsen, *Insecure Gulf,* p. 41.

8. Ibid., p. 8.

9. K.M. Fierke, *Critical Approaches to International Security* (Cambridge, UK: Polity, 2007), p. 18.

10. Graeme Cheeseman, "Military Force(s) and In/security," in *Critical Security Studies and World Politics,* Ken Booth, ed. (Boulder, CO: Lynne Rienner, 2005), p. 64. For a summary of some of the definitions of *security dilemma,* see Ken Booth and Nicholas J. Wheeler, *The Security Dilemma: Fear, Cooperation, and Trust in World Politics* (New York: Palgrave Macmillan, 2008), p. 8.

11. John J. Mearsheimer, *The Tragedy of Great Power Politics* (New York: W.W. Norton, 2001), p. 36.

12. Booth and Wheeler, *The Security Dilemma,* pp. 2, 1, 4.

13. Charles L. Glaser, "The Security Dilemma Revisited," *World Politics,* Vol. 50, No. 1 (October 1997), p. 184.

14. Ibid., p. 175.

15. Booth and Wheeler, *The Security Dilemma,* pp. 9, 5.

16. Robert O. Keohane, *Power and Governance in a Partially Globalized World* (London: Routledge, 2002), p. 91.

17. Janice Gross Stein, "The Security Dilemma in the Middle East: A Prognosis for the Decade Ahead," in *The Many Faces of National Security in the Arab World,* Bahgat Korany, Paul Noble, and Rex Brynen, eds. (London: Macmillan, 1993), p. 62.

18. Booth and Wheeler, *The Security Dilemma,* p. 5.

19. Robert Jervis, "Cooperation under the Security Dilemma," *World Politics,* Vol. 30, No. 2 (January 1978), p. 194.

20. Shiping Tang, "The Security Dilemma: A Conceptual Analysis," *Security Studies,* Vol. 18, No. 3 (October 2009), p. 590.

21. Booth and Wheeler, *The Security Dilemma,* p. 5.

22. Ibid., p. 7.

23. Glaser, "The Security Dilemma Revisited," p. 193.

24. Booth and Wheeler, *The Security Dilemma,* p. 9.

25. Fred H. Lawson, "Neglected Aspects of the Security Dilemma," in *The Many Faces of National Security in the Arab World,* Bahgat Korany, Paul Noble, and Rex Brynen, eds. (London: Macmillan, 1993), p. 119.

26. Kenneth Waltz, *Realism and International Relations* (London: Routledge, 2008), p. 197.

27. Kenneth Waltz, *Theory of International Politics* (Long Grove, IL: Waveland, 1979), p. 121.

28. Joseph S. Nye, *Bound to Lead: The Changing Nature of American Power* (New York: Basic Books, 1990), p. 181.

29. David A. Lake, *Hierarchy in International Relations* (Ithaca, NY: Cornell University Press, 2009), p. 174.

30. Hedley Bull, *The Anarchical Society: A Study of Order in World Politics*, 3rd. ed. (New York: Columbia University Press, 2002), p. 49.

31. Tang, "The Security Dilemma," pp. 594–595.

32. Booth and Wheeler, *The Security Dilemma*, pp. 61, 70.

33. Ibid., pp. 80, 137–138.

34. Glenn H. Snyder, "The Security Dilemma in Alliance Politics," *World Politics*, Vol. 36, No. 4 (July 1984), p. 462.

35. Snyder, "The Security Dilemma in Alliance Politics," p. 465.

36. Ibid., p. 472.

37. Stephen M. Walt, *The Origins of Alliances* (Ithaca, NY: Cornell University Press, 1987), p. 181.

38. Snyder, "The Security Dilemma in Alliance Politics," p. 471.

39. Walt, *The Origins of Alliances*, p. 29.

40. Lake, *Hierarchy in International Relations*, p. 11.

41. Walt, *The Origins of Alliances*, p. 21.

42. Snyder, "The Security Dilemma in Alliance Politics," p. 467.

43. Ibid., p. 470.

44. Peter Hough, *Understanding Global Security*, 3rd ed. (London: Routledge, 2013), p. 3.

45. Keohane, *Power and Governance in a Partially Globalized World*, p. 89.

46. Deborah Welch Larson, T. V. Paul, and William C. Wohlforth, "Status and World Politics," in *Status in World Politics*, T. V. Paul, Deborah Welch Larson, and William C. Wohlforth, eds. (Cambridge, UK: Cambridge University Press, 2014), pp. 7, 22.

47. Tang, "The Security Dilemma," pp. 591–592.

48. Columba Peoples and Nick Vaughn-Williams, *Critical Security Studies: An Introduction* (London: Routledge, 2010), p. 70.

49. Snyder, "The Security Dilemma in Alliance Politics," pp. 467–468.

50. Alexander Wendt, *Social Theory of International Politics* (Cambridge, UK: Cambridge University Press, 1999), p. 362.

51. Briefly, states that *bandwagon* try to appease a more dominant, potentially threatening power in order to either help *balance* against a closer threat or to share in the spoils of a winning coalition. *Omnibalancing* refers to a state's efforts to address different and often fluctuating threats and needs that are located in its multiple environments, both domestic and international. And *hedging* refers to a strategy of placing one big bet one way (usually in the field of security) and a number of smaller bets the opposite way. For more on bandwagoning, see Walt, *The Origins of Alliances*, pp. 147–180. On omnibalancing, see Gerd Nonneman, "Determinants and Patterns of Saudi Foreign Policy: 'Omnibalancing' and 'Relative Autonomy' in Multiple Environments," in *Saudi Arabia in the Balance: Political Economy, Society, Foreign Affairs*, Paul Aarts and Gerd Nonneman, eds. (London: Hurst, 2005), pp. 317–318. And for more on Qatar's employment of hedging strategy, see Mehran Kamrava, *Qatar: Small State, Big Politics* (Ithaca, NY: Cornell University Press, 2015), pp. 51–52.

52. Janice Gross Stein, "The Security Dilemma in the Middle East: A Prognosis for the Decade Ahead," in *The Many Faces of National Security in the Arab World*, Bahgat Korany, Paul Noble, and Rex Brynen, eds. (London: Macmillan, 1993), p. 57.

53. Fred H. Lawson, "Neglected Aspects of the Security Dilemma," in *The Many Faces of National Security in the Arab World*, Bahgat Korany, Paul Noble, and Rex Brynen, eds. (London: Macmillan, 1993), p. 118.

54. Raymond Hinnebusch, "Foreign Policy in the Middle East," in *The Foreign Policies of Middle East States*, 2nd ed., Raymond Hinnebusch and Anoushiravan Ehteshami, eds. (Boulder, CO: Lynne Rienner, 2014), p. 1.

55. Ibid., p. 34. For more on omnibalancing in the Persian Gulf, see above, chapter 1.

56. Raymond Hinnebusch, "The Middle East Regional System," in *The Foreign Policies of Middle East States*, 2nd ed., Raymond Hinnebusch and Anoushiravan Ehteshami, eds. (Boulder, CO: Lynne Rienner, 2014), p. 49.

57. Louise Fawcett, "Alliances and Regionalism in the Middle East," in *International Relations of the Middle East*, 3rd ed., Louise Fawcett, ed. (Oxford: Oxford University Press, 2013), pp. 187–188.

58. F. Gregory Gause, "Threats and Threat Perceptions in the Persian Gulf Region," *Middle East Policy*, Vol. 14, No. 2 (Summer 2007), p. 122.

59. Hinnebusch, "Foreign Policy in the Middle East," p. 4.

60. Anoushiravan Ehteshami, "Making Foreign Policy in the Midst of Turmoil," in *The Foreign Policies of Middle East States*, 2nd ed., Raymond Hinnebusch and Anoushiravan Ehteshami, eds. (Boulder, CO: Lynne Rienner, 2014), p. 339.

61. Hinnebusch, "The Middle East Regional System," p. 68.

62. Raymond Hinnebusch, "The Politics of Identity in Middle East International Relations," in *International Relations of the Middle East*, 3rd ed., Louise Fawcett, ed. (Oxford: Oxford University Press, 2013), p. 157.

63. Peter Mandaville, "Islam and International Relations in the Middle East: From *Umma* to Nation State," in *International Relations of the Middle East*, 3rd ed., Louise Fawcett, ed. (Oxford: Oxford University Press, 2013), p. 181.

64. Anoushiravan Ehteshami, "The Middle East's New Power Dynamics," *Current History*, December 2009, p. 396.

65. Mohammed Ayoob, "American Policy toward the Persian Gulf," in *The International Politics of the Persian Gulf*, Mehran Kamrava, ed. (Syracuse, NY: Syracuse University Press, 2011), p. 141.

66. Ibid., p. 133.

67. Michael C. Hudson, "The United States in the Middle East," in *International Relations of the Middle East*, 2nd ed., Louise Fawcett, ed. (Oxford: Oxford University Press, 2009), pp. 308–309.

68. Hinnebusch, "The Middle East Regional System," pp. 59–67.

69. Ayoob, "American Policy toward the Persian Gulf," p. 131.

70. Ehteshami, "The Middle East's New Power Dynamics," p. 395.

71. Gause, "Threats and Threat Perceptions in the Persian Gulf Region," p. 120.

72. Adham Saouli, "The Foreign Policies of Iraq and Lebanon," in *The Foreign Policies of Middle East States*, 2nd ed., Raymond Hinnebusch and Anoushiravan Ehteshami, eds. (Boulder, CO: Lynne Rienner, 2014), p. 107.

73. Anoushiravan Ehteshami and Raymond Hinnebusch, "Foreign Policymaking in the Middle East," in *The Foreign Policies of Middle East States*, 2nd ed., Raymond Hinnebusch and Anoushiravan Ehteshami, eds. (Boulder, CO: Lynne Rienner, 2014), p. 243.

74. F. Gregory Gause, *The International Relations of the Persian Gulf* (Cambridge, UK: Cambridge University Press, 2010), p. 9.

75. Fred H. Lawson, "Security Dilemma in the Contemporary Persian Gulf," in *The International Politics of the Persian Gulf*, Mehran Kamrava, ed. (Syracuse, NY: Syracuse University Press, 2011), p. 53.

76. Paul Gallagher, "British Arms Sales to Bahrain Total £45m since Arab Spring," *The Independent* (London), February 13, 2016, http://www.independent.co.uk/news/uk/politics/bahrain-protesters-tortured-while-britain-signs-45m-arms-deal-a6872166.html. Among other things, the arms included machine guns, assault rifles, and anti-armor ammunition.

77. Lawson, "Security Dilemma in the Contemporary Persian Gulf," p. 51.

78. Gawdat Bahgat, "Security in the Gulf: The View from Oman," *Security Dialogue*, Vol. 30, No. 4 (1999), p. 446.

79. Personal interview with Yusuf bin Alawi bin Abdullah, minister of foreign affairs of Oman, Muscat, April 6, 2015.

80. Ibid.

81. Personal interview with Behzad Khoshandam, researcher at Center for Strategic Research, Tehran, June 17, 2014.

82. For more on Iran's relations with the South Caucasus, see Mehran Kamrava, ed. *The Great Game in West Asia: Iran, Turkey, and the South Caucasus* (New York: Oxford University Press, 2018), especially chapters 1, 3, and 5.

83. Zalmay Khalilzad, *The Envoy* (New York: St. Martin's, 2016), pp. 164–165.

84. Personal interview with Behzad Khoshandam.

85. Saouli, "The Foreign Policies of Iraq and Lebanon," p. 130.

86. The Mahdi Army, under the leadership of Muqtada al-Sadr, was set up in 2003 in the wake of the U.S. invasion and was officially disbanded in 2008. The militia was reconstituted in 2014 in response to the rise of Daesh and rebranded itself as the Peace Companies (Sarāyā al-Salām).

87. Personal interview with Kazem Sajjadpour, director of the School of International Relations, Tehran, June 17, 2014.

88. Ibid.

89. Keyhan Barzegar, "Iran-US Relations in Light of the Nuclear Negotiations," *The International Spectator*, Vol. 49, No. 3 (July 2014), pp. 1–7.

90. Personal interview with Abbas Maleki, deputy director of the Center for Strategic Research, Tehran, June 17, 2014. As discussed in chapter 3, Iran nevertheless continues to develop "anti-access and area denial" capabilities in order to have the ability the control approaches to the Strait.

91. Mohammad Javad Zarif, "What Iran Really Wants: Iranian Foreign Policy in the Rouhani Era," *Foreign Affairs*, Vol. 93, No. 3 (May/June 2014), pp. 49–59.

92. See, for example, Thomas Erdbrink, "Iranian Leader Expresses Skepticism on Nuclear Talks," *The New York Times*, January 8, 2015, p. 4; and Thomas Erdbrink, "Iran's Supreme Leader Backs Missile Program," *The New York Times*, March 31, 2016, p. 8.

93. Personal interview with Mohammad Farazmand, director of the Persian Gulf Department, Iranian Ministry of Foreign Affairs, Tehran, June 18, 2014.

94. Ibid.

95. Ibid.

96. Mohammad Javad Zarif, "Why Iran Is Building Up Its Defenses," *The Washington Post*, April 21, 2016, p. 17.

97. Personal interview with Kazem Sajjadpour.

98. Personal interview with Behzad Khoshandam.

99. Personal interview with Kazem Sajjadpour.

100. Ibid.

101. Ibid.

102. Ibid.

103. Quoted in Jeffrey Goldberg, "The Obama Doctrine," *The Atlantic*, April 2016, p. 75.

104. Personal interview with Kazem Sajjadpour.

105. Tom Coghlan, Aimal Yaqubi, and Sara Elizabeth Williams, "Assad Recruits Afghan Mercenaries to Fight Isis," *The Times* (London), June 2, 2015, p. 30.

106. Bebnam Ben Taleblu, "Enemy of Convenience: Iran's Fight against Daesh," *FRIDE Policy Brief*, No. 2013 (December 2015), p. 1.

107. Ibid.

108. Ibid.

109. Kenneth Katzman and Carla E. Humud, "Iraq: Politics and Government," Congressional Research Service, 7-5700 (September 16, 2015), pp. 10–11.

110. Saouli, "The Foreign Policies of Iraq and Lebanon," p. 125.

111. Taleblu, "Enemy of Convenience," p. 2.

112. Sam Perlo-Freeman et al., "Trends in World Military Expenditure, 2014," *SIPRI Fact Sheet*, April 2015, p. 2.

113. "SIPRI Military Expenditure Database," http://www.sipri.org/research/armaments/milex/milex_database. See also table 2.1, in chapter 2.

114. Michael Herb, *All in the Family: Absolutism, Revolution, and Democracy in the Middle Eastern Monarchies* (Albany: State University of New York Press, 1999), pp. 237–238.

115. F. Gregory Gause, "Kings for All Seasons: How the Middle East's Monarchies Survived the Arab Spring," *Brookings Doha Center Analysis Paper*, No. 8 (September 2013), pp. 3, 18–20, 27.

116. Tim Niblock, *Saudi Arabia: Power, Legitimacy, and Survival* (London: Routledge, 2006), p. 70.

117. Madawi Al-Rasheed, *Muted Modernists: The Struggle over Divine Politics in Saudi Arabia* (New York: Oxford University Press, 2015), pp. 52–53.

118. Leigh Nolan, "Managing Reform? Saudi Arabia and the King's Dilemma," *Brookings Doha Center Policy Briefing*, May 2011, p. 2.

119. Gause, "Kings for All Seasons," p. 1.

120. Steve A. Yetiv, "Oil, Saudi Arabia, and the Spring That Has Not Come," in *The Arab Spring: Change and Resistance in the Middle East*, Mark L. Hass and David W. Lesch, eds. (Boulder, CO: Westview Press, 2013), pp. 99–113.

121. Jamal Abdullah, "Motives and Consequences of Ambassador Withdrawals from Doha," Aljazeera Center for Studies, 10 April 2014, p. 3.

122. Simon Henderson, "Saudi Arabia Ups Pressure on Qatar," *Policy Analysis*, The Washington Institute, August 27, 2014, http://www.washingtoninstitute.org/policy-analysis/view/saudi-arabia-ups-pressure-on-qatar.

123. "HH the Emir Arrives in Saudi Arabia," Qatar News Agency, July 22, 2014; and "Qatari Emir in Jeddah for Talks with King Abdullah," *Arab News*, October 14, 2014, http://www.arabnews.com/featured/news/643711.

124. Maha El Dahan, "Saudi Arabia Considering Further Steps against Iran, Foreign Minister Says," *The Washington Post*, January 10, 2016, p. 11.

125. Adel bin Ahmed Al-Jubeir, "Why Iran Is Still Dangerous," *The New York Times*, January 20, 2016, p. 25.

126. In January 2016, Sudan, which was once close to Iran, cut diplomatic ties with the Islamic Republic. It received $5 billion in military aid from Saudi Arabia. The kingdom, however, withheld $4 billion from Lebanon a sum earmarked for military and police training assistance, because it claimed that the pro-Iranian Hezbollah group remained powerful in the country. Although not necessarily close to Iran, Djibouti and the Maldives also cut diplomatic ties with Iran under Saudi pressure in 2016. See Jeremy Binnie, "Saudi-Sudanese Alliance Reportedly Cemented with $5bn in Military Aid," *IHS Jane's Defense Weekly*, 23 February 2016, http://www.janes.com/article/58299/saudi-sudan-alliance-reportedly-cemented-with-5bn-in-military-aid; and Bernedetta Berti, "Saudi Brinkmanship in Lebanon," *Sada Journal*, Carnegie Endowment for International Peace, March 24, 2016.

127. This included eleven million dollars in direct lobbying in 2015. According to *The Christian Science Monitor*, "The lobbying extends to US media outlets. By providing media time and interviews to pro-Saudi analysts, sponsoring op-eds, and hosting Congressional aids at lavish gala dinners—including one attended by King Salman himself last

September—the anti-Iran messaging is amplified." Taylor Luck, "To Counter Iranian Rival, Saudi Arabia Steps up Washington Lobbying," *The Christian Science Monitor*, February 8, 2016, https://www.csmonitor.com/World/Middle-East/2016/0208/To-counter-Iranian-rival-Saudi-Arabia-steps-up-Washington-lobbying.

128. Lawson, "Security Dilemma in the Contemporary Persian Gulf," p. 56.

129. Ben Hubbard, "Despite Displeasure with U.S., Saudis Face Long Dependency," *The New York Times*, May 15, 2015, p. 8.

130. Quoted in ibid.

131. Al-Jubeir, "Why Iran Is Still Dangerous."

132. Prince Turki al-Faisal, director of the kingdom's intelligence service (1979–2001) and later Saudi ambassador to the United States (2005–2007), delivered the following warning in 2011: "Saudi Arabia will no longer be able to cooperate with America in the same way it historically has. With most of the Arab world in upheaval, the "special relationship" between Saudi Arabia and the United States would increasingly be seen as toxic by the vast majority of Arabs and Muslims, who demand justice for the Palestinian people.

"Saudi leaders would be forced by domestic and regional pressures to adopt a far more independent and assertive foreign policy. Like our recent military support for Bahrain's monarchy, which America opposed, Saudi Arabia would pursue other policies at odds with those of the United States, including opposing the government of Prime Minister Nuri al-Maliki in Iraq and refusing to open an embassy there despite American pressure to do so. The Saudi government might part ways with Washington in Afghanistan and Yemen as well" (Turki al-Faisal, "Veto a State, Lose an Ally," *The New York Times*, September 12, 2011, p. 27).

It should be noted, however, that since Prince Turki had retired from public service in 2007, it is not clear to what extent his views are representative of official Saudi thinking, or, for that matter, how much influence he carried within Saudi policy circles at the time of *The New York Times* op-ed piece.

133. See, for example, Elisabeth Bumiller, "Defense Chief Is in Mission to Mend Saudi Relations," *The New York Times*, April 7, 2011, p. 12; Mark Landler and Steven Lee Myers, "Healing a Rift, U.S. Agrees to $30 Billion Fighter Jet Sale to Saudi Arabia," *The New York Times*, December 30, 2011, p. 10; and Helene Cooper and Gardiner Harris, "An Arms Deal Is Aimed at Saudis' Iran Worries," *The New York Times*, September 4, 2015, p. 11.

134. F. Gregory Gause, "The Foreign Policy of Saudi Arabia," in *The Foreign Policies of Middle East States*, 2nd ed., Raymond Hinnebusch and Anoushiravan Ehteshami, eds. (Boulder, CO: Lynne Rienner, 2014), p. 191.

135. Al-Jubeir, "Why Iran Is Still Dangerous," p. 25.

136. Personal interview with Turki M. Saud al-Kabeer, deputy minister for Multilateral Affairs, Ministry of Foreign Affairs, Kingdom of Saudi Arabia, Riyadh, September 11, 2014.

137. Quoted in Matthew Rosenberg and Ben Hubbard, "Middle East Allies See Heightened Peril in Newly Empowered, Emboldened Tehran," *The New York Times* (July 15, 2015), p. 9.

138. Personal interview with Turki M. Saud al-Kabeer.

139. Personal interview with Saleh Al-Rajhi, Center for American Studies, Ministry of Foreign Affairs, Kingdom of Saudi Arabia, Riyadh, September 11, 2014.

140. Helene Cooper, Rod Nordland, and Neil MacFarquhar, "New Saudi King and U.S. Face Crucial Point in Relationship," *The New York Times*, January 24, 2015, p. 1.

141. The documents can be accessed at https://wikileaks.org/saudi-cables/.

142. For a concise discussion of the cables, see Ben Hubbard and Mayy El Sheikh, "A Saudi Obsession with Politics and Religion," *The New York Times*, July 17, 2015, p. 1.

143. Personal interview with Saleh Al-Rajhi.

144. Banafsheh Keynoush, *Saudi Arabia and Iran: Friends or Foes?* (New York: Palgrave Macmillan, 2016), pp. 132–133.

145. Ibid. p. 18.

146. For a compelling account of the rise of violent religious extremism in Saudi Arabia, see Robert Lacey, *Inside the Kingdom: Kings, Clerics, Modernists, Terrorists, and the Struggle for Saudi Arabia* (New York: Viking, 2009), especially pp. 119–123. See also Ben Hubbard, "ISIS Undermines Saudi State, Remaking Creed as a Weapon," *The New York Times,* April 1, 2016, p. 1.

147. For an insightful analysis of the profile of Saudi recruits into Al Qaeda in the Arabian Peninsula, see Thomas Hegghammer, "Terrorist Recruitment and Radicalization in Saudi Arabia," *Middle East Policy,* Vol. 13, No. 4 (Winter 2006), pp. 39–60.

148. Nolan, "Managing Reform?," p. 6.

149. Gause, "Kings for all Seasons," p. 31.

150. Cole Bunzel, *The Kingdom and the Caliphate: Duel of the Islamic States* (Washington, DC: Carnegie Endowment for International Peace, 2016), pp. 3, 14, 24, 15–17.

151. Ibid., p. 18.

152. For a discussion of Iran-UAE relations, see Stephanie Cronin and Nur Masalha, "The Islamic Republic of Iran and the GCC States: Revolution or Realpolitik?" London School of Economics, Kuwait Programme on Development, Governance and Globalisation in the Gulf States, No. 17 (November 2011), pp. 26–31.

153. Personal interview with Abdulkhaleq Abdulla.

154. Personal interview with Jamal Sanad Al-Suwaidi, director general of the Emirates Center for Strategic Studies and Research, Abu Dhabi, March 12, 2016.

155. Personal interview with Abdulkhaleq Abdulla.

156. Ibid.

157. Personal interview with Jamal Sanad Al-Suwaidi.

158. Personal interview with Abdulkhaleq Abdulla.

159. Ibid.

160. Personal interview with Jamal Sanad Al-Suwaidi.

161. Personal interview with Abdulkhaleq Abdulla.

162. Ibid.

163. Personal interview with Jamal Sanad Al-Suwaidi.

164. Anoushiravan Ehteshami, *Globalization and Geopolitics in the Middle East: Old Games, New Rules* (London: Routledge, 2007), p. 58.

165. Leonard Binder, "Introduction: The International Dimensions of Ethnic Conflict in the Middle East," in *Ethnic Conflict and International Politics in the Middle East,* Leonard Binder, ed. (Gainesville: University Press of Florida, 1999), p. 5.

Chapter 5. Insecurity in the Persian Gulf

1. Kristian Coates Ulrichsen, *Insecure Gulf: The End of Certainty and the Transition to the Post-oil Era* (New York: Columbia University Press, 2011), p. 3.

2. David Held and Kristian Ulrichsen, "The Transformation of the Gulf," in *The Transformation of the Gulf: Politics, Economics, and the Global Order,* David Held and Kristian Ulrichsen, eds. (London: Routledge, 2012), p. 14.

3. An example is the work of Andrew Rathmell, Theodore Karasik, and David Gompert, who as far back as 2003 were arguing that a viable security system in the Persian Gulf needs to entail two synergetic components: a multilateralism that encompasses a GCC-Iran-Iraq balance of power and internal reforms within the GCC states. Andrew Rathmell, Theodore Karasik, and David Gompert, "A New Persian Gulf Security System," *Rand Issue Paper* (2003), p. 10.

4. On the resource course, see Michael L. Ross, *The Oil Curse: How Petroleum Wealth Shapes the Development of Nations* (Princeton, NJ: Princeton University Press, 2012); on the rise of global cities along the Persian Gulf, see Mehran Kamrava, ed. *Gateways to the World: Port Cities in the Persian Gulf* (New York: Oxford University Press, 2016).

5. Held and Ulrichsen, "The Transformation of the Gulf," p. 8.

6. Ulrichsen, *Insecure Gulf*, p. 76.

7. According to estimates by the U.S. Energy Information Administration, oil prices are likely to hover around $47 per barrel in 2017. See U.S. Energy Information Administration, "Short-Term Energy Outlook (STEO)," May 2016, https://www.eia.gov/forecasts/steo/report/prices.cfm.

8. Anthony Cordesman, "The Coming Petroleum Revenues Crisis in the MENA," Center for Strategic and International Studies, March 11, 2016, p. 2.

9. Ulrichsen, *Insecure Gulf*, p. 11.

10. The Iraqi Shia militia Al-Muqawama Al-Islamiya is popularly known as Al-Hashad Al-Sha'abi (the Popular Mobilization). For a report on Iran's alleged relationship with the Taliban, see Barbara Slavin, "Iran's 'Marriage of Convenience' with Taliban," *Al-Monitor*, May 31, 2016, http://www.al-monitor.com/pulse/originals/2016/05/iran-marriage-convenience-taliban-isis.html#ixzz4AghBfzML.

11. Mohammed Ayoob, "The Iranian Nuclear Deal: Long-Term Implications for the Middle East," *Insight Turkey*, Vol. 17, No. 3 (Summer 2015), p. 50.

12. See also Frederic Wehrey and Richard Sokolsky, *Imagining a New Security Order in the Persian Gulf* (Washington, DC: Carnegie Endowment for International Peace, 2015), p. 1.

13. Rathmell, Karasik, and Gompert, "A New Persian Gulf Security System," p. 5.

14. Caspar Weinberger, "A Report to the Congress on Security Arrangements in the Persian Gulf," United States Department of Defense, June 15, 1987, p. 1.

15. Gary Sick. "US Persian Gulf Policy in Obama's Second Term," March 19, 2013, http://garysick.tumblr.com.

16. Anoushiravan Ehteshami, "Making Foreign Policy in the Midst of Turmoil," in *The Foreign Policies of Middle East States*, 2nd ed., Raymond Hinnebusch and Anoushiravan Ehteshami, eds. (Boulder, CO: Lynne Rienner, 2014), p. 349.

17. See Jim Lobe, "The Neocon-Liberal Hawk Convergence Is Worse Than I Thought," *LobeLog*, May 25, 2016, http://lobelog.com/the-neocon-liberal-hawk-convergence-is-worse-than-i-thought/.

18. Rathmell, Karasik, and Gompert, "A New Persian Gulf Security System," pp. 1–2.

19. Ibid., p. 7.

20. Robert E. Hunter, "Securing the Persian Gulf: Diplomacy, Not Arms," *LobeLog*, December 18, 2013, https://lobelog.com/securing-the-persian gulf diplomacy-not-arms/

21. Sick, "US Persian Gulf Policy in Obama's Second Term."

22. Michael Ryan Kraig, "Forging a New Security Order for the Persian Gulf," *Policy Analysis Brief*, The Stanley Foundation, January 2006, p. 13.

23. Wehrey and Sokolsky, *Imagining a New Security Order in the Persian Gulf*, p. 5.

24. Michael Kraig, "Assessing Alternative Security Frameworks for the Persian Gulf," *Middle East Policy*, Vol. 15, No. 3 (Fall 2004), p. 154.

BIBLIOGRAPHY

Books and Articles

Abdullah, Jamal. "Motives and Consequences of Ambassador Withdrawals from Doha," Aljazeera Center for Studies, April 10, 2014.

Akbarzadeh, Shahram. "Why Does Iran Need Hizbollah?" *The Muslim World*, Vol. 106 (January 2016), pp. 127–140.

Alker, Hayward. "Emancipation in the Critical Security Studies Project," in *Critical Security Studies and World Politics*. Ken Booth, ed. Boulder, CO: Lynne Rienner, 2005, pp. 181–188.

Al-Rasheed, Madawi. *Muted Modernists: The Struggle over Divine Politics in Saudi Arabia*. New York: Oxford University Press, 2015.

——. "Saudi Arabia's Foreign Policy: Loss without Gain?" *The New Politics of Intervention of Gulf Arab States*, LSE Middle East Center, Vol. 1 (April 2015), pp. 32–40.

Alsultan, Fahad M. "The Saudi King: Power and Limitations in the Saudi Arabian Foreign Policy Making," *International Journal of Social Science and Humanity*, Vol. 3, No. 5 (September 2013), pp. 457–460.

Anthony, John Duke. "Saudi Arabian-Yemeni Relations: Implications for U.S. Policy," *Middle East Policy*, Vol. 7, No. 3 (June 2000), pp. 78–96.

Antoniades, Alexis. "The Gulf Cooperation Council Monetary Union," in *The Political Economy of the Persian Gulf*. Mehran Kamrava, ed. London: Hurst, 2012, pp. 173–191.

Ayoob, Mohammed. "American Policy toward the Persian Gulf: Strategies, Effectiveness, and Consequences," in *The International Politics of the Persian Gulf*. Mehran Kamrava, ed. Syracuse, NY: Syracuse University Press, 2011, pp. 120–143.

——. "The Iranian Nuclear Deal: Long-Term Implications for the Middle East," *Insight Turkey*, Vol. 17, No. 3 (Summer 2015), pp. 45–52.

Ayub, Fatima. "Introduction," in *Post-Nuclear: The Future for Iran and Its Neighbourhood*. European Council on Foreign Relations, ed. London: ECFR, 2014, pp. 1–5.

Bahgat, Gawdat. "Security in the Gulf: The View from Oman," *Security Dialogue*, Vol. 30, No. 4 (1999), pp. 445–458.

Bailey, Rob, and Robin Willoughby. "Edible Oil: Food Security in the Gulf," *Chatham House Briefing Paper*, November 2013.

Bâli, Aslı Ü. "A Turkish Model for the Arab Spring?" *Middle East Law and Governance*, Vol. 3 (2011), pp. 24–42.

Barnett, Michael N. *Dialogues in Arab Politics: Negotiations in Regional Order*. New York: Columbia University Press, 1998.

Barzegar, Keyhan. "Iran-US Relations in Light of the Nuclear Negotiations," *The International Spectator*, Vol. 49, No. 3 (July 2014), pp. 1–7.

Bergen, Peter, and Daniel Rothenberg, eds. *Drone Wars: Transforming Conflict, Law, and Policy*. Cambridge, UK: Cambridge University Press, 2014.

Berti, Bernedetta. "Saudi Brinkmanship in Lebanon," *Sada Journal*, Carnegie Endowment for International Peace, March 24, 2016.

Binder, Leonard. "Introduction: The International Dimensions of Ethnic Conflict in the Middle East," in *Ethnic Conflict and International Politics in the Middle East*. Leonard Binder, ed. Gainesville, FL: University Press of Florida, 1999, pp. 1–40.

Booth, Ken. "Emancipation," in *Critical Security Studies and World Politics*. Ken Booth, ed. Boulder, CO: Lynne Rienner, 2005, pp. 181–187.

Booth, Ken, and Nicholas J. Wheeler. *The Security Dilemma: Fear, Cooperation, and Trust in World Politics*. Basingstoke, UK: Palgrave Macmillan, 2008.

Brand, Laurie A. *Official Stories: Politics and National Narratives in Egypt and Algeria*. Stanford, CA: Stanford University Press, 2014.

Bristol-Rhys, Jane. "Socio-spatial Boundaries in Abu Dhabi," in *Migrant Labor in the Persian Gulf*. Mehran Kamrava and Zahra Babar, eds. New York: Columbia University, 2011, pp. 59–84.

Bull, Hedley. *The Anarchical Society: A Study of Order in World Politics*. 3rd ed. New York: Columbia University Press, 2002.

Bunzel, Cole. *The Kingdom and the Caliphate: Duel of the Islamic States*, Washington, DC: Carnegie Endowment for International Peace, 2016.

Burke, Edward, and Sara Bazoobandi. "The Gulf Takes Charge of the MENA Region," *FRIDE Working Paper*, No. 97 (April 2010), pp. 1–15.

Buzan, Barry, and Lene Hansen. *The Evolution of International Security Studies*. Cambridge, UK: Cambridge University Press, 2009.

Buzan, Barry, and Olea Waever. *Regions and Powers: The Structure of International Security*. Cambridge, UK: Cambridge University Press, 2003.

Buzan, Barry, Ole Waever, and Jaap de Wilde. *Security: A New Framework for Analysis*. Boulder, CO: Lynne Rienner, 1998.

Cheeseman, Graeme. "Military Force(s) and In/security," in *Critical Security Studies and World Politics*. Ken Booth, ed. Boulder, CO: Lynne Rienner, 2005, pp. 63–87.

Clark, Victoria. *Yemen: Dancing on the Heads of Snakes*. New Haven, CT: Yale University Press, 2010.

Colombo, Silvia. "The GCC and the Arab Spring: A Tale of Double Standards," *The International Spectator*, Vol. 47, No. 4 (December 2012), pp. 110–126.

Cooper, Andrew F. and Bessma Momani. "Qatar and Expanded Contours of Small State Diplomacy," *The International Spectator*, Vol. 46, No. 3 (September 2011), pp. 113–128.

Cooper, Andrew, and Daniel Flemes. "Foreign Policy Strategies of Emerging Powers in a Multipolar World: An Introductory Review," *Third World Politics*, Vol. 34, No. 6 (2013), pp. 943–962.

Cooper, Andrew, Richard A. Higgot, and Kim Richard Nossal. *Relocating Middle Powers: Australia and Canada in a Changing World Order*. Vancouver: University of British Columbia Press, 1993.

Cordesman, Anthony. "The Coming Petroleum Revenues Crisis in the MENA," *Center for Strategic and International Studies*, March 11, 2016.

———. *Saudi Arabia: National Security in a Troubled Region*. Washington, DC: Center for Strategic and International Studies, 2009.

Cronin, Stephanie, and Nur Masalha. "The Islamic Republic of Iran and the GCC States: Revolution or Realpolitik?" London School of Economics, Kuwait Programme on Development, Governance and Globalisation in the Gulf States, No. 17, November 2011.

Davidson, Christopher M. "Dubai and the United Arab Emirates: Security Threats," *British Journal of Middle Eastern Studies*, Vol. 36, No. 3 (2009), pp. 431–447.

de Mesquita, Ethan Bueno. "Correlates of Public Support for Terrorism in the Muslim World," *United States Institute of Peace Working Paper*, May 17, 2007.

Downs, Kevin. "A Theoretical Analysis of the Saudi-Iranian Rivalry in Bahrain," *Journal of Politics and International Studies*, Vol. 8 (Winter 2012/13), pp. 203–237.

Ehteshami, Anoushiravan. *Dynamics of Change in the Persian Gulf: Political Economy, War and Revolution*. London: Routledge, 2013.

———. "GCC Foreign Policy: From the Iran-Iraq War to the Arab Awakening," *The New Politics of Intervention of Gulf Arab States*, LSE Middle East Center, Vol. 1 (April 2015), pp. 13–22.

———. *Globalization and Geopolitics in the Middle East: Old Games, New Rules*. London: Routledge, 2007.

———. "Making Foreign Policy in the Midst of Turmoil," in *The Foreign Policies of Middle East States*. 2nd ed. Raymond Hinnebusch and Anoushiravan Ehteshami, eds. Boulder, CO: Lynne Rienner, 2014, pp. 339–350.

———. "The Middle East's New Power Dynamics," *Current History* (December 2009), pp. 395–401.

———. "Security and Strategic Trends in the Middle East," in *The Transformation of the Gulf: Politics, Economics, and the Global Order*. David Held and Kristian Coates Ulrichsen, eds. London: Routledge, 2011, pp. 261–277.

Ehteshami, Anoushiravan, and Raymond Hinnebusch, "Foreign Policymaking in the Middle East: Complex Realism," in *International Relations of the Middle East.* 3rd ed. Louise Fawcett, ed. Oxford: Oxford University Press, 2013, pp. 225–245.

Ennis, Crystal A., and Bessma Momani. "Shaping the Middle East in the Midst of the Arab Uprisings: Turkish and Saudi Foreign Policy Strategies," *Third World Quarterly*, Vol. 34, No. 6 (July 2013), pp. 1127–1144.

Entessar, Nader. "Iran's Security Challenges," *The Muslim Quarterly*, Vol. 94, No. 4 (October 2004), pp. 537–554.

Fawcett, Louise. "Alliances and Regionalism in the Middle East," in *International Relations of the Middle East.* 3rd ed. Louise Fawcett, ed. Oxford: Oxford University Press, 2013, pp. 185–204.

Fierke, K. M. *Critical Approaches to International Security.* London: Polity, 2007.

Foley, Sean. "The UAE: Political Issues and Security Dilemmas," *Middle East Review of International Affairs*, Vol. 3, No. 1 (March 1999), pp. 25–45.

Forstenlechner, Ingo, Emilie Rutledge, and Rashed Salem Alnuaimi. "The UAE, the 'Arab Spring' and the Different Types of Dissent," *Middle East Policy*, Vol. 29, No. 4 (Winter 2012), pp. 54–67.

Friedman, Brandon. "The Arab Gulf States: Balancing Regional Security and Domestic Political Changes," *Bustan: The Middle East Book Review*, Vol. 4 (2013), pp. 43–56.

Gause, F. Gregory. "Beyond Sectarianism: The New Middle East Cold War," *Brookings Doha Center Analysis Paper*, No. 11, July 2014.

——. "The Foreign Policy of Saudi Arabia," in *The Foreign Policies of Middle East States.* 2nd ed. Raymond Hinnebusch and Anoushiravan Ehteshami, eds. Boulder, CO: Lynne Rienner, 2014, pp. 185–206.

——. "The Illogic of Dual Containment," *Foreign Affairs*, Vol. 73, No. 2 (March–April 1994), pp. 56–66.

——. "The International Politics of the Gulf," in *International Relations of the Middle East.* 2nd ed. Louise Fawcett, ed. Oxford: Oxford University Press, 2009, pp. 263–281.

——. *The International Relations of the Persian Gulf.* Cambridge, UK: Cambridge University Press, 2010.

——. "Saudi Arabia's Regional Security Strategy," in *The International Politics of the Persian Gulf.* Mehran Kamrava, ed. Syracuse, NY: Syracuse University Press, 2011, pp. 169–183.

——. "Systemic Approaches to Middle East International Relations," *International Studies Review*, Vol. 1, No. 1 (Spring 1999), pp. 11–31.

——. "Threats and Threat Perceptions in the Persian Gulf Region," *Middle East Policy*, Vol. 14, No. 2 (Summer 2007), p. 119–124.

Glaser, Charles L. "The Security Dilemma Revisited," *World Politics*, Vol. 50, No. 1 (October 1997), pp. 171–201.

Goldberg, Jeffrey. "The Obama Doctrine," *The Atlantic* (April 2016), pp. 70–90.

Gray, Kevin, and Craig N. Murphy. "Introduction: Rising Powers and the Future of Global Governance," *Third World Politics*, Vol. 34, No. 6 (2013), pp. 183–193.

Halliday, Fred. *The Middle East in International Relations: Power, Politics, and Ideology.* Cambridge, UK: Cambridge University Press, 2005.

Hassan, Bassem Ahmed. "The American-Saudi-Iranian Triangle: Limitations of Confrontation," *Reports*, Aljazeera Center for Studies, October 8, 2011.

Haykel, Bernard. "Saudi Arabia and Qatar in a Time of Revolution," *Gulf Analysis Paper*, Center for Strategic and International Studies, February 2013.

Hegghammer, Thomas. "Terrorist Recruitment and Radicalization in Saudi Arabia," *Middle East Policy*, Vol. 13, No. 4 (Winter 2006), pp. 39–60.

Held, David, and Kristian Ulrichsen, "The Transformation of the Gulf," in *The Transformation of the Gulf*. David Held and Kristian Ulrichsen, eds. London: Routledge, 2012, pp. 1–25.

Henderson, Simon. "Desert Stretch: Saudi Arabia's Ambitious Military Operations," *Policy Watch*, No. 2559, The Washington Institute for Near East Policy, February 16, 2016.

Herb, Michael. *All in the Family: Absolutism, Revolution, and Democracy in the Middle Eastern Monarchies*. Albany, NY: SUNY Press, 1999.

Hinnebusch, Raymond, "Foreign Policy in the Middle East," in *The Foreign Policies of Middle East States*. 2nd ed. Raymond Hinnebusch and Anoushiravan Ehteshami, eds. Boulder, CO: Lynne Rienner, 2014, pp. 1–34.

——. "The Middle East Regional System," in *The Foreign Policies of Middle East States*. 2nd ed. Raymond Hinnebusch and Anoushiravan Ehteshami, eds. Boulder, CO: Lynne Rienner, 2014, p. 35–72.

——. "The Politics of Identity in Middle East International Relations," in *International Relations of the Middle East*. 3rd ed. Louise Fawcett, ed. Oxford: Oxford University Press, 2013, pp. 148–166.

——. "Order and Change in the Middle East: A Neo-Gramscian Twist on the International Society Approach," in *International Society and the Middle East: English School Theory at the Regional Level*. Barry Buzan and Ana Gonzalez-Pelaez, eds. New York: Palgrave Macmillan, 2009, pp. 201–225.

Hough, Peter. *Understanding Global Security*. 3rd ed. London: Routledge, 2013.

Hudson, Michael C. "The United States in the Middle East," in *International Relations of the Middle East*. 3rd ed. Louise Fawcett, ed. Oxford: Oxford University Press, 2013, pp. 308–330.

Hunter, Robert E. *Building Security in the Persian Gulf*. Santa Monica, CA: Rand, 2010.

——. "Securing the Persian Gulf: Diplomacy, Not Arms," December 18, 2013, www.lobelog.com.

Ismael, Tareq Y. *International Relations of the Contemporary Middle East: A Study in World Politics*. Syracuse, NY: Syracuse University Press, 1986.

Jervis, Robert. "Cooperation under the Security Dilemma," Vol. 30, No. 2 (January 1978), pp. 167–214.

Johnson, Robert H. "The Persian Gulf in U.S. Strategy: A Skeptical View," *International Security*, Vol. 14, No. 1 (Summer 1989), pp. 122–160.

Juneau, Thomas. "Iran's Policy towards the Houthis in Yemen: A Limited Return on a Modest Investment," *International Affairs*, Vol. 92, No. 3 (May 2016), pp. 647–663.

Kahler, Miles. "Rising Powers and Global Governance: Negotiating Change in a Resilient Status Quo," *International Affairs*, Vol. 89, No. 3 (2013), pp. 711–729.

Kamrava, Mehran. "The Arab Spring and the Saudi-Led Counterrevolution," *Orbis*, Vol. 56, No. 1 (Winter 2012), pp. 96–104.

——, ed. *Fragile Politics: Weak States in the Greater Middle East*. New York: Oxford University Press, 2016.

——, ed. *Gateways to the World: Port Cities in the Persian Gulf*. New York: Oxford University Press, 2016.

——, ed. *The Great Game in West Asia: Iran, Turkey, and the South Caucasus*. New York: Oxford University Press, 2018.

——. *The Modern Middle East: A Political History since the First World War*. 3rd ed. Berkeley: University of California Press, 2013.

——. "The Political Economy of Rentierism in the Persian Gulf," in *The Political Economy of the Persian Gulf*. Mehran Kamrava, ed. New York: Oxford University Press, 2012, pp. 39–68.

——. "Preserving Non-Democracies: Leaders and State Institutions in the Middle East," *Middle Eastern Studies*, Vol. 46, No. 2 (March 2010), pp. 231–250.

——. *Qatar: Small State, Big Politics*. Ithaca, NY: Cornell University Press, 2015.

Kamrava, Mehran, and Zahra Babar, eds. *Migrant Labor in the Persian Gulf*. New York: Columbia University Press, 2011.

Katzman, Kenneth. "The United Arab Emirates (UAE): Issues for U.S. Policy," *Congressional Research Services*, 7-5700, September 14, 2015.

Katzman, Kenneth, and Carla E. Humud. "Iran, Gulf Security, and U.S. Policy," *Congressional Research Services*, 7-5700, May 19, 2015, and March 30, 2016.

——. "Iraq: Politics and Government," *Congressional Research Services*, 7-5700, September 16, 2015.

Kechichian, Joseph. "Trends in Saudi National Security," *The Middle East Journal*, Vol. 53, No. 2 (Spring 1999), pp. 232–253.

Keohane, Robert O. *Power and Governance in a Partially Globalized World*. London: Routledge, 2002.

Keynoush, Banafsheh. *Saudi Arabia and Iran: Friends or Foes?* New York: Palgrave Macmillan, 2016.

Khalilzad, Zalmay. *The Envoy*. New York: St. Martin's, 2016.

Khouri, Nadim. "Food Security Strategies in the GCC Region," UN-ESCWA and IFPRI, 2012.

Korany, Bahgat. "The Middle East since the Cold War: Initiating the Fifth Wave of Democratization," in *International Relations of the Middle East*. 3rd ed. Louise Fawcett, ed. Oxford: Oxford University Press, 2013, pp. 77–100.

Kostiner, Joseph. "GCC Perceptions of Collective Security in the Post-Saddam Era," in *The International Politics of the Persian Gulf*. Mehran Kamrava, ed. Syracuse, NY: Syracuse University Press, 2011, pp. 94–119.

Kraig, Michael Ryan. "Assessing Alternative Security Frameworks for the Persian Gulf," *Middle East Policy*, Vol. 15, No. 3 (Fall 2004), pp. 139–156.

——. "Forging a New Security Order for the Persian Gulf," *Policy Analysis Brief*, The Stanley Foundation (January 2006), pp. 1–16.

Lacey, Robert. *Inside the Kingdom: Kings, Clerics, Modernists, Terrorists, and the Struggle for Saudi Arabia*. New York: Viking, 2009.

Lake, David A. *Hierarchy in International Relations*. Ithaca, NY: Cornell University Press, 2009.

Laney, Christopher. "From Preponderance to Offshore Balancing: America's Future Grand Strategy," *International Security*, Vol. 22, No. 1 (Summer 1997), pp. 86–124.

Larson, Deborah Welch, T. V. Paul, and William C. Wohlforth. "Status and World Order," in *Status in World Politics*. T. V. Paul, Deborah Welch Larsen, and William C. Wohlforth, eds. Cambridge, UK: Cambridge University Press, 2014, pp. 3–29.

Lawson, Fred H. *Constructing International Relations in the Arab World*. Stanford, CA: Stanford University Press, 2006.

——. "Neglected Aspects of the Security Dilemma," in *The Many Faces of National Security in the Arab World*. Bahgat Korany, Paul Noble, and Rex Brynen, eds. London: Macmillan, 1993, pp. 100–126.

——. "Security Dilemma in the Contemporary Persian Gulf," in *The International Politics of the Persian Gulf*. Mehran Kamrava, ed. Syracuse, NY: Syracuse University Press, 2011, pp. 50–71.

LeBaron, Richard. "Hagel's Meeting with GCC Defense Ministers: How to Measure Results," Atlantic Council, May 14, 2014.

——. "The Jordan-Morocco Solution for GCC Defense Makes Bigger Issues," Atlantic Council, April 18, 2014.

Legrenzi, Matteo, and Marina Calculli. "Middle East Security: Continuity amid Change," in *International Relations of the Middle East*. 3rd ed. Louise Fawcett, ed. Oxford: Oxford University Press, 2013, pp. 205–221.

Linklater, Andrew. "Political Community and Human Security," in *Critical Security Studies and World Politics*. Ken Booth, ed. Boulder, CO: Lynne Rienner, 2005, pp. 113–131.

Lippman, Thomas W. "The U.S. Dilemma in Bahrain," *POMED Policy Brief* (September 22, 2011), pp. 1–6.

Lustick, Ian S. "The Absence of Middle Eastern Great Powers: Political 'Backwardness' in Historical Perspective," *International Organization*, Vol. 51, No. 4 (Autumn 1997), pp. 653–683.

Lynch, Marc. "Obama and the Middle East: Rightsizing the U.S. Role," *Foreign Affairs*, Vol. 94, No. 5 (September/October 2015), pp. 18–27.

Malvig, Helle. "Power, Identity, and Securitization in Middle East: Regional Order after the Arab Uprisings," *Mediterranean Politics*, Vol. 19, No. 1 (2014), pp. 145–148.

Mandaville, Peter. "Islam and International Relations in the Middle East: From *Umma* to Nation State," in *International Relations of the Middle East*. 3rd ed. Louise Fawcett, ed. Oxford: Oxford University Press, 2013, pp. 167–184.

Mathews, Jessica. "The New Deal," *The New York Review of Books*, Vol. 62, No. 8 (May 7, 2015), p. 4.

Matthiesen, Toby. *Sectarian Gulf: Bahrain, Saudi Arabia, and the Arab Spring That Wasn't*. Stanford, CA: Stanford University Press, 2013.

Mearsheimer, John J. *The Tragedy of Great Power Politics*. New York: W. W. Norton, 2001.

Menaldo, Victor. *The Institutions Curse: Natural Resources, Politics, and Development*. Cambridge, UK: Cambridge University Press, 2016.

Milani, Mohsen. "Why Tehran Won't Abandon Assad(ism)," *The Washington Quarterly*, Vol. 36, No. 4 (Fall 2013), pp. 79–93.

Mitchell, Timothy. *Carbon Democracy: Political Power in the Age of Oil.* London: Verso, 2011.

Mousseau, Michael. "Market Civilization and Its Clash with Terror," in *New Global Dangers: Changing Dimensions of International Security.* Michael Brown, Owen Cote Jr., Sean M. Lynn-Jones, and Steven Miller, eds. Cambridge, MA: MIT Press, 2004, pp. 421–447.

Munro, Alan. "The Dilemma for Saudi Foreign Policy," *RUSI Journal*, Vol. 147, No. 5 (October 2002), p. 46–50.

Nephew, Richard. "The Grand Bargain: What Iran Conceded in the Nuclear Talks," *Brookings Markaz: Middle East Politics & Policy*, April 18, 2015.

Niblock, Tim. *Saudi Arabia: Power, Legitimacy, and Survival.* London: Routledge, 2006.

Nolan, Leigh. "Managing Reform? Saudi Arabia and the King's Dilemma," *Brookings Doha Center Policy Briefing*, May 2011.

Nonneman, Gerd. "Determinants and Patterns of Saudi Foreign Policy: 'Omnibalancing' and 'Relative Autonomy' in Multiple Environments," in *Saudi Arabia in the Balance: Political Economy, Society, Foreign Affairs.* Paul Aarts and Gerd Nonneman, eds. London: Hurst, 2005, pp. 315–351.

Nye, Joseph S. *Bound to Lead: The Changing Nature of American Power.* New York: Basic Books, 1990.

Obaid, Nawaf. "A Saudi Arabian Defense Doctrine: Mapping the Expanded Force Structure the Kingdom Needs to Lead the Arab World, Stabilize the Region, and Meet Its Global Responsibilities," Belfer Center for Science and International Affairs, Harvard Kennedy School, May 2014.

Olson, Robert. *Turkey-Iran Relations, 1979–2004: Revolution, Ideology, War, Coups, and Geopolitics.* Costa Mesa, CA: Mazda, 2005.

Ozbaran, Salih. "The Ottoman Turks and the Portuguese in the Persian Gulf, 1534–1581." *Journal of Asian History* Vol. 6, No. 1 (1972), pp. 45–87.

Paris, Roland. "Human Security: Paradigm Shift or Hot Air?" in *New Global Dangers: Changing Dimensions of International Security.* Michael Brown, Owen Cote Jr., Sean M. Lynn-Jones, and Steven Miller, eds. Cambridge, MA: MIT Press, 2004, pp. 249–264.

Parsi, Trita. *Treacherous Alliance: The Secret Dealings of Israel, Iran, and the U.S.* New Haven, CT: Yale University Press, 2007.

Patrick, Neil. "Saudi Arabia's Problematic Allies against the Houthis," *Sada Journal*, Carnegie Endowment for International Peace, February 12, 2016, http://carnegie endowment.org/sada/?fa=62753.

——. "Saudi Arabia's Yemen Gambit," *Sada Journal*, Carnegie Endowment for International Peace, October 1, 2015, http://carnegieendowment.org/sada/?fa=61475.

Peoples, Columba, and Nick Vaughan-Williams. *Critical Security Studies: An Introduction.* London: Routledge, 2010.

Perlo-Freeman, Sam, et al. "Trends in World Military Expenditure, 2014," *SIPRI Fact Sheet*, April 2015, pp. 1–7.

Pettman, Jan Jindy. "Questions of Identity: Australia and Asia," in *Critical Security Studies and World Politics*. Ken Booth, ed. Boulder, CO: Lynne Rienner, 2005, pp. 159–177.

Pew Research Center. *Saudi Arabia's Image Falters among Middle East Neighbors*. Washington, DC: Pew Research Center, 2013.

Phillips, Christopher. "Gulf Actors and the Syrian Crisis," *The New Politics of Intervention of Gulf Arab States*, LSE Middle East Center, Vol. 1 (April 2015), pp. 41–51.

Posen, Barry. "Command of the Commons: The Military Foundation of U.S. Hegemony," in *New Global Dangers: Changing Dimensions of International Security*. Michael Brown, Owen Cote Jr., Sean M. Lynn-Jones, and Steven Miller, eds. Cambridge, MA: MIT Press, 2004, pp. 3–44.

Potter, Lawrence G. ed. *Sectarianism in the Persian Gulf*. New York: Oxford University Press, 2014.

Qadiri, Abbas. "President Hassan Rouhani's Defense Policy," Atlantic Council, February 11, 2016, http://www.atlanticcouncil.org/blogs/new-atlanticist/president-hassan-rouhani-s-defense-policy.

Ramazani, R.K. "Security in the Persian Gulf," *Foreign Affairs*, Vol. 57, No. 4 (Spring 1979), pp. 821–835.

Rathmell, Andrew, Theodore Karasik, and David Gompert. "A New Persian Gulf Security System," *Rand Issue Paper*, 2003, pp. 1–10.

Ross, Michael. "Does Oil Hinder Democracy?" *World Politics*, Vol. 53 (April 2001), pp. 325–361.

——. *The Oil Curse: How Petroleum Wealth Shapes the Development of Nations*. Princeton, NJ: Princeton University Press, 2012.

Rovner, Joshua, and Caitlin Talmadge. "Less Is More: The Future of the U.S. Military in the Persian Gulf," *The Washington Quarterly*, Vol. 37, No. 3 (Fall 2014), pp. 47–60.

Rugh, William A. "The Foreign Policy of the United Arab Emirates," *Middle East Journal*, Vol. 50, No. 1 (Winter 1996), pp. 57–70.

Russell, James A., "Environmental Security and Regional Stability in the Persian Gulf," *Middle East Policy*, Vol. 16, No. 4 (Winter 2009), pp. 90–101.

Saouli, Adham. "The Foreign Policies of Iraq and Lebanon," in *The Foreign Policies of Middle East States*. 2nd ed. Raymond Hinnebusch and Anoushiravan Ehteshami, eds. Boulder, CO: Lynne Rienner, 2014, pp. 105–132.

Sirriyeh, Hussein. "A New Version of Pan-Arabism?" *International Relations*, Vol. 15, No. 3 (December 2000), pp. 53–66.

Smith, Steve, "The Contested Concept of Security," in *Critical Security Studies and World Politics*. Ken Booth, ed. Boulder, CO: Lynne Rienner, 2005, pp. 27–62.

Snyder, Glenn H. "The Security Dilemma in Alliance Politics," *World Politics*, Vol. 36, No. 4 (July 1984), pp. 461–495.

Sowell, Kirk H. "Saudi Arabia and Iran: Rouhani Fades as Riyadh Focuses on Containment," in *Post-Nuclear: The Future for Iran and its Neighborhood*. European Council on Foreign Relations, ed. London: ECFR, 2014, pp. 5–8.

Springborg, Robert. "GCC Countries as 'Rentier States' Revisited," *Middle East Journal*, Vol. 67, No. 2 (Spring 2013), pp. 301–309.

Stein, Janice Gross. "The Security Dilemma in the Middle East: A Prognosis for the Decade Ahead," in *The Many Faces of National Security in the Arab World*. Bahgat Korany, Paul Noble, and Rex Brynen, eds. London: Macmillan, 1993, pp. 56–75.

——. "War and Security in the Middle East," in *International Relations of the Middle East*. 3rd ed. Louise Fawcett, ed. Oxford: Oxford University Press, 2013, pp. 208–227.

Strategy&. "Achieving a Sustainable Water Sector in the GCC: Managing Supply and Demand, Building Institutions," Beirut, 2014.

Taleblu, Behnam Ben. "Enemy of Convenience: Iran's Fight against Daesh," *FRIDE Policy Brief*, No. 2013 (December 2015), pp. 1–5.

Tammen, Ronald L., et al. *Power Transitions: Strategies for the 21st Century*. New York: Seven Bridges, 2000.

Tang, Shiping. "The Security Dilemma: A Conceptual Analysis," *Security Studies*, Vol. 18, No. 3 (October 2009), pp. 587–623.

Twinam, Joseph Wright. *The Gulf, Cooperation, and the Council*. Washington, DC: Middle East Policy Council, 1992.

Ulrichsen, Kristian Coates. "The GCC States and the Shifting Balance of Global Power," *CIRS Occasional Paper*, No. 6. Doha: Center for International and Regional Studies, 2010.

——. *Insecure Gulf: The End of Certainty and the Transition to the Post-oil Era*. New York: Columbia University Press, 2011.

——. "Internal and External Security in the Arab Gulf States," *Middle East Policy*, Vol. 16, No. 2 (Summer 2009), pp. 39–58.

United States Department of Defense. *Sustaining U.S. Global Leadership: Priorities for 21st Century Defense*. Washington, DC: U.S. Defense Department, 2012.

——. Unclassified Executive Summary, "Annual Report on Military Power of Iran," 2014.

United States Department of State. *Country Reports on Terrorism 2013, Executive Summary*. Washington, DC: US Department of State Bureau of Counterterrorism, 2014.

United States Joint Chiefs of Staff. *The National Military Strategy of the United States of America, 2015*. Washington, DC: Department of Defense, 2015.

Vakhshouri, Sara. *Iran's Energy Policy after the Nuclear Deal*. Washington, DC: The Atlantic Council, 2015.

Valeri, Marc. "Summering Unrest and Succession Challenges in Oman," Carnegie Endowment for International Peace, January 2015.

Yetiv, Steve A. "Oil, Saudi Arabia, and the Spring That Has Not Come," in *The Arab Spring: Change and Resistance in the Middle East*. Mark L. Hass and David W. Lesch, eds. Boulder, CO: Westview Press, 2013, pp. 97–115.

Young, Karen. "Foreign Policy Analysis of the Gulf Cooperation Council: Breaking Black Boxes and Explaining New Interventions," *The New Politics of Intervention of Gulf Arab States*, LSE Middle East Center, Vol. 1 (April 2015), p. 4–12.

Walt, Stephen M. *The Origins of Alliances*. Ithaca, NY: Cornell University Press, 1987.
——. "The Renaissance of Security Studies," *International Studies Quarterly*, Vol. 35, No. 2 (1991), pp. 211–239.
Waltz, Kenneth. *Realism and International Relations*. London: Routledge, 2008.
——. *Theory of International Politics*. Long Grove, IL: Waveland, 1979.
Wang, Hongying, and Erik French. "Middle Range Powers in Global Governance," *Third World Politics* 34, no. 6 (2013), pp. 985–999.
Wehrey, Frederic, and Richard Sokolsky. *Imagining a New Security Order in the Persian Gulf*. Washington, DC: Carnegie Endowment for International Peace, 2015.
Wehrey, Frederic M. *Sectarian Politics in the Gulf: From the Iraq War to the Arab Uprisings*. New York: Columbia University Press, 2014.
Weinberger, Caspar. "A Report to the Congress on Security Arrangements in the Persian Gulf," United States Department of Defense, June 15, 1987.
Weiner, Myron. "Security, Stability, and International Migration," in *New Global Dangers: Changing Dimensions of International Security*. Michael Brown, Owen Cote Jr., Sean M. Lynn-Jones, and Steven Miller, eds. Cambridge, MA: MIT Press, 2004, pp. 301–336.
Wendt, Alexander. *Social Theory of International Politics*. Cambridge, UK: Cambridge University Press, 1999.
Zambelis, Chris. "Royal Rivalry in the Levant: Saudi Arabia and Qatar Duel over Syria," *Terrorism Monitor*, Vol. 11, No. 16 (August 9, 2013), pp. 9–11.
Zarif, Mohammad Javad. "Overcoming Regional Challenges in the Middle East: An Iranian Perspective," Chatham House, February 4, 2016.
——. "What Iran Really Wants: Iranian Foreign Policy in the Rouhani Era," *Foreign Affairs*, Vol. 93, No. 3 (May/June 2014), pp. 49–59.
Zayani, Mohamed. "Al Jazeera's Complex Legacy: Thresholds for an Unconventional Media Player from the Global South," *International Journal of Communication*, Vol. 10 (2016), pp. 3554–3569.
Zimmerman, Katherine. "AQAP: A Resurgent Threat," *CTCSentinel*, Vol. 8, No. 9 (September 2015), pp. 19–23.

Personal Interviews

Abdulla, Abdulkhaleq. Chairman of the Arab Council for the Social Sciences, Dubai, March 28, 2016.
al-Kabeer, Turki M. Saud. Deputy Minister for Multilateral Affairs, Saudi Ministry of Foreign Affairs, Riyadh, September 11, 2014.
Al-Rajhi, Saleh. Director of the Center for American Studies, Saudi Ministry of Foreign Affairs, Riyadh, September 11, 2014.
Al-Suwaidi, Jamal Sanad. Director General of the Emirates Center for Strategic Studies and Research, Abu Dhabi, March 12, 2016.
bin Abdullah, Yusuf bin Alawi. Minister of Foreign Affairs of Oman, Muscat, April 6, 2015.
Farazmand, Mohammad. Director of the Persian Gulf Department, Iranian Ministry of Foreign Affairs, Tehran, June 18, 2014.

Khoshandam, Behzad. Researcher at the Center for Strategic Research, Office of the Presidency, Tehran, June 17, 2014.

Maleki, Abbas. Deputy director of the Center for Strategic Research, Office of the Presidency, Tehran, June 17, 2014.

Sajjadpour, Kazem. Director of the School of International Relations, Tehran, June 17, 2014.

INDEX